Caribbean Development in the New Multipolar World Order

This book addresses the subject of critical development alternatives for the Caribbean Community (CARICOM) states in a post-neoliberal, new multipolar world order based on competition and co-operation by the United States, the European Union, China, and Russia for natural resources and markets. Neoliberal globalization has traditionally restricted economic and political activities in the Caribbean region to Western-style free-market capitalism and liberal democracy. However, through an exploration of the new multipolar world order, which replaces the US-led unipolar global order that existed since the collapse of the former Soviet Union, the author argues that today, the Caribbean Community states now have real economic and political options for development alternatives. Through examining how countries such as China and Russia have risen to economic success in recent years, the book seeks to explore how the Caribbean Community states might adopt such features which would allow them to formulate "another" development, such as introducing measures which can bring about a reconciliation between resource use and endowment, and reduce inequalities. As such, it will appeal to scholars of sociology and development studies with interests in the Caribbean region and world order.

Dennis C. Canterbury is Professor of Sociology at Eastern Connecticut State University, USA.

Capitalism, Power and the Imperial State

In an increasingly turbulent political landscape, this series addresses disputed theoretical and conceptual issues within the realms of political sociology and political economy, to evaluate the shifting dynamics of global power in the modern age. With attention to the ever-changing contours of economic and political world power, Capitalism, Power and the Imperial State invites contributions from scholars looking to advance the debate between theorists of globalization and advocates of class analysis and imperialism, as well as those interested in unpacking the economic configurations of power. Focusing on how power affects, and is affected by, both the higher and lower ranks of society, it seeks to investigate the relationship between the capitalist state and imperial power, the rise of emerging regional rivalries, and polarization within the imperial state between sectors of the "deep state" and the regime. A timely and important opportunity to review the ongoing crisis of the capitalist state, and to evaluate the social and political factors that influence the balance of global power in the twenty-first century, this series invites research which pays attention to the impact of the class struggle on global alignments of power, and the impact of such power on the global class war between capital and labour.

Series Editors

Henry Veltmeyer is Senior Research Professor of Development Studies at the Autonomous University of Zacatecas, Mexico; and Professor Emeritus of International Development Studies at Saint Mary's University, Canada.

James Petras is Bartle Professor Emeritus of Sociology at Binghamton University, USA.

Titles in this series

Latin America in the Vortex of Social Change
Development and Resistance Dynamics
Henry Veltmeyer and James Petras

For more information about this series, please visit:
www.routledge.com/Capitalism-Power-and-the-Imperial-State/book-series/CPIS

Caribbean Development in the New Multipolar World Order

Dennis C. Canterbury

LONDON AND NEW YORK

First published 2022
by Routledge
2 Park Square, Milton Park, Abingdon, Oxon OX14 4RN

and by Routledge
605 Third Avenue, New York, NY 10158

Routledge is an imprint of the Taylor & Francis Group, an informa business

© 2022 Dennis C. Canterbury

The right of Dennis C. Canterbury to be identified as author of this work has been asserted by him in accordance with sections 77 and 78 of the Copyright, Designs and Patents Act 1988.

All rights reserved. No part of this book may be reprinted or reproduced or utilised in any form or by any electronic, mechanical, or other means, now known or hereafter invented, including photocopying and recording, or in any information storage or retrieval system, without permission in writing from the publishers.

Trademark notice: Product or corporate names may be trademarks or registered trademarks, and are used only for identification and explanation without intent to infringe.

British Library Cataloguing-in-Publication Data
A catalogue record for this book is available from the British Library

Library of Congress Cataloging-in-Publication Data
A catalog record has been requested for this book

ISBN: 9780367552039 (hbk)
ISBN: 9780367552046 (pbk)
ISBN: 9781003092414 (ebk)

DOI: 10.4324/9781003092414

Typeset in Times NR MT Pro
by KnowledgeWorks Global Ltd.

To the memory of Abayomi Seitu Osaze (Charles Waldron)
November 5th, 1948 – July 15th, 2020
Comrade and Revolutionary Artist in the
Working People's Alliance, Guyana

Contents

1 Introducing an alternative development idea   1

2 The imperialist frameworks of Caribbean development   14

3 The Caribbean in the "New American Century"   25

4 The Caribbean making America great again   39

5 The new multipolar world order   60

6 Theoretical advances with Caribbean capitalist development   77

7 The CARIFORUM-EU EPA and Brexit   95

8 Neoliberal financialization in the Caribbean   112

9 Caribbean agriculture in the new multipolar world order   133

10 PetroCaribe and the CARICOM–China development alternative   151

11 China–US policies and the CARICOM   167

12 Conclusion: Economic policy for the new multipolar world order   185

Index   202

1 Introducing an alternative development idea

Introduction

This book employs a historical critical development studies method to undertake a post-neoliberal globalization analysis of development alternatives for the Caribbean in the new multipolar world order (NMWO). The goal is to shift the analysis of Caribbean political economy off the deconstructionist perch it occupied in the neoliberal era, to new constructionist explorations in the NMWO. The analysis, therefore, falls under the purview of the critical tradition of the "golden age" in Caribbean political economy that vigorously searched for and attempted to construct development alternatives to colonial capitalist exploitation. The Caribbean Community countries are in the political independence stage of their evolution, from their status as colonies of imperial European powers to autonomous self-governing nation-states. Political independence however was a mechanism to continue the utilization of the new countries' economic resources for capital accumulation in the imperial European economies. These countries have had half a century to transcend that neocolonial trap set for them at the time of their political independence. Also, the neoliberal globalization era that constrained their economic and political behaviors within the boundaries of free-market fundamentalism and neoliberal democratization is over. Their political and economic actions must now reflect the evolutionary phase of their development. The Caribbean states are at a historical conjuncture at which they have had 50 years to unshackle neocolonial relations, and neoliberal globalization economic relations that fettered them for three decades. They must now embark on a new course of development in the post-neoliberal NMWO.

The Caribbean cannot stand idly by while the post-war liberal and neoliberal economic structures that control it but which it had no part in creating, are being dismantled. The gravity of international power is shifting from the West to the East, and new international institutional structures are emerging. The politically independent Caribbean states collectively through the CARICOM have an opportunity and obligation to contribute at the level of ideas and practice to shape the vision of the NWMO. They were merely passive

DOI: 10.4324/9781003092414-1

albeit important participants in hitherto economic orders such as neocolonialism and neoliberal globalization created by Western powers. The leading Eastern country shaping the NMWO is not doing so from the perspective of a colonizer modeling an economic order for its colonies. Countries are being invited to determine for themselves the extent of their economic participation in the NMWO. This idea is at the core of China's Belt and Road Initiative that is reordering international economic transactions away from the Western-centered institutions created at Bretton Woods and the policies they prescribe.

The question is: what are the Caribbean states going to do about the new situation in which they have found themselves? Are they brave and practical enough to realign their economies with China and the BRICS, and renegotiate their economic relations with the United States (US) and European Union (EU)?

The immediate post-independence period was the golden age for alternative models of political economy in the Caribbean. But, the region slipped into a deconstructionist mode in the neoliberal era when it was constrained only to operate in the free-market model. Caribbean scholarship lost its way to generate original critical ideas on how to provide working people their basic needs. A wide chasm emerged between the subject matters of Caribbean scholarship and solutions to the poverty conditions in which working people live. Thomas (2001) expressed the need for the Caribbean to return to its ways of constructing alternative development models. This book about development in the Caribbean Community in the NMWO is intended as a contribution toward that need. It is a premeditated return to the sources, as it were, in the furtherance of the tradition of independent critical thinking in the Caribbean.

The globe has transitioned to a NMWO comprising four poles of power – China, the EU, Russia, and the US. China and Russia are a part of the BRICS with Brazil, India, and South Africa. The BRICS, which at times is identified as a separate pole of power, constitute about 42 percent of the world's population, 23 percent of its GDP, 30 percent of the territory, and 18 percent of global trade, and are larger than were all of the advanced countries at the end of World War II (Stiglitz, 2018). The transition to the NMWO is based on the assumption that the US-led unipolar neoliberal global order has collapsed. This global order was in place since the demise of the former Union of Soviet Socialist Republics (USSR).

The Caribbean Community comprises 15 member states – Antigua and Barbuda, The Bahamas, Barbados, Belize, Dominica, Grenada, Guyana, Haiti, Jamaica, Montserrat, St. Kitts and Nevis, Saint Lucia, St. Vincent, and the Grenadines, Suriname, and Trinidad, and five associate members – Anguilla, Bermuda, British Virgin Islands (BVI), Cayman Islands, and Turks and Caicos Islands (TCI) (CARICOM, 2018). The 15 member countries of the CARICOM had a total population of approximately 18,848,730 persons in 2020 covering a land mass 177,000 square miles or 458,428 square kilometers. These countries are relatively small considering their diverse population, size, geography, culture, and economic and social development.

Introducing an alternative development idea 3

They are located in the Americas that give them close access to North and Latin American markets. The economies in several of these countries depend on tourism, financial services, agricultural, and natural resources extraction. Their primary constraints are periodic natural disasters – hurricanes, floods, and mudslides, and their small size, dearth of scale economies, and vulnerabilities to external shocks.

These small island developing states (SIDS) and mainland countries have evolved within the historical frameworks of capitalist theory and practice since their encounter with European feudalism and mercantile capitalism. They have been subjected to mercantile, classical political economy, neo-classical, Keynesian, and neoliberal theories; experimented with Marxism, and advanced their own theoretical approaches to explain and advance their social, political, and economic realities. They have actively participated as colonies and independent countries in different international environments and orders – multipolar, bipolar, unipolar and now a NMWO which is the product of a contradictory process. Neoliberal economic policies intended to universalize the free market, catapulted communist China to superpower status. China now wants to have more state-led free market policies in the NMWO, while the US through Trumpian "America first" policies is implementing protectionist measures in the form of tariffs. Stiglitz's (2018) analysis of the new protectionism demonstrates the extent to which neoliberal free market fundamentalism has lost its way.

Another dimension of the NMWO is that the world has traversed imperialism and colonialism and has arrived at a stage where there is not a preponderance of colonies directly owned by imperial or colonial powers. The age of those imperial empires is gone (Harvey, 2003), although, imperialism continues to be manifested in different forms other that direct ownership of one country by another (Canterbury, 2012; Harvey, 2003; Noonan, 2017; Petras and Veltmeyer, 2001; 2014). The former European colonizers, now with the exception of the UK due to Brexit, have merged as a single force the EU on the world stage. The US is disengaging from neoliberal globalization under Trumpian "America first" nationalist doctrine labeled "patriotism." The US and UK seem ready to take the world into newer forms of imperialism as the US disengages from neoliberal globalization and the UK from the EU. The vast majority of the nation-states in the world are politically independent, save for the small number of existing UK and US colonies.

The CARICOM countries emerged from colonies that had no say in their insertion into the world capitalist economic system. Today they are independent states and do have a say about the direction of their economic policies in the NMWO. They do not have to conform to the false dichotomy of having to choose between state-led and market-led economic policies to develop their economies. The capitalist state is controlled by business interests that elect political representatives that make laws that govern the economy. The Caribbean can choose to replace the capitalist multinationals with state-owned companies supported by economic policies of the domestic political elites. The difference is whether state elites or private individuals control the commanding heights of the economy and not about the economy being state-led or market-led.

The economic model that has emerged in China combines several large state-owned companies with privately owned businesses under the aegis of the Chinese state to lead the economic development process. These companies partake in domestic and international markets as directed by the state and in accordance with market conditions. China has implemented market reforms but in a sequenced gradual manner rather than in a chaotic way as happened in Russia where liberalization was rapid (Stiglitz, 2018). Stiglitz (2018) speaks of a multipolar globalization in which China can circumscribe the abuse of market power by the advanced countries and their companies but warned that the interests of these companies and those of China may converge in the future to limit competition.

The Caribbean has had a very violent beginning marked by the decimation of pre-Colombian peoples and their economic, political, and social organizations and the burden of slavery. European conquest, plunder, and colonial settlement from the late fifteenth century to the early seventeenth century was followed by the imposition of a colonial slave mode of production or slavery-cum-capitalism from the mid-seventeenth century to the early nineteenth century. The emancipation of slaves, introduction of indentured labor, collapse of the colonial slave mode of production, transformation of the planter class and slave labor into full-fledged capitalist and working classes, and the emergence of the US as a major capitalist power, shaped capitalist development in the Caribbean.

The book addresses the subject of critical development alternatives for the CARICOM states in a post-neoliberal globalization new multipolar world order. The NMWO is based on competition and co-operation between the US, EU, China, and Russia for natural resources and markets. The CARICOM states have real economic and political options for development alternatives. Neoliberal globalization restricted their economic and political activities to Western-styled free-market capitalism and liberal democracy. Economic prosperity in the NMWO is derived through different styles of economic and political organization. There are the Chinese, Russian, US, and European paths to economic success. The US and EU succeeded through imperialism and colonialism, unlike current successes in China and Russia which have not been imperial powers in the Caribbean.

Caribbean development is about the people and they are the ones to choose the economic path they wish to pursue. The economic prosperity of the Caribbean is being held back by four key factors. The first are the historical constraints placed on the region by its role as former European colonies and by European and US imperialisms. Second, the consumption patterns do not satisfy the basic needs of the population. Third, there is a disjuncture in the pattern of resource use and resource endowment. Fourth, the inequalities associated with property ownership and the social relations it engenders are worsening (Thomas, 1988). The solution to these problems requires the CARICOM states to pursue development alternatives. The principal challenge for Caribbean states in constructing another development in the twenty-first century is for them to engage in a win-win navigation of the NMWO in the furtherance of their self-interest. The Caribbean must recognize the NMWO as a framework for the creation of paths to alternative development. What are the prospects for the Caribbean engaging the NMWO as a means to construct another development?

Selected economic indicators in the CARICOM

The CARICOM emerged after the British West Indies Federation which existed between 1958 and 1962, was aborted. Various heads of government meetings on regional cooperation from 1963 led to the establishment of the Caribbean Free Trade Area (CARIFTA) in 1965. The CARIFTA was transformed into a Common Market and the Caribbean Community was established in 1972. The Treaty of Chaguaramas founded the CARICOM in 1973. The Treaty of Chaguaramas was revised between 1993 and 2000 and is now officially entitled, The Revised Treaty of Chaguaramas Establishing the Caribbean Community, Including the CARICOM Single Market and Economy. The main purpose of the revision was to create a new version of the Treaty, to bring it in line with the neoliberal free trade ideology.

The CARICOM (2018) has identified the objectives of the agency as that of improving the standard of living and work of Caribbean people. The CARICOM promotes full employment of the productive factors, as well as accelerated, coordinated, and sustained economic development and convergence, the expansion of trade and economic relations with third states, and enhanced levels of international competitiveness. Its objective includes organizing member-states for increased production and productivity, the achievement of a greater measure of economic leverage and effectiveness in dealing with third states, groups of states and entities of any description, and enhancing the co-ordination of their foreign and international economic policies. The CARICOM's objective is to enhance functional cooperation which includes the stimulation of more efficient operation of common services and activities for the benefit of Caribbean peoples, accelerated promotion of greater understanding among Caribbean peoples and the advancement of their social, cultural and technological development, and the intensification of activities in health, education, transportation and telecommunications (CARICOM, 2018).

Currently, the CARICOM economies are in a pretty bad shape which requires the region to recalibrate its development strategy within the framework of the NMWO. The community has failed to reach a 2 percent annual growth rate in gross domestic product (GDP) at constant prices between 2010 and the preliminary reporting on the statistic for 2018. The percent annual growth rate in GDP at constant prices ranged between −1.7 and 1.9 percent

6 *Introducing an alternative development idea*

(ECLAC, 2019). The annual growth rate in per capita GDP was preliminarily reported to grow 1.4 percent in 2018 but it failed to reach 1 percent in the entire period between 2010 and 2017. It was as low as −2.3 percent in 2016 and only recovered to −0.5 in 2017 (ECLAC, 2019). New resource transfers remained in the negative quadrant through the period 2010–2018 which indicated that outflows to service debt continue to exceed inflows which come primarily from direct foreign investment. When net resource transfers are considered in conjunction with the precipitous decline in foreign direct investment from US$2,500M in 2010 to US$596M in 2018, the economic situation is even more dismal.

Meanwhile, the total gross external public debt increased from US$18,567M in 2011 to US$25,805M in 2018 (ECLAC, 2019). The gross international reserves declined from US$18,262M in 2010 to US$15,773M in 2018. The average non-financial public sector gross public debt as a percentage of GDP fluctuated between a high of 82.5 percent in 2013 and a low of 78.6 percent in 2018. The average gross central government public debt as a percentage of GDP increased from 69.8 percent in 2011 to 71.8 percent in 2018 but was at its highest point 74.3 percent in 2017 (ECLAC, 2019). Neoliberal economic theory holds, a debtor country cannot grow out of debt when the debt stock is over 75 percent of GDP (Bernal, 2017). Thus, the economic plight of the CARICOM states is revealed by the debt/GDP ratio which in 2014 was 130.5 percent for Jamaica, 108.5 percent for Barbados, 99.1 percent for Grenada, 96.4 percent for Antigua, 82.4 percent for the Bahamas, 79.4 percent for St. Vincent, 78.4 percent for St. Lucia, 78.0 percent for St. Kitts, 77.3 percent for Belize, and 74.1 percent for Dominica (Bernal, 2017).

The data on the balance of payments showed that exports of goods free on board (f.o.b.) recovered from US$−5,193M in 2016 to US$199M in 2018, while the balance on the export of services was US$−2,177M in 2016 and US$−2,020M in 2017, and US$−831M in 2018. The imports of goods f.o.b. declined precipitously from US$12,697M in 2016 to US$3,333M in 2018, as did the import of services from US$8,581M to US$2,022M in the same period. The goods and services balance improved from US$−5,193M in 2016 to US$199M in 2018 and income balance from US$-2,177M to US$−831M. The current transfer balance declined from US$2,803M in 2016 to US$73M in 2018, while the current account balance changed from US$−4567M to US$−558M in the same period (ECLAC, 2019).

Meanwhile, the capital balance including omissions and errors declined from US$4,548M in 2016 to US$638M in 2018, and the overall balance improved from US$−19M to US$127M in the same period (ECLAC, 2019). Reserve assets varied from US$118M to US$−166M in the period indicating an increase in reserve assets. The negative sign (−) in reserve assets variations indicates an increase in reserve assets meaning countries were spending funds to buy reserves. Meanwhile, other financing declined from US$62M to US$−12M in the period. The data showed that the actual fiscal primary balance as a percentage of GDP improved slightly from 0.7 percent to 1.6 percent between 2015 and 2018. The actual overall fiscal balance however was negative being −2.5 percent and −1.2 percent in 2015 and 2018, respectively (ECLAC, 2019).

Global realignment of economic power

The dismal economic situation in the Caribbean is a direct result of the region's continued economic entanglement with the US and EU. Meanwhile, there is a major global realignment of economic power taking place from the US and Europe to the BRICS (Petras and Veltmeyer, 2018). Simultaneously, the financial capitalists at the center of the system are embroiled in efforts to protect their interests while maintaining their hegemony over the world capitalist production processes (Petras and Veltmeyer, 2018). The transfer of economic power is taking place concurrently with significant political and cultural events and processes across the globe. The nationalist doctrines exhibited by the far-right in Europe and the authors of Brexit, the consolidation of the EU in spite of Brexit, Trumpian nationalism in the US, the economic, political, and military rise of China, and the restoration of Russia on the world stage, indicate that the US-led neoliberal global order has ended.

Some scholars analyzed the US-led unipolar global order in terms of a transition from US and Soviet Union spheres of influence, to a de facto American sphere at the end of the cold war (Allison, 2020). The US now acknowledges however that its de facto unipolar global order is over and claims that the world has entered into a new era of great power competition. According to Mattis (2018), "inter-state strategic competition, not terrorism, is now the primary concern in the US national security." This means that there is a transition from a de facto American sphere at the global level to a new international order characterized by multiple spheres of influence. The US has to share the world stage with China, Russia, and the EU that are increasingly using their power to assert their interests and values that often are in conflict with those of the US (Allison, 2020; Saunders, 2020; Wong, 2019). The US has to contend with three important facts – Russia has been restored as a central actor in international affairs; the EU is a bloc that behaves as a nation-state which exercises imperialist powers in Africa, Asia, the Caribbean, and Latin America; and China has joined the ranks of great powers.

The US neoconservatives designated the twenty-first century as a new American century in which they positioned the US as the pre-eminent global power (DeMuth and Kristol, 1995; Kagan, 2003; Kagan and Kristol, 2000; Kagan, Schmitt, and Donnelly, 2000). This doctrine was replaced by Trumpism, a retreat to right-wing nationalism in the US. The colossal change from unipolar neoliberal globalization or a de facto American sphere, to a multipolar world order is on the same scale as the collapse of the former Soviet Union. The Soviet Union lost power to US-led neoliberal globalization, but now the US has lost power to the new multipolar world order.

The Caribbean in the moment

The Caribbean states are in a new multipolar world order in which the US, EU, China, and Russia are in competition for resources and influence. Seemingly, China and Russia's interests have converged in their challenge to US and EU historic dominance in the Caribbean. Some observers believe that the challenge is not ideological but economic (CSIS, 2019). The ideological nature of the challenge however seem to concern the state-driven economic approached displayed by China and Russia compared with the market-driven approach supported by the US and EU. Nonetheless, even this distinction is problematic considering the role of the state in implementing capitalist market measures in the US and EU. The possible difference is the political structures in China and Russia that have presidents for life, compared with the US and EU that have well-established political parties that share presidencies in entrenched capitalist power structures.

Seemingly, China's primary concerns in the Caribbean include the procurement of long-term access to natural resources such as oil and bauxite, securing its trade route to the US through infrastructure investments in port development, and promoting its one-china policy under the Belt and Road Initiative (BRI). Meanwhile, Russia's diplomatic profile and its economic presence are on the rise evidenced by its expanding tourism, reengaging Cuba in trade and economic development, investing in resource extraction in Jamaica and Guyana, and its proposal to explore the Caribbean Sea with respect to oil and gas research, seismic activities, fisheries, and climate changes (Jessop, 2017). The primary mechanisms through which the US and EU, respectively, engage the Caribbean are the Caribbean Basin Initiative (CBI) and the Caribbean Forum-European Union Economic Partnership Agreement (CARIFORUM-EU EPA).

The principal problem for the CARICOM states in the twenty-first century is the creation of an autonomous economic and social development strategy in this NMWO. Two obvious stumbling blocks in this endeavor are the region's historic ties with Europe and its geographic proximity to the US which considers the Caribbean its "front yard" or "back yard," or "third border." The US exercises its military and economic power and leverage to rein in recalcitrant Caribbean states. Guyana, Jamaica, and Grenada are recent examples. The Caribbean does not have to be confrontational or apologetic in declaring its intent to pursue appropriate strategies to take advantage of the global realignment of economic power in the NMWO. In theory, the CARICOM states are not bound to confirm to neoliberal free-market capitalism and liberal democracy. The practice however is that even as Trumpism dismantles neoliberal globalization, the US continues to destabilize countries trying to pursue an independent path to development.

European medieval imperial powers created Caribbean colonies as a part of the then newly emerging international capitalist system. Ever since, as colonies and neocolonial states the Caribbean has been on a roller coaster ride with capitalist crises and reforms that ended the colonial-slave-mode of production, and inaugurated center-periphery relations simultaneously as US imperialism arose in the region. Crisis and reforms forged nationalist struggles for political and economic change and independence, and restructured economies on the bases of neoliberal free market principles. These former colonies entered the twenty-first century as independent states under the EU- and US-led neoliberal globalization – the new imperialism. The NMWO challenges the Caribbean to move beyond center-periphery relations and the new imperialism into an era of greater economic independence.

Regional economic policies in the NMWO have to transcend those implemented in the era of neoliberal globalization. They must reverse neoliberal financialization and pursue a more win-win self-reliant financial architecture, use Brexit as a means to put an end to the EU bloc imperialist economic partnership agreement, and be pro-working people by providing them with ample social protection that sustainably guarantee their right to work, decent income, equality, and food security. Caribbean academics and policymakers however continue to espouse a pro-neoliberal globalization economic perspectives such as "critical insertion" (Nogueira, 1997) and "strategic global repositioning" (Bernal, 2000) that have not been recanted. These viewpoints hold that Caribbean states will maximize their economic development through the critical insertion and strategic global repositioning of their economies within the framework of neoliberal globalization.

The proponents of "critical insertion" advocate neoliberal globalization and plans for a hemispheric free-trade bloc (FTAA), and rendered as anachronistic the state-centered economic integration approaches pursued by the CARICOM and the Association of Caribbean States (ACS). The challenge identified for the region was to determine the roles of the CARICOM and ACS in bringing about the competitive insertion of the Caribbean into the global economy dominated by trading blocs. "Strategic global repositioning" was identified as the process involving the relocating of a country in the global economy and world affairs through the implementation of a strategic medium- to long-term plan framed around continuous dialogue among the public, private, and social sectors, and the academic community (Bernal, 2000). Regarded as different to structural adjustment, it purports to involve improving among other things the competitiveness and productivity in existing Caribbean export in industries. Like its counterpart idea about "competitive insertion" it supports the notion that neoliberal globalization is well advanced in irreversibly reducing or eliminating national barriers to the international flow of goods, services, capital, money, and information (Bernal, 2000).

Neither of these perspectives on Caribbean development demonstrates any sensible understanding of capital-labor class relations and the structure of power in the Caribbean. A proper estimation and appreciation of the class relations and power structure are absolutely necessary to formulate effective transformative economic policies. The Caribbean scholars holding on to the old ideas of neoliberal globalization are keeping company with the global institutions created at Bretton Woods. These institutions were established to maintain macro-economic stability in the world capitalist system, but the neoliberal counter-revolutionaries remodeled them to become debt collectors. They have lost their focus but are holding on to their failed economic theories and policies (Stiglitz, 2018).

Trumpism and Brexit are disemboweling neoliberal globalization, but the IMF and World Bank continue to pedal their "snake oil" policies in the developing countries. The Caribbean states must support the break-up of neoliberal globalization for selfish reasons. They will gain a new lease on life to exercise their economic independence in the NMWO. It is not far-fetched for Caribbean states to actively create an alternative future or another development in the NMWO. These states did not have a voice in formulating the economic policies of neoliberal globalization, but they can definitely play a role in shaping their economic future in the NMWO.

Caribbean academics, political activists, policymakers, working people and their organizations must embrace the challenges of economic realignment. This is critical to redress the class disparities in capital-labor relations and the structure of power in the region. Poverty alleviation, closing the income gap, food security, human rights, agricultural self-sufficiency, industrialization, and social and economic transformation are core issues that economic realignment must redress. Economic realignment must not replace EU and US domination with Chinese or Russian hegemony. This is hardly likely to be the case however because the CARICOM states will have a seat at the table to express their views and to accept or reject the conditions of economic alignment with the BRICS countries. The goal must be a win-win situation that furthers the economic development interests of the Caribbean. The constant US attacks on China and Russia however pose the strongest challenge to Caribbean economic realignment. US media networks are filled with articles, blogs, reports, and shows that target China as a negative force in the Caribbean. The CARICOM states have to sift through this deluge of information while being aware that the US is at war with its principal competitors.

Structure of book

Chapter 2 sets out the imperialist frameworks of capitalist development in the Caribbean that propelled the CARICOM states into the NMWO. Since their creation as colonies by medieval European feudal powers the CARICOM states have experienced five phases of US imperialism. These phases are analyzed focusing on the rise of the Monroe Doctrine, the US' capture of economic dominance in Latin America from European powers after World War I, the period between the end of the World War II and the end of the cold war, the neoliberal era in which the US was the sole superpower, and the current period of the new multipolarity. It critiques the erroneous claim that the US is disengaging from the globe, and analyses the emergence of the Caribbean as a periphery entrapped by center-periphery relations. It takes the position that the new multipolarity places the politically independent Caribbean states in the best position since their creation to shape the political economy of the region in their self-interest. The NMWO provides an opportunity for the CARICOM countries to transcend center-periphery relations and enter into a new era of social and economic development.

Chapter 3 assesses US imperialism in the CARICOM under the "new American century" doctrine. That period was characterized by a US-led unipolar neoliberal global order, in which the "Project for the New American Century" (PNAC) a US neoconservatives thinktank outlined the blueprint for America's global hegemony. The ideals of the new American century included the defeat of terrorism as defined by America, the US' preemptive military strikes against rouge states, and a financial war to starve terrorist organizations of resources. The US dragged the Caribbean states and their institutions into its war on terrorism. But, the US itself is engaged in terrorist acts in the region which Caribbean counter-terrorism strategies must address.

Chapter 4 focuses attention on the CARICOM in the era of US imperialism depicted as "make America great again." The MAGA doctrine emerged in the new multipolar world order, and seemingly is reflective of the recognition that the US has lost ground globally and must share power on the world stage with China, Russia, and the EU. It is dismantling the neoliberal global order, fueling white supremacy, American nationalism, and promoting divisions in the CARICOM over Venezuela and China's belt and road initiative.

Chapter 5 explores the dynamic nature of the theoretical debates on the new multipolar world order and analyzes its characteristic features. It outlines the proposition and argument in support of the emergence of the new multipolarity. Chapter 6 analyzes some pertinent theoretical frameworks that accompanied capitalist development in the Caribbean. The theoretical trajectory and corresponding policies associated with capitalist development in the Caribbean evolved through mercantilism, classical political economy, Marxism, neo-classicism, and Keynesianism. Theoretical challenges to the ideas underlying colonial policy, the neoliberal counter-revolution that derailed development theory, and the new thinking on development are analyzed.

The focus shifts in Chapter 7 to a discussion on the CARIFORUM-EU EPA and Brexit. A descriptive analysis is presented on the social, economic, and political circumstances that stimulated the formation of the EU, CARIFORUM, the EPA, and Brexit. It presents a case for the renegotiation of the CARIFORUM-EU EPA on the basis that Brexit has changed the dynamics of Caribbean representation in the EU.

The topic of neoliberal financialization in the Caribbean is explored in Chapter 8. There it is argued that the Caribbean has erected a subservient

12 *Introducing an alternative development idea*

financial architecture in accordance with neoliberal financialization, whereas the community is better served by recalibrating its financial system in line with the BRICS' New Development Bank (NDB) and China's BRI.

Caribbean agriculture in the new multipolar world order is analyzed in Chapter 9, where the focus is on the problems of the sector as the region remains trapped in the colonial agricultural framework, and trade arrangements such as the Caribbean Basin Initiative (CBI), and the CARIFORUM-EU EPA. Caribbean agricultural policy needs to be brought into the NMWO by embracing the terms provided by the BRI.

The focus in Chapter 10 is on PetroCaribe and the CARICOM-China development alternatives. The US utilizes its entire arsenal of weapons – military intervention, economic sanctions, political propaganda, destabilization, sabotage, diplomacy, and military threats to defeat development alternatives in the Caribbean. The US' efforts to destroy PetroCaribe must sound warning to the CARICOM-China development alternative projects.

Chapter 11 analyzes the policies formulated by China and the US for the Caribbean and possible effects of US–China relations on the CARICOM. Security concerns dominate US policy toward the Caribbean, unlike China's which is more focused on economic development. Negative US–China relations can have a debilitating effect on CARICOM–China relations and development projects.

The concluding Chapter 12 presents ideas on the Caribbean economic policies for the new multipolar world order. The view is that a state directed private sector model driven by a true concern for economic development rather than profit has to form the foundation of the CARICOM's economic policy in the new multipolarity. The state has to remain in the control of working people which must systematically guide economic expansion to eradicate inequality, poverty and advance the economic well-being of Caribbean people.

References

Allison, G. (2020). "The New Spheres of Influence: Sharing the Globe with other Great Powers," *Foreign Affairs*, March/April: 30–40.

Bernal, R.L. (2000). "The Caribbean in the International System: Outlook for the First 20 Years of the 21st Century," pp. 295–325 in Kenneth Hall, K. and D. Benn (eds.) *Contending with Destiny: The Caribbean in the 21st Century*. Kingston: Ian Randle.

Bernal, R.L. (2017). *A Caribbean Policy for the Trump Administration*. Washington DC: Center for Strategic and International Studies.

Canterbury, D.C. (2012). *European Bloc Imperialism*. Chicago, IL: Haymarket Publishers.

CARICOM. (2018). *Annual Report of the Secretary-General 2013*. Turkeyen Guyana: Caribbean Community Secretariat.

Center for Strategic and International Studies (CSIS). (2019). *Are the United States and China in an Ideological Competition?* Washington DC. 13 December.

DeMuth, C. and W. Kristol (eds.) (1995). *The Neoconservative Imagination: Essays in Honor of Irvine Kristol.* Washington: The AEI Press.

ECLAC. (2019). *Economic Survey of Latin America and the Caribbean 2019. The New Global Financial Context: Effects and Transmission Mechanisms in the Region.* Santiago: United Nations.

Harvey, D. (2003). *The New Imperialism.* Oxford and New York: Oxford University Press.

Jessop, D. (2017). "Russia's Growing Interest in the Caribbean," *Caribbean Intelligence,* 10 October.

Kagan, R. (2003). *Of Paradise and Power: America and Europe in the New World Order.* New York: Vintage Books.

Kagan, R. and W. Kristol (eds.) (2000). *Present Dangers: Crisis and Opportunity in American Foreign and Defense Policy.* New York: Encounter Books.

Kagan, D., G. Schmitt, and T. Donnelly (2000). *Rebuilding America's Defenses: Strategy, Forces and Resources for a New Century.* Washington DC: Project for a New American Century.

Mattis, J. (2018). *Summary of the 2018 National Defense Strategy of the United States of America: Sharpening the American Military's Competitive Edge.* US Department of Defense Washington DC.

Nogueira, U.B. (1997). *The Integration Movement in the Caribbean at Crossroads: Towards a New Approach of Integration.* Buenos Aires, Argentina: Inter-American Development Bank, Institute for the Integration of Latin America and the Caribbean, Working Paper Series 1.

Noonan, M. (2017). *Marxist Theories of Imperialism: A History.* London and New York: I.B. Tauris and Company, Limited.

Petras, J. and H. Veltmeyer. (2001).). *Globalization Unmasked: Imperialism in the 21st Century.* London: Zed Boks.

Petras, J. and H. Veltmeyer (with Contributions by P. Bowles, D. Canterbury, N. Girvan, and D. Tetreault). (2014). *Extractive Imperialism in the Americas: Capitalism's New Frontier.* Leiden and Boston: Brill.

Petras, J. and H. Veltmeyer (2018). *Imperialism and Capitalism in the Twenty-First Century: A System in Crisis.* London and New York: Routledge.

Saunders, P. (2020). "US Embrace of Great Power Competition Also Means Contending With Spheres of Influence," *Russia Matters,* Harvard Kennedy School, Belfer Center for Science and International Affairs, 13 February.

Stiglitz, J.E. (2018). *Globalization and Its Discontents Revised: Anti-Globalization in the Era of Trump.* London and New York: W.W. Norton.

Thomas, C.Y. (1988). *The Poor and the Powerless: Economic Policy and Change in the Caribbean.* New York: Monthly Review.

Thomas, C.Y. (2001). "On Reconstructing a Political Economy of the Caribbean," pp. 498–520 in Meeks, B. and F. Lindahl (eds.) *New Caribbean Thought: A Reader.* Jamaica, Barbados Trinidad and Tobago: The University of the West Indies Press.

Wong, E. (2019). "US Versus China: A New Era of Great Power Competition, but Without Boundaries," *The New York Times,* 26 June.

2 The imperialist frameworks of Caribbean development

Introduction

The political economy of English-speaking Caribbean Community states has been molded within the frameworks of European and US imperialisms. Without much fanfare however, the English-speaking Caribbean Community states were propelled into the new multipolar world order (NMWO) in the early twenty-first century. The imperialist frameworks through which they traveled to arrive at the current stage of their historical evolution as nation-states are the subject of analysis in this chapter. They started off as colonies of European feudal imperial powers in the post-Columbian era entrapped in a mercantilist colonial slave economy or colonial slave mode of production and subsequently center–periphery relations in the industrial capitalist epoch (Thomas 1974, 1984, 1988). The US joined in the imperialist domination of the Caribbean simultaneously as the transition occurred from the colonial slave mode of production to center–periphery relations. The broader theoretical issue here concerns the development of capitalist center–periphery relations concurrently with US imperialism. This issue is addressed through an analysis of the trajectory of Caribbean development in its transition from the colonial slave mode of production to center–periphery relations.

The argument is the Caribbean Community and Common Market (CARICOM) states grew-up in five phases of US imperialism, the first beginning in the nineteenth century up to the end of World War I. The second period immediately followed that war when the US positioned itself to create a situation of dependence by European imperial powers on American capital in the then imperialist multipolar world order as the US took power from Europe in Latin America. In the third phase from the close of World War II to the end of the cold war US imperialism operated in a bipolar world order in which it competed with the former Union of Soviet Socialist Republics (USSR) for global hegemony. The collapse of the former Soviet Union ushered in the fourth phase when the US became the sole hyper-imperial power in a unipolar world order founded on US-led neoliberal globalization. The fifth and current phase of US imperialism is characterized by the dismantling of neoliberal globalization under Trumpian nationalism, and power-sharing in the NMWO.

DOI: 10.4324/9781003092414-2

The argument is presented in three parts beginning with an analysis of the rise and evolution of US imperialism. Thereafter, the analysis pivots to the alleged US disengagement from the globe because Trumpian nationalism is dismantling neoliberal globalization (Chollet, 2016; Kapalan, 2017). The argument here is that Trumpian nationalism is the current manifestation of US imperialism. Center–periphery relations and US imperialism are analyzed in the following section in which it is propositioned inter alia that the Caribbean only became a periphery, and Europe and the US centers in political and economic relations, to facilitate capitalist development in general and in the Caribbean in particular. In the NMWO, despite Zala's (2017) redefinition of polarity, the CARICOM states can transcend the center–periphery enigma and enter into a new win–win era of even, equal and just, social and economic development.

Rise and evolution of US imperialism

US imperialism was a late comer on the stage of global capitalism whose first phase includes ideas associated with the Monroe Doctrine, Charles A. Conant, the Platt Amendment, and the Roosevelt Corollary. Conant (1898) presented the best known economic justification for US imperialism, even before J.A. Hobson's (1902) treatise on the subject. Conant (1898) believed finding employment for US capital was the greatest problem US capitalism faced. The solution to ease the "congestion of capital" in the US was for America to use its military power to pry-open and maintain overseas territories (Conant, 1898). According to Conant (1898), the international economic environment was founded on Darwinian notions of "the law of self-preservation" and "the survival of the fittest." This required the US to use its military to force other countries to do business with American corporations to boost capital accumulation in the US (Conant, 1898). Conant (1898) believed that imperialism was "a natural law of economic and race development" which was necessary to employ surplus saving accrued from mechanized production. In his view, Africa, Asia, Latin America, and the Caribbean were the destinations of US surplus capital or outlets for investments and therefore the areas to be pried-open by US military forces to maintain social stability and thwart social revolution in America (Conant, 1898).

According to Conant (1898), the added advantage of US imperialism was that it brought socio-economic prosperity to the underdeveloped states in those geographic regions. The pursuit of imperial policies was the surest way the US would end its isolation and join the scramble by European powers to command new markets around the world. The survival of US capitalism depended on these new markets and new opportunities to invest American surplus capital. Advocacy of US imperialism had nothing to do with "sentiment," it was the means for the US to assert its right to free markets opened up around the world (Conant, 1898).

According to Conant (1898), it was debatable whether American imperialism required US "direct government" of foreign lands, however "on the economic side of the question there is but one choice." The economic argument for US imperialism was outlined as follows: the US must either enter by various means the competition for the employment of American capital and enterprise in foreign countries, or alternatively "continue the needless duplication of existing means of production and communication" (Conant, 1898). If the latter option was adopted the glut of unconsumed products will invoke trade stagnation and a "steadily declining return upon investments" (Conant, 1898). American imperialism operates on the basis of US self-preservation and Trumpian nationalism is vocal about this fact with its "America first" stance.

US imperialist designs on the Western Hemisphere promulgated in the Monroe Doctrine in 1823, were cemented by Conant (1898). The Monroe Doctrine determined that European powers could not increase their influence or re-colonize any independent country in the Western Hemisphere. Then, the Platt Amendment in 1901 outlined the guidelines for US–Cuba relations, which were incorporated into the 1902 Cuban constitution which effectively made Cuba a US colony. The Platt Amendment was abrogated in 1934, but not before the US used it on occasions to invade Cuba, install friendly governments, or protect US investments in the island.

Meanwhile, with the Roosevelt Corollary in 1904, the US applied a "big stick" in its economic and political relations with Latin America and the Caribbean. The US arrogated for itself the role of regional police in the Western Hemisphere. It pledged to intervene in any country in the region to ensure it paid its debt to international creditors, did not violate the rights of the US, or invited "foreign aggression to the detriment of the entire body of American nations" (Roosevelt, 1904). The US increased its use of military force in Latin American and the Caribbean, under the pretext of maintaining hemispheric stability. President Roosevelt declared the US would exercise international police power in "flagrant cases of wrongdoing or impotence" in the world (Roosevelt, 1904). The Roosevelt Corollary had little to do with the relations between the US and Europe. It served as justification for US military interventions in Cuba, Nicaragua, Haiti, and the Dominican Republic (DR).

The second phase of American imperialism was characterized by the US taking over the political economy of Latin America from European powers in particular England and France. The US was outside the global imperialist arena until after the Spanish American War in 1898, the same year that Conant (1898) justified US military actions abroad as a means to spread American capital. The US invasion of Mexico and Central America at the beginning of the twentieth century under the aegis of "dollar diplomacy" and the "big stick" policy were key indicators that America had arrived as an imperialist power. But, it was only during and after World War I America became a first-rate industrial power, when America positioned itself to bring European imperial powers into a state of dependence on US capital, and took power from the Europeans in South America.

According to Novack (1941), the US portrayed itself as a "guardian of peace, an apostle of civilization, the defender of democracy, the patron of humanity" (Novack, 1941), as it intervened toward the close of World War I to decide the outcome and dictate the terms of peace. Then, "Washington-Wall Street played the role of 'benevolent dictator' toward defeated Europe" (Novack, 1941). The US emerged from the war as the chief capitalist victor and its ruling class rushed to the rescue of European capitalism by helping to thwart social revolution in Europe, stabilizing European economies, and repairing their vital structures (Novack, 1941). American banks forced Europe to "acknowledge Wall Street's financial supremacy and to pay a heavy tribute," and "usurped England's lordship over the world market and stock exchanges" (Novack, 1941). The US harvested golden fruits from this policy until the stock market crash in 1929 when American assets in Europe became liabilities and the US turned its focus on its domestic economy (Novack, 1941).

Novack (1941), argues the stock market crash freed European capital from American enslavement and created an opening for the rise of German, Italian, and Japanese imperialisms primarily through militarization. The US joined in the militarization process and shifted to a wartime basis in the 1940s under the impact of the spread of inter-imperialist conflict. The militarization speedup reached "all departments of national activity: domestic and foreign politics, military affairs, industry, culture, entertainment, domestic life" (Novack, 1941).

As British capital declined due to the imperialist war of 1914–1918, US imperialism gained momentum in South America. Justo (1940) noted that prior to the war British capital controlled railroads, banks, insurance companies, ports, and lines of maritime and river navigation across the continent. They controlled the extraction of petroleum in Peru, tin in Bolivia, the nitrate industry in Chile, abattoirs, ranches, lumbering, waterpower companies, telephones, trolley cars in Argentina, coffee in Brazil, and electric companies, and provided the greater part of the national, provincial, and municipal loans in those countries.

According to Justo (1940), the US gained huge petroleum concessions in Venezuela, Bolivia, and Peru, began large-scale exploitation in the copper mines of Chile and Peru and acquired from the British control of the Chilean nitrate industry. It started to compete with Argentina and Uruguay for the industrialization of the meat industry, began to finance coffee plantations in Colombia, and established tanneries in Paraguay. It seized large parts of South America's electric industry, gained enormous concessions in Brazil's rubber industry, and acquired the interests of British telephone companies in some Latin American countries (Justo, 1940). Its automobiles and buses invaded the South American market in competition with British railroads, as did the industrial plants its corporations built in the region (Justo, 1940). It established maritime navigation boundaries in South America as well as an extensive network of aerial communications spanning the entire continent, while the leading US banks started branches in various countries in the subcontinent (Justo, 1940).

Justo (1940) noted that the US became the principal exporter to South America, US capital there increased, by 1200 percent from 1919 to 1930,

18 The imperialist frameworks

and the subcontinent became the US' principal "sphere of influence." The US began militarizing Latin America through military missions in several countries, providing them with warships, building extensive network of aerial communications extending throughout Latin America, and using its aerial squadrons to carry out raids on the continent (Justo, 1940). The US created "good neighbor fleets" to stimulate the US–Latin America carrying trade, and loans were granted to Latin American governments for highway construction on the continent (Justo, 1940). The US exerted pressure on these countries to implement measures against its European and Asian rivals (Justo, 1940).

In its third phase from the close of World War II to the end of the cold war US imperialism operated in a bipolar world order. The collapse of European empires created international power vacuums that the US and USSR rivaled each other to fill in the aftermath of the war. Luce (1999) saw the opportunity for a new American century (Meyer, and Steinberg (2004). The competition ushered in the cold war two years following the end of World War II (Sullivan, 2008). Sullivan (2008) chronicled several iterations of US imperialism since the end of World War II. US imperialism extended into Europe, Greece, Italy, the Middle East, and East Asia, Indochina or South Asia, Africa, South America, the Caribbean, and Central America during the cold war (Sullivan, 2008). Competing with the USSR, the US engaged in coups, counter-coups, military invasions, sabotage, assassinations, arm-twisting, threats, and intimidation in these countries and geographic areas.

Neoliberal globalization constituted the fourth phase of US imperialism in which America became the sole hyper-power in a unipolar world order. This phase emerged after the collapse of European communism between 1989 and 1991 which signaled the end of the cold war. The US emerged as global hegemon coercing socialist/communists states, and Third World dictatorships it propped-up as buffers to socialism/communism, to convert to liberal democracy and free market economies. Francis Fukuyama (1992) hailed this development as the "end of history," while Henry Kissinger opined that no other great empire had ever achieved the preeminence that America enjoyed (Bellamy-Foster, 2003).

The US ruling class declared that a "New World Order" had emerged after the collapse of Eastern European communism. The US attempted to redefine international political and economic relations to reflect the end of three worlds – first (capitalist), second (communists), and third (former European colonies in Africa, Asia Pacific, and Latin America and the Caribbean) – and the beginning of a new unipolar globe under its single will and hegemony in a new American century (Kagan et al., 2000; Mian, 2005). President George Bush, Jr., took US hegemony to new heights in his second-term inaugural speech when he linked US national security to global "freedom."

President Bush's policy to preemptively launch military attacks on countries the US determined "rogue states" requiring "regime change" was a precursor to his declaration that linked "freedom" and US national security. These anti-terrorism measures were a particular dimension of the new imperialism represented as globalization especially after the attacks on the US on September 11, 2001. The US imperial "war on terrorism" was and remains compatible with the expansionary agendas of the US business classes. Evidently, US companies reaped significant economic gains in the imperialist "war on terrorism" against Iraq (Petras and Veltmeyer, 2001).

The US imperialist strategy linked with its "war on terrorism" operated on the bases that "regime change" required the total destruction and rebuilding of "rogue states." The US seizes assets, eliminate opposition, establish favorable governments, and control markets and natural resources, in foreign countries. Direct military intervention and informal control through favorable governments such as in Afghanistan and Iraq are not the only techniques used by US imperialism. The US continues cold war tactics such as intimidating political opponents, fomentation of social unrest, and economic sabotage and blackmail. Since 2000, for example, the US influenced the results of elections in Guyana (Canterbury, 2018), Latin American countries, and former Soviet republics, and staged coups in Haiti, Venezuela, and Egypt. Operation Desert Storm in 1991, US military intervention in Somalia 1992–1993, the bombing of the Serbia, and the occupation of Afghanistan and Iraq in 2003, were the strongest indicators the US was the sole global hegemonic power (Noonan, 2017).

The fifth and current phase of US imperialism is manifested under the doctrine of Trumpian nationalism in the NMWO. This is the latest form of US imperialism alleged to be founded on a policy of principled realism, and which gives the false impression that the US is disengaging from the globe (Kaplan, 2017). It holds that the US "will not be held hostage to old dogmas, discredited ideologies, and so-called experts who have been proven wrong over the years" (Kirkey, 2018; Trump, 2018). It supports a slew of pragmatic policy measures, prescriptions, and actions that place US interests first. It is rooted in great powers competition, rabidly anti-communist, anti-terrorist, pro-liberal-democracy, and pro-free market capitalism. It opposes globalism by supporting pretensive actions such as US withdrawals and threats of withdrawals from global agencies and alliances, and international trade and other agreements.

Center–periphery relations and US imperialism

The origin of capital accumulation or primitive accumulation and therefore class distinctions in the Caribbean was in the colonial slave economy or colonial slave mode of production. Primitive accumulation was realized through conquest, plunder, and enslavement rendering it different from its origins in Europe. The European peasantry was estranged from the land that created large pools of labor available for exploitation as an industrial proletariat in the emerging factory system. Thus commenced the process of primitive accumulation in Europe founded on capital–labor relation based on the factory system which transformed the means by which wealth was accumulated with the associated social and property relations.

Capital–labor relations developed in Europe were transferred to the Caribbean, but primitive accumulation in the region took a different path determined by the colonial slave mode of production – slavery with capitalism. In Europe, peasants were driven off the land to work in factories, but the Caribbean never really developed a peasantry in the classical definition of the term. In the Caribbean, the natives were enslaved and exterminated and African slaves and indentured servants brought to replace them and to work the agricultural plantations.

Thus, the Caribbean has not experienced a process where peasants were transformed into an industrial proletariat. Slaves were imported from Africa, and indentured laborers from Africa, China, Europe, and India, to produce agricultural crops and work in sugar factories. The colonial economy was based on slavery and a factory system in which slaves labored. Primitive accumulation, the stage before the development of full-fledged capitalist production relations, therefore, resulted from the exploitation of slaves and indentured labor working in plantation agriculture involving the cultivation of sugar cane and its manufacture in factories into sugar. It was only after the abolition of that system with the elimination of the slave component that full-fledged capitalist capital–labor relations emerged. Thus, primitive accumulation does not only emerge from the evolution of peasants into industrial workers. It also took the form slaves and indentured laborers working in agricultural and factory settings.

Capital accumulation based on the exploitation of freed labor commenced after the collapse of the colonial slave mode of production. That was the first time capital–labor relations in the Caribbean were placed on an equal footing with those in Europe. Then, in both Europe and the Caribbean capital and labor were free to seek employment as their respective owners saw fit. The purchase and sale of labor-power as the principal form of commodity production in the Caribbean took almost 100 years to be accomplished. The process commenced in 1834 with the abolition of slavery, and ended in 1921 when the final batch of indentured servants served out their contracts. The capitalist was free to invest in the most profitable ventures, and the worker was free to sell his labor-power to the purchaser who paid the highest wage. Social and property relations, the accumulation of capital, and capital–labor relation were placed on a different footing in the emergent capitalist mode of production.

The Caribbean became a peripheral region in the international capitalist system at that stage. Hitherto, the colonies were merely extensions of Europe subjected to colonial laws and economic policy. The dynamics of capitalist development incorporates the Caribbean's passage from a colonial slave mode of production, to peripheral status. These dynamics included Europe's acceptance of America's emergence as an imperial power, and the Caribbean's advancement from colony to center–periphery relations, which was a positive development similar to the progression from feudalism to capitalism.

Peripheralization meant the Caribbean was left economically to fend for itself in the international capitalist environment while simultaneously coming under neocolonial oppression. The dynamics of peripheralization involved the struggle for self-rule, political independence, and economic freedom. The struggle comprised various forms of social unrest but primarily strikes and street demonstrations. Its two conflicting dimensions were the Caribbean's fight for freedom, and England's intentions to keep the colonies as neocolonial entities.

Center–periphery relations are therefore based on the conflicting interests of the former colonies seeking economic and political independence, and center states wishing to maintain the status quo of economic and political dominance over the newly independent states. The Caribbean was entrapped in European political and economic molds as it transitioned from the colonial slave mode of production in which it supplied raw materials to Europe. When it entered into center–periphery relations it depended on the very production, consumption, and export–import trade arrangements that existed under the colonial slave mode of production. The politics of the region were also founded on the periphery of the international capitalist system, while those of Europe were at its center. That was the political economy arrangement in which Caribbean countries pursued nationhood.

The conflict over the domestic economy and state power was broadened to include working people. The principal actors in this conflict included the colonial authorities, domestic plantation interests, and the emergent middle and working classes. Hitherto, agricultural interests dominated the colonial state and the conflict over state power was between local plantation farmers and the colonial authorities in Europe. The social dynamics began to change as former slaves and indentured servants staked their claims in the political and economic affairs of the colonies. It was clear that economic and political power over the Caribbean resided in Europe, while domestic power was merely an appendage in that colonial power-dynamics.

The transition to full-fledged capital–labor relations brought about changes in social and property relations and capital accumulation in which independent Caribbean states became mere appendages to European colonial powers. The Caribbean could be classified as peripheral with a different set of economic and political interests in the international economic system, compared with those of the European colonial powers at the center. The imperial relations reflected the emergent center–periphery dynamics that sped up the long, painful demise of the plantation agriculture system. Economic diversification however has hardly come about through domestic economic planning but has largely been in response to changes in the capitalist world economy.

The Caribbean's entry into center–periphery relations coincided with the rise of US imperialism. The development of capitalist center–periphery relations in the Caribbean and the historical origins of US imperialism are coterminous. The transition to full-fledged capitalist relations in the Caribbean between 1834 and 1921 went hand-in-hand with the first phase of the rise of US imperialism. The Monroe Doctrine in 1823, the Spanish American War in 1898, Conant's ideas on US imperialism, the Platt

Amendment in 1901, the Roosevelt Corollary in 1904, and the rise of US capital in South America as a consequence of World War I, were early building blocks of US imperialism and the peripheralization of the Caribbean.

Conclusion

There is indication that individual Caribbean countries are willing to step outside the imperialist framework in which they were created and entraps them, to cultivate economic relations with the BRICS (Brazil, Russia, India, China, South Africa) countries. Seemingly, Caribbean states are waking up to the new multipolarity, but the bigger issue is the formulation of a CARICOM-wide development strategy that embraces the opportunities the BRICS provide. A CARICOM regional approach to the BRICS versus individual countries going it alone can strengthen the collective contributions of the Caribbean in defining the region's economic realignment toward an alternative development framework.

About a third of Caribbean countries have joined China's Belt and Road Initiative (BRI), having bilateral investment treaties with China (Devonshire-Ellis, 2019). China has signed Double Tax Treaties with Barbados, Cuba, Jamaica, and Trinidad and Tobago to prevent profit from being taxed twice on either side. This reduces the taxes and duties paid on specific products and services and "allow profits tax to be mitigated against by use of withholding taxes rates which are typically lower" (Devonshire-Ellis, 2019).

Antigua and Barbuda, Barbados, Dominica, Dominican Republic (DR), Guyana, Jamaica, Suriname, and Trinidad and Tobago have individually signed on to the Belt and Road Initiative (BRI). In the case of Antigua and Barbuda the BRI signed in 2018 is intended to open up "unimpeded trade and investment flows," expand "the use of local currency in investment and trade," and encourage "industry to build industrial parks and special economic and trade zones" (Devonshire-Ellis, 2019). Through the BRI roads, bridges, civil aviation, ports, energy, and telecommunications will be built in Antigua and Barbuda. Barbados has been considering providing financial services for Chinese businesses, and its financial sector has been lobbying the Barbados government to allow development in this area (Devonshire-Ellis, 2019). Dominica, the smallest of the regional BRI partners, is seeking assistance with protection against global warming and climate change (Devonshire-Ellis, 2019). The DR negotiated a US$600M loan with the China Export–Import Bank to upgrade power distribution, and it is believed the figure could reach US$3.1Bn through a package of investments and low-interest loans (Devonshire-Ellis, 2019).

Grenada participated in BRI forums but has not signed on to an agreement, while Guyana signed on in 2018 with provisions for cooperation in the areas of policy coordination, facilities connectivity, trade and investment, finance and integration, and the national broadband network (Devonshire-Ellis, 2019). Projects in Guyana for BRI funding include design and construction of roads, harbors, the Linden–Lethem highway, and a new Demerara Harbor Bridge. Previously China funded marine vessels that ply the Essequibo River between Parika and Supenaam, constructed the Guyana International Conference Center, and provided vehicles and equipment for the Guyana Police Force (Devonshire-Ellis, 2019).

Jamaica joined the BRI in 2018 but had previously received approximately US$2.1Bn in funding from China. The funding was primarily for infrastructure including US$400M for road construction, US$300M for road and bridge rehabilitation in 2013, US$457M for the north-south toll road construction, US$327M for road network in 2016, and US$326M for the Southern Coastal Highway Improvement Project in 2017 (Devonshire-Ellis, 2019).

The recent visit by Jamaican Prime Minister Holness to China was hailed as one of the clearest signals of a new era in bilateral relations, made even more evident by the prompt US response to the trip (MacDonald, 2019). US Ambassador to Jamaica Donald Tapia criticized China's role in Jamaica arguing that China will control the narrative when Jamaica fails to keep up with repayment on its loans. The Ambassador's intervention caused *The Gleaner* to editorialized in displeasure that Mr. Tapia "should be given a message about where Jamaica's foreign policy is formulated" (MacDonald, 2019).

Suriname signed on to the BRI in 2018 to enhance cooperation in the fields of infrastructure construction, agriculture, forestry, fishing, law enforcement, human resources, and public health (Devonshire-Ellis, 2019). Trinidad and Tobago also signed the BRI in 2018 to promote practical cooperation in areas such as financing investment, industrial parks, infrastructure, and tourism, reshaping Trinidad and Tobago as the regional center for shipping, logistics, and financing (Devonshire-Ellis, 2019). The BRI Trinidad and Tobago cover the economy, medicine and health, and human resources.

The CARICOM has formed the Caribbean–China Economic and Trade Forum, the Caribbean–China Consultations process and a new mechanism, a standing meeting in the United Nations General Assembly (Devonshire-Ellis, 2019). There is also the China–Community of Latin American and Caribbean States (CELAC) Forum that brings together under a formal banner, China and the CELAC.

It is quite evident that a huge change in the political economy dynamics is occurring in the Caribbean, whose future will be quite different from domination by European powers and the US. The region seems to be evolving along a different path they and their US and European traditional allies have been accustomed to (Devonshire-Ellis, 2019).

The CARICOM and Caribbean ruling elites and academics have thus far failed to provide clear leadership and understanding of the changing dynamics of the new multipolarity, much more to formulate strategies for the region's engagement with it. Instead, individual countries are forging ahead at their own peril, with bilateral agreements with China.

References

Bellamy-Foster, J. (2003). "Imperial America and War," *Monthly Review* 55 (1): 1–10.
Canterbury, D.C. (2018). *Neoextractivism and Capitalist Development*. London and New York: Routledge.
Chollet, D. (2016). "The Myth of American Disengagement," *Defense One*, 20 May.
Conant, C.A. (1898). "The Economic Basis of 'Imperialism,'" *North American Review* 326–340.
Devonshire-Ellis, C. (2019). "China's Belt and Road – The Caribbean and West Indies," *Silk Road Briefing*, 24 May.
Fukuyama, F. (1992). *The End of History and the Last Man*. New York: Free Press.
Hobson, J.A. (1902). *Imperialism: A Study*. New York: James Pott and Company.
Justo, L. (1940). "Inter-Imperialist Struggle for South America," *Fourth International* 1 (7): 182–187.
Kagan, D., G. Schmitt, and T. Donnelly (2000). *Rebuilding America's Defenses: Strategy, Forces and Resources for a New Century*. Washington, DC: Project for a New American Century.
Kaplan, R.D. (2017). "Why Trump Can't Disengage America From the World," *The New York Times*, 6 January.
Kirkey, S. (2018). "Is Donald Trump's 'Principled Realism' a Real Doctrine?" *National Post*, 26 September.
Luce, H.R. (1999). "The American Century," *Diplomatic History* 23 (2): 159–171.
MacDonald, S.B. (2019). "The Shifting Tides in Caribbean International Relations: Jamaica, China and the United States," *Global Americans*, 19 December.
Meyer, S.P., and J. Steinberg (2004). "Henry Luce's Empire of Fascism," *Executive Intelligence Review (EIR)* 31 (25), 25 June.
Mian, Z. (2005). "A New American Century?" Silver City, NM and Washington, DC: *Foreign Policy in Focus*, 4 May.
Noonan, M. (2017). *Marxist Theories of Imperialism: A History*. London and New York: I.B. Tauris and Company.
Novack, W.F. (1941). "The Aims of American Imperialism," *Fourth International* 2 (8): 236–239.
Petras, J., and H. Veltmeyer (2001). *Globalization Unmasked: Imperialism in the 21st Century*. London: Zed Press.
Roosevelt, T. (1904). Annual Message to Congress, 6 December.
Sullivan, M.J. III (2008). *American Adventurism Abroad: Invasions, Interventions, and Regime Changes since World War II*. Malden, MA: Blackwell Publishing.
Thomas, C.Y. (1974). *Dependence and Transformation: The Economics of the Transition to Socialism*. New York: Monthly Review.
Thomas, C.Y. (1984). *Plantations, Peasants and State: A Study of the Mode of Sugar Production in Guyana*. Los Angles: UCLA Center for Afro-American Studies.
Thomas, C.Y. (1988). *The Poor and the Powerless: Economic Policy and Change in the Caribbean*. London and New York: Monthly Review.
Trump, D. (2018). *Remarks to the 73rd Session of the United Nations General Assembly*, New York: *Foreign Policy*, 25 September.
Zala, B. (2017). "Polarity Analysis and Collective Perceptions of Power: The Need for a New Approach," *Journal of Global Security Studies* 2 (1): 2–17.

3 The Caribbean in the "New American Century"

Introduction

The Project for the New American Century (PNAC) a US neoconservatives think tank outlined the blueprint for America to maintain global hegemony in a US-led unipolar global order in the twenty-first century. The neoconservatives occupied key policy positions in the US government and global institutions to implement their plans. They assessed the present dangers in terms of crisis and opportunity in American foreign and defense policy, and identified the strategy, forces, and resources for rebuilding America's defenses for a new American century. The US war on terrorism became central to the ideals of the new American century. The US defined "terrorism" to suit its interest, declared the policy of preemptive military strikes, and launched a financial war on terrorism. The Caribbean was dragged into the US fight against "terrorism" a term also defined especially to suit regional conditions. The Caribbean Financial Action Task Force (CFATF) embraced the war, as the US arm-twisted the Caribbean Community and Common Market (CARICOM) states to join in the fight. Meanwhile, the US has been involved in terrorist activities in the Caribbean prompting the need for a regional strategy to counter US terrorism.

The condition of unipolarity in the CARICOM is elucidated including US terrorism, bullying, threats, and sanctions that existed before the transition to the new multipolar world order. It is argued that the US war on terrorism had two main political effects on the CARICOM states. First, the unilateral declaration of war on Iraq by the US, and America's positions on maritime security and Haiti divided the CARICOM states. Second, in a *quid pro quo* America promised economic assistance to CARICOM states if they supported the war on terrorism, and when failed to do so the US arm-twisted them to secure their backing.

The global hegemon

Toward the close of the twentieth century as the cold war ended the US was catapulted into a position of unprecedented global hegemonic power. This new situation for America led the neoconservatives to create the PNAC that formulated a statement of principles in which they pledged to confidently advance a strategic vision of America's role in the world and global leadership. They declared the twenty-first century, as the "new American century" meaning the US will dominate the globe for the next 100 years and beyond (DeMuth and Kristol, 1995; Kagan, 2003; Kagan and Kristol, 2000; Kagan, Schmitt, and Donnelly, 2000; PNAC, 1997). The PNAC doctrine represented the arrogance US neoconservative harbored against non-Americans whom they intended to dominate in a world characterized by a community of nation-states. The grand vision of the PNAC was to promote their moral principles globally, and cleanse humanity of ethical intransigence. The community of nation-states would then come under US political, economic, and military control in a single global order in which America alone is hegemon.

The PNAC supported three principal propositions – "American leadership is good both for America and the world; that such leadership requires military strength, diplomatic energy, and commitment to moral principle; and that too few [American] political leaders [were] making the case for global leadership" (PNAC, 1997). The PNAC ideologues occupied senior policy positions in President George W. Bush, Jr., Administration and global institutions where they had the opportunity to implement their sinister plans for US global domination. The PNAC argued the US led the West to victory in the cold war and now stood as the world's most preeminent power. This position provided the US with an opportunity and a challenge exemplified in two key questions. "Does the United States have the vision to build upon the achievement of past decades? Does the United States have the resolve to shape a new century favorable to American principles and interests?" (PNAC, 1997).

The PNAC reasoned that the US needed a strong military "ready to meet both present and future challenges," with corresponding foreign policy to "boldly and purposefully promote American principles abroad," along with "a national leadership that accepts the United States' global responsibility" (PNAC, 1997). The PNAC believed the "history of the past century should have taught" the US "it was important to shape circumstances before crises emerge, and to meet threats before they become dire," and "to embrace the cause of American leadership" (PNAC, 1997).

The PNAC creed was pursued in a historical period demarcated by the end of a bipolar world order. That order was characterized by the capitalist economic system and its attendant liberal political institutions, and the socialist/communist economic approach and its associated political organizations. The struggle between these two blocs for global dominance was referred to as the cold war which commenced in the early years after World War II ended. The triumph of capitalism over communism in the cold war was celebrated as the "end of history" (Fukuyama, 1992). The "clash of civilizations" thesis emerged in which European and Anglo-American cultural hegemony was predicted to be maintained in the aftermath of communism's defeat, through conquest of Muslims and Chinese, and suppression of anti-western tribal skirmishes in India and Africa (Huntington, 2011)

The PNAC was not the first time that class forces in the US presented formal proposals for America's domination of the globe. The PNAC merely echoed Henry Robinson Luce's manifesto in 1941 (Luce, 1999; Meyer and Steinberg, 2004; Mian, 2005). The anticipated defeat of fascism and power vacuum post-World War II led Luce to a startling conclusion: "Americans must accept whole-heartedly our duty and our opportunity as the most powerful and vital nation in the world and in consequence to exert upon the world the full impact of our influence for such purpose as we see fit and by such means as we see fit" (quoted in Meyer and Steinberg, 2004).

Luce, an ardent admirer and promoter of Benito Mussolini, formed the Congress for Cultural Freedom (CCF) to implement his plan for the American century. According to Meyer and Steinberg (2004), the "explicit purpose" of the CCF "was to launch a fascist assault on truth as science and on Classical culture." The American century in Luce's view was essential, what he perceived as the duty and responsibility of Anglo-Americans to dominate the globe. Luce is therefore considered the patriarch of the neoconservatives that controlled political power in the US under the Bush administration. The goal of US dominance is still in vogue but disguised as nationalism under the Trump Administration which has launched an assault on science, facts, and basic Western values it purports to be defending.

The US neoconservatives ideologues believe 9/11 marked "the end of the age of geopolitics and the advent of a new age – the era of global politics" (Daalder and Lindsay, 2003). This change presented the US with the challenge to use its "unrivaled military, economic, and political power to fashion an international environment conducive to its interests and values" (Daalder and Lindsay, 2003). Geography, was no longer the pivot of US foreign policy, but "America's unrivalled power in world affairs and the extensive and growing globalization of world politics" (Daalder and Lindsay, 2003). The US was "the only truly global power" with "military reach – whether on land, at sea, or in the air – to every point on the globe" (Daalder and Lindsay, 2003). The US "economic prowess [fueled] world trade and industry," and its "political and cultural appeal ... is so extensive that most international institutions reflect American interests" (Daalder and Lindsay, 2003).

The US war on terrorism

The US military and financial war on terrorism was an important dimension of the PNAC doctrine which privileged politics over economics with the argument that democratic freedom was essential for economic prosperity. Terrorism was considered an obstacle to freedom, democracy, and economic prosperity. Its defeat and replacement with democracy was essential for economic development. There is no universally acceptable definition of terrorism, and the United Nations does not have a general convention on the term. The US however has its own definitions of terrorism and terrorists which it imposes on the globe.

US definitions of terrorism

The US State Department Counterterrorism Office in its report on patterns of global terrorism in 2000 states "no one definition of terrorism has gained universal acceptance" (US Department of State, 2001). Nevertheless, the US State Department used "the definition of terrorism contained in Title 22 of the United States Code, Section 2656 f (d)" to compile its global terrorism report – a definition the US government has used for statistical and analytical purposes since 1983 (US Department of State, 2001). That US Statute defines terrorism in the following ways: "The term 'terrorism' means premeditated, politically motivated violence perpetrated against noncombatant targets by sub national groups or clandestine agents, usually intended to influence an audience. The term 'international terrorism' means terrorism involving citizens or the territory of more than one country. The term 'terrorist group' means any group practicing, or that has significant subgroups that practice, international terrorism" (US Department of State, 2001).

The four pillars of US counterterrorism policy are first no concessions and deals are to be made with terrorists. Second, the terrorists must be brought to justice for their crimes. Third, states that sponsor terrorism must be isolated and pressure applied to them to force them to change their behavior. Fourth, the counterterrorism capabilities of states that work with the US and require assistance must be bolstered (US Department of State, 2001). The US pledged its commitment to implement its National Strategy for Combating Terrorism to defeat terrorist organizations that have a global reach by attacking their sanctuaries; leadership; command, control, and communications; material support; and finances (US Department of State, 2001). The strategy involved the denial of sponsorship, support and sanctuary for terrorists, and diminishing the underlying conditions that terrorists seek to exploit (US Department of State, 2001). The US intended to use all the tools at its disposal – diplomatic, law enforcement, intelligence, financial, and military to defend America, its citizens and interests at home and abroad (US Department of State, 2001).

Preemptive military strikes

In the aftermath of the 9/11 attacks, the Bush administration recast its national security policy by placing greater emphasis on preemptive military strikes that is to attack the preceived enemy first before they attack the US (Mueller et al., 2006). Preemptive military strikes were advocated as a strategy in the Bush war on terror. The doctrine of preemption was formally launched by President Bush in his speech at a graduating class of cadets at West Point in 2002. The problem with this policy is the US could strike another country without necessarily doing so in response to an imminent danger of attack (Daalder and Lindsay, 2004). The US arrogated to itself the right to use force to oust leaders of foreign countries it dislikes long before they could threaten America (Daalder and Lindsay, 2004).

The preemptive strike doctrine was based on two assumptions the first being US technology would make it easy for Americans to defeat their adversaries and second it is cheaper to pursue war with those advance technologies. The new technologies allow the US to have "access to reliable intelligence about the intentions and capabilities of potential adversaries" (Daalder and Lindsay, 2004). Modern spy technology would allow the US to look into secret weapons sites from the air, and listen to conversations and other communications without being detected (Daalder and Lindsay, 2004). But, that assumption was laid bare by the war in Iraq, which was executed on false intelligence. The belief that the technological edge by the US lowered the cost of war, was also falsified by the high cost of the war in Iraq (Daalder and Lindsay, 2004).

The financial war on terrorism

The financial war on terrorism aimed to defeat terrorist organizations by cutting their sources of funding through banking regulations and by denying organizations suspected of financing terrorists access to banks (Warde, 2008). Terrorist organizations were treated like any commercial endeavor that needed access to finance and means of money transfer to sustain their activities. They were assumed to need funds to procure and use weapons and to pay for their daily operations (Ryder, 2015). The Patriot Act gives US authorities power to monitor financial institutions for money laundering (US Department of Justice, 2001). The institutional structure of the financial war on terror include the Terrorist Financing Tracking Program (TFTP) and the Financial Crimes Enforcement Network (FinCEN) that focus their attention on money laundering and financial crimes.

The US authorities used the TFTP to covertly access financial transactions on the international Society for Worldwide Interbank Financial Telecommunication (SWIFT) network (Lichtblau and Risen, 2006). Financial institutions legally obtain secure, standardized, and reliable information on financial transactions globally, through the SWIFT network. They are provided with SWIFT Codes – Business Identifier Codes previously known as Bank Identifier Codes to facilitate the legal sending and receiving of money. The TFTP was accused of violating financial privacy laws in the US and European Union by accessing information on financial transactions without obtaining in advance search warrants to access financial data (Köppel, 2011).

FinCEN a bureau of the US Treasury Department through the US Patriot Act, collects and analyzes information about financial transactions to combat domestic and international money laundering, terrorist financing, and other financial crimes. Its mission is to thwart the unlawful use of the financial system to launder money and promote US national security.

The UN's Security Council Resolution 1373 which calls on all states to prevent and suppress the financing of all terrorist acts is another mechanism in the financial war on terror (United Nations, 2001). Also, the Financial Action Task Force (FATF) established as an intergovernmental organization by the G-7 in 1989, develops policies to fight against money laundering. The mandate of the FATF was expanded after the 9/11 attacks to embrace the fight against the financing of terrorism. The FATF's recommendations are recognized as the global anti-money laundering and counter-terrorist financing standards (FATF, 2019).

The Caribbean in the US "war on terrorism"

This section focuses on the definition of terrorism in the Caribbean, the US' arm-twisting of CARICOM states for support, the issue of US terrorism in the Caribbean, and the notion of counterterrorism.

Defining terrorism in the Caribbean

The CARICOM states were regarded as soft targets for terrorism oriented toward the US, requiring a definition of term suitable to the region. It incorporates "organized criminal gangs whose stated intentions [were] to instill fear and disrupt or change social and work patterns through activity, which usually [involved] drug, firearm, or people smuggling" (Kelshall, 2005). It covers "politically-motivated acts of violence often involving innocent individuals and with drama and fear as main ingredients" (Griffith, 2004). Drug and firearm smuggling, kidnapping, piracy, human trafficking, and internal de-stabilizing groups with international linkages were identified as part of the problem (Kelshall 2005).

These activities are monitored by multiple police, defense force, and intelligence communities. According to Kelshall (2004a), the problem was that these agencies in individual CARICOM countries had different responsibilities in the war on terrorism, each had unique systems, used their own methods, and retained information with little or no sharing of real intelligence. The Caribbean countries were encouraged to develop a united regional approach to fight terrorism to overcome such problems (Kelshall, 2004a).

The rationale for fighting terrorism in the Caribbean is the fortification of the US economic and political interests, and not to safeguard the Caribbean states and peoples. The Caribbean's fight against terrorism was linked to then US dependence on Trinidad and Tobago for liquefied natural gas (LNG) (Kelshall, 2004a, 2004b, 2005). The US reliance on LNG was predicted to constitute about 10 percent of its total energy consumption by 2010, and almost 80 percent of its imports of the product came from Trinidad and Tobago (Kelshall, 2004b). The economics of energy in America was therefore a major factor in the US war on terrorism in the Caribbean. The economic and human resources allocated to fight terrorism in the Caribbean's energy sector were seen to be insufficient and needed to be buttressed (Kelshall, 2004b).

The Caribbean Financial Action Task Force

The CFATF was created to combat money laundering in the region. The CFATF's secretariat was hosted by Trinidad and Tobago, funded by five FATF donor countries, and directed by an official seconded from the UK (CFATF, 1995). The work program of the CFATF Secretariat has three core elements – self-assessment, mutual evaluation, and technical assistance and training (CFATF, 1995). The Secretariat helps to co-ordinate the work carried out to combat money laundering by the United Nations Drug Control Program (UNDCP), the Inter-American Drug Abuse Commission (OAS-CICAD), the United Nations Latin American Institute for the Prevention of Crime and the Treatment of Offenders (ILANUD) and the Commonwealth Secretariat (CFATF, 1995).

The CFATF was brought in line with the US war on terrorism after the 9/11 attacks when extended its mandate to include terrorism and terrorist financing. The CFATF Annual Report for 2001–2002 for the first time since 1994 had a section on "Combating the Financing of Terrorism" (CFATF, 2002). In 2002, the CFATF "collectively considered both the FATF 8 Special Recommendations on Terrorist Financing and the attendant global Self-Assessment Exercise" (CFATF, 2002). The CFATF membership committed to "the enactment of anti-terrorist financing legislation in keeping with the Special Recommendations and completion of the FATF Self-Assessment Questionnaire" (CFATF, 2002). It endorsed the FATF 8 Special Recommendations on Terrorist Financing, and agreed to "participate in the global FATF Self-Assessment Exercise against the FATF Special Recommendations on Terrorist Financing. The CFATF agreed that the remit of the Secretariat to facilitate the provision of technical assistance and training to Member States should be extended to include terrorist financing. The CFATF members agreed to give their consent to the agreement in writing rather than await the Ministerial meeting in October 2002 (CFATF, 2002: 22).

US arm-twisted the CARICOM

The CARICOM expressed its "deepest sympathy and solidarity with the Government and people of the United States of America and with all other countries which lost nationals in the [9/11] attacks, and extend condolences to their families, friends and associates" (CARICOM, 2001). Things soon went downhill as the US arm-twisted Caribbean states to support its positions on maritime security, Iraq and Haiti. The US resorted to threats of economic and political sabotage and destabilization commonly referred to as "sanctions," to force Caribbean states to support its war on terrorism. The US Congress passed the Maritime Transport Security Act (MTSA) in 2002 that increased penalties on vessels and ports that failed to comply with the new rules from the UN International Ship and Port Facility Security (ISPS). The ISPS required all ships and ports to adopt standard security measures to be in compliance with the rules of the agency. Caribbean countries that did not comply had their ports blacklisted which restricted sea trade in the area particularly in perishable agricultural produce, coffee, sugar, bananas, tourist and cruise ship passengers, fuel, and food (Kenney and Meyer, 2004). The arm-twisting of Caribbean countries took another turn with the US invasion of Iraq.

The CARICOM leaders supported the UN's position against the unilateral invasion of Iraq (CARICOM, 2003). They "expressed their profound concern at the escalation of global tensions and their grave implications for the preservation of international peace and security" (CARICOM, 2003). The US responded by dispatching by Mr. Otto Reich the Assistant Secretary of State for the Western Hemisphere to strong-arm regional leaders. Reich threatened Caribbean leaders to get them to change their position on Iraq. On Barbados national television he said: "I would urge CARICOM to study very carefully not only what it says, but also the consequences of what it says. What do I tell a member of Congress, if I go asking for increased access for Caribbean products, 'Well, they did not support us in our time of need?'" (Conkling and Goble, 2004). The CARICOM leaders were also bullied to support the US position on Haiti.

The US wanted the CARICOM to support the illegal Latortue regime in Haiti that overthrew the democratically elected President Jean-Bertrand Aristide (Jasor and Morrow, 2005). US officials Otto Reich, Roger Noriega, and Daniel Fisk threatened CARICOM leaders that "opposition to US foreign policies would not pass unnoticed and could result in unfavorable consequences" (Jasor and Morrow, 2005). The then Bahamian foreign affairs minister remarked that the US had "been pressuring CARICOM countries to invite the interim administration back to the table, arguing that this will help the stability of the Government in Haiti" (Jasor and Morrow, 2005). Barbados, Jamaica, Grenada, the Bahamas, and Antigua and Barbuda broke with the CARICOM on Haiti in support of the US (Jasor and Morrow, 2005).

The Bush Administration demanded that the CARICOM states assured immunity for US citizens before the International Criminal Court due to the illegal war in Iraq (Jamaica Observer, 2003). The Clinton Administration signed the treaty to establish the ICC but the Bush administration nullified the signature, and sought permanent exemption from prosecution (Jamaica Observer, 2003). The US cut military aid to Antigua and Barbuda, Barbados, Belize, Dominica, St Vincent and the Grenadines, and Trinidad and Tobago, because they failed to grant such immunity to its citizens before the July 1, 2003 deadline (Jamaica Observer, 2003).

The Trump Administration is bullying the region on support for Venezuela claiming the US and Caribbean face common terrorist threats by small, but significant, numbers of violent extremists from the region who joined ISIS (Islamic State of Iraq and Syria) (US State Department, 2020). The US reasons that high murder rates, rising crime, and endemic corruption threatens security and good governance in the Caribbean (US State Department, 2020). These factors the US believes drive irregular Caribbean migration to America. The US must "prepare for transnational criminal organizations to shift more of their operations to the Caribbean as a transit point for drugs, migrants, weapons, and other illicit activity" (US State Department, 2020). The Trump State Department promotes partnership with Caribbean governments to strengthen their mutual national security and advance safety "by pursuing programs to dismantle transnational criminal and terrorist organizations, curb the trafficking and smuggling of illicit goods and people, strengthen the rule of law, improve citizen security, and counter vulnerability to terrorist threats" (US State Department, 2020).

President Trump proposes to counter transnational criminal and terrorist organizations by focusing on law enforcement and defense forces. The plan is to support "law enforcement and border-control agencies, defense forces, and regional security institutions with training, equipment, institution-building programs, technical assistance, and operational collaboration" to deter terrorism (US State Department, 2020). The idea is to strengthen US partnership in the fight against transnational criminal and terrorist organizations and improve cooperation, accountability, and trust between the security forces and the public (US State Department, 2020).

Transnational criminal and terrorist organizations will be countered through government, the justice system, and civil society. The plan is to "bolster partnerships with governments and civil society to prevent, investigate, and prosecute terrorism; counter terrorist financing and facilitation networks; reduce the vulnerability to radicalization; and improve border security" (US State Department, 2020). The US government will "increase governments' capacity to investigate and prosecute domestic and transnational crime, assist victims, dismantle criminal organizations, and expand rehabilitation options for juvenile offenders" (US State Department, 2020).

To promote regional cooperation America "will define a common operational framework to tackle shared threats, including combating maritime drug trafficking and promoting law enforcement information sharing" (US State Department, 2020). With regard to advancing citizen security, crime and violence prevention will be stepped up through partnering with "governments to build the resilience of at-risk youth and communities by providing educational, economic, and social opportunities" (US State Department, 2020). Finally, measures to improve governance include support of "efforts to prevent and prosecute corruption, increase government effectiveness, and build national and regional crime monitoring institutions to ensure crime prevention programs are well-targeted" (US State Department, 2020).

US terrorism in the Caribbean

The US does not discuss the terrorist acts it has committed and the terrorist groups it organized, financed, fought alongside, and harbored in the Caribbean. Some examples of the key terrorist acts committed and or sponsored/supported by the US in the Caribbean are presented below with examples from Guyana, Grenada, Haiti, and Jamaica. US terrorism in Guyana can be traced back to the overthrow of the democratically elected government of Dr. Cheddi Jagan in 1953 and then again with British imperialist collusion in his removal from office in 1964 (Agee, 1981; Jagan, 1997; Slichsinger, 2002). The Burnham dictatorship in Guyana supported by the US was responsible for the murders of its political opponents from the Working People's Alliance (WPA) party including Edward Dublin, Ohene Koama, and its co-leader world renowned historian Dr. Walter Rodney (Canterbury, 2019).

The US invaded Grenada a tiny CARICOM island-state of 110,000 people in 1983 killing hundreds. The US-trained police and counter-insurgence forces implanted in Grenada after the invasion became involved in brutality, arbitrary arrest, abuse of authority, and eroded the civil rights of Grenadians (Blum, 1995, 2000; Chomsky, 1993). The US used air, sea, and ground forces to crush an attempt by a small group of Haitians, aided by some Cubans and other Latin Americans, to overthrow the dictator Francois Duvalier in Haiti in 1959 (Blum, 2000). It supported the Duvalier family dictatorship for 30 years and worked intimately with death squads, torturers, and drug traffickers in Haiti. US state-sponsored terrorism in Haiti reached new heights with the overthrow of Aristide in February 2004. The US placed a 13-years full-scale arms embargo on Haiti during the reign of President Aristide but supplied weapons to the coup leaders who engaged in the deliberate slaughter of innocent civilian women, children, and Aristide supporters (Globe and Mail, 2005; Kurzban, 2005).

The Michael Manley government in Jamaica was destabilized by US covert action during the 1970s because it pursued a democratic socialist agenda by using tax measures to increase government revenue from leading economic sectors in Jamaica. The country was engulfed in political violence and food shortages due to hoarding by the business community. The Manley government was eventually voted out and replaced by the pro-US Edward Seaga Administration in 1980.

Counterterrorism in the Caribbean

Counterterrorism in the Caribbean does not focus on preventing future US terrorism in the CARICOM states. US terrorism does not feature in the current regional strategy to fight terrorism. Instead, the counterterrorism strategy is in cahoots with the US war on terrorism. The Declaration of Port of Spain on Strengthening Cooperation on Strategies to Sustain and Advance the Hemispheric Fight against Terrorism, in February 2005, mentioned nothing about American terrorism in the region. The declaration was made by the Organization of American States' Inter-American Convention against Terrorism.

Counterterrorism in the Caribbean is merely against what the US classifies as terrorists or terrorism. There is therefore some urgency for progressive civil society agencies to formulate a strategy against American terrorism in the Caribbean. Countering US terrorism in the Caribbean is indeed a very difficult task for these predominantly island nation-states and mainland countries. The military might of the US and the political and economic leverage it has over the region has created a "David and Goliath" type situation. The Caribbean cannot hope to have a military victory against the US, but it can study the various terrorist techniques the US utilizes in order to formulate an effective counter-strategy.

The point of departure of a Caribbean counterterrorism strategy against US terrorism is the unequivocal understanding that there could be no war against US terrorism. The adoption of such a position would mean that the region would be in a permanent state of war with the US. The premise of counterterrorism in the Caribbean has to be changed, based on the definition of terrorism to include US terrorism. The first goal of the strategy must be to consistently expose in regional and international forums US terrorist acts in the region. The usefulness of this exposure is to shame the US and make the US more unpopular around the globe. The US power would be challenged, in every country and region around the globe, and it would be impossible for America to maintain its level of global terrorist operations. Sustained exposure and resistance to US terrorism could eventually lead to a decline in US terrorism.

Second, essentially the strategy has to be an anti-imperialist. US terrorism is an integral component of its imperialist domination of the region. The Caribbean region represents a classic case of the use of US terrorism to secure economic resources for America, to control territory, and fashion political systems in the American way. Third, counterterrorism in the Caribbean requires regional political commitment to steer the course of activities to expose US terrorism. Caribbean civil society must play an important role in the fight against US terrorism, and not just preach message fed to them by the US.

Conclusion

The new American century doctrine was an important ideological component of the US-led unipolar neoliberal global order. Its political motive to build democracy by defeating terrorism was only an appearance. In reality, the US imperialists require the foreign countries in which they invest to protect their capital, which the expectation is that democratic government will do. Thus, there was an economic motive behind the US neoconservatives political and military actions to defeat terrorism and build democracy. The push by the US for democracy in the global south was to create the conditions that would allow the US transnational corporations to freely plunder these terrorist-free democratic states. The pro-US governments formulated policies that were favorable to the financial and business interests of US corporations.

The PNAC doctrine promoted the equivalent of a one-party state, but at the global level – rule by a single country in a community of nation-states. The party in power that ruled the globe would be either the Democrats or Republicans. The Hobbesian Leviathan would rule in the arenas of international political and economic relations and militarily. It encouraged global leadership by a single country – the US, global dominance by one political ideology – liberal democracy, and global dominance by a single economic system – neoliberal capitalism. Thus, in like manner that a one-party state suppresses political opposition and rewards supporters, the US punishes its enemies, compensates, and defends its obedient friends. The freedom of choice that free market capitalism and democracy promised is nothing but the tyranny of freedom, meaning freedom within a single economic and political system. It does not represent free choice between contending economic and political systems.

The PNAC doctrine suppressed the freedom of choice between competing political and economic systems in a unipolar world order. It is authoritarian at its core but presented itself as its democratic opposite. It locked neoliberal economic theory in a political box and threatened to put a halt to further theoretical searches to achieve the neoclassical free trade ideal. It placed a break on economic theorizing as only neoliberal economic theory was tolerated, and gave its participants the false sense that they would catch-up economically, politically, and socially with the rich capitalist countries. The neoconservatives were adamant that the US will not allow any other country to match its military power. That meant no other country would be allowed to match US economic power since economic and military power go hand in hand – what some observers described as the military-industrial complex (Turley, 2014). In practice, the PNAC doctrine protected US domestic and foreign economic and political interests, by promoting free trade and US-styled democracy abroad. The US war on terrorism in the heyday of the doctrine provides further evidence of the link between US national interests and America's endeavors to promote democracy in the global south.

References

Agee, P. (1981). *Inside the Company: CIA Diaries*. New York: Bantam Books.
Blum, W. (1995). *Killing Hope: U.S. Military and CIA Interventions since World War II*. Monroe, ME: Common Courage.

Blum, W. (2000). *Rouge State: A Guide to the World's Only Superpower.* Monroe, ME: Common Courage.
Canterbury, D.C. (2019). *Neoliberal Democratization and New Authoritarianism.* London and New York: Routledge.
CFATF (1995). *Annual Report 1994–1995.* Port of Spain Trinidad and Tobago: Caribbean Financial Action Task Force.
CFATF (2002). *Annual Report 2001–2002.* Port of Spain Trinidad and Tobago: Caribbean Financial Action Task Force, 17 October.
CARICOM (2001). *The Nassau Declaration on International Terrorism: The CARICOM Response.* Nassau Bahamas, 11–12 October.
CARICOM (2003). Statement on the War in Iraq Issued by the *Sixteenth Meeting of the Bureau of the Conference of Heads of Government of the Caribbean Community 5 April*, Montego Bay Jamaica, 6 April.
Chomsky, N. (1993). *What Uncle Sam Really Wants.* Tucson Arizona: Odonian Press.
Conkling, W. and S. Goble. (2004). *Otto Reich: A Career in Disservice.* Washington DC: Council on Hemispheric Affairs, 13 July.
Daalder, I.H. and J.M. Lindsay. (2003). *The Globalization of Politics: American Foreign Policy for a New Century.* Washington: The Brookings Institution, 1 January.
Daalder, I.H. and J. Lindsay. (2004). *The Preemptive-War Doctrine Has Met an Early Death in Iraq.* Washington: The Brookings Institution, 30 May.
DeMuth, C. and W. Kristol (eds.) (1995). *The Neoconservative Imagination: Essays in Honor of Irvine Kristol.* Washington: The AEI Press.
FATF (2019). International Standards on Combating Money Laundering and the Financing of Terrorism and Proliferation: The FATF Recommendations, June.
Fukuyama, F. (1992). *The End of History and the Last Man.* New York: Free Press.
Globe and Mail (2005). "U.S. Funnels $7 Million in Arms to Haiti's Puppet Regime, Death Squads," *Globe and Mail*, 7 April.
Griffith, I.L. (ed.) (2004). *Caribbean Security in the Age of Terror: Challenge and Change.* Kingston Jamaica: Ian Randle.
Huntington, S.P. (2011). *The Clash of Civilizations and the Remaking of World Order.* New York: Simon and Schuster.
Jagan, C.B. (1997). *The West on Trial: My Fight for Guyana's Freedom.* London: Hansib Publications.
Jamaica Observer (2003). "US Cuts Aid to CARICOM Six," *Jamaica Observer*, International Edition, 2 July.
Jasor, O. and P. Morrow (2005). *Barbados Creates Rift Within CARICOM: Who Are the Heroes and Who Are the Knaves?* Washington DC: Council on Hemispheric Affairs, 6 June.
Kagan, R. (2003). *Of Paradise and Power: America and Europe in the New World Order.* New York: Vintage Books.
Kagan, R. and W. Kristol (eds.) (2000). *Present Dangers: Crisis and Opportunity in American Foreign and Defense Policy.* New York: Encounter Books.
Kagan, D., G. Schmitt, and T. Donnelly (2000). *Rebuilding America's Defenses: Strategy, Forces and Resources for a New Century.* Washington DC: Project for a New American Century.
Kelshall, C.M. (2004a). "Radical Islam and LNG in Trinidad and Tobago," *Energy Security.* Washington, DC: Institute for the Analysis of Global Security (IAGS), 15 November.

Kelshall, C.M. (2004b). *LNG Tanker Terrorism: A Case Study.* London: Global Facilitation Network for Security Sector Reform (GFN-SSR) GFN-SSR, 16 August.

Kelshall, C.M. (2005). *Countering Maritime Terrorism in the Caribbean.* London: Global Facilitation Network for Security Sector Reform (GFN-SSR), 18 April.

Kenney, E. and L. Meyer (2004). *Anti-Terrorism Costs Could Bring Caribbean to Its Knees.* Washington: Council on Hemispheric Affairs, 12 August.

Köppel, J. (2011). *The SWIFT Affair: Swiss Banking Secrecy and the Fight against Terrorist Financing.* Geneva: The Graduate Institute.

Kurzban, I. (2005). "Diplomacy Death Squad: How Bolton Armed Haiti's Thugs and Killers," *Looking Glass News*, 7 May.

Lichtblau, E. and J. Risen. (2006). "Bank Data Is Sifted by US in Secret to Block Terror," *The New York Times*, 23 June.

Luce, H.R. (1999). "The American Century," *Diplomatic History* 23 (2): 159–171.

Meyer, S.P. and J. Steinberg (2004). "Henry Luce's Empire of Fascism," *Executive Intelligence Review (EIR)* 31 (25): 28–29, 25 June.

Mian, Z. (2005). *A New American Century?* Silver City, NM & Washington DC: Foreign Policy in Focus, 4 May.

Mueller, K.P., J.J. Castillo, F.E. Morgan, N. Pegahi, and B. Rosen (2006). *Striking First: Preemptive and Preventive Attack in US National Security Policy.* Arlington VA: RAND Corporation.

PNAC (1997). *Statement of Principles.* Washington DC: Project for a New American Century.

Ryder, N. (2015). *The Financial War on Terrorism: A Review of Counter-Terrorist Financing Strategies.* London and New York: Routledge.

Slichsinger, A.M. Jr. (2002). *A Thousand Days: JFK in the White House.* New York: Mariner Books.

Turley, J. (2014). *Big Money behind War: The Military-Industrial Complex.* Doha, Qatar: Aljazeera, 11 January.

United Nations (2001). Resolution 1373 Adopted by the Security Council at Its 4385th Meeting. S/RES/1373 28 September.

US Department of Justice (2001). *The US Patriot Act (2001): Preserving Life and Liberty (Uniting and Strengthening America by Providing Appropriate Tools Required to Intercept and Obstruct Terrorism), H.R.3162.* Washington DC: US Department of Justice.

US Department of State (2001). *Patterns of Global Terrorism 2000.* Washington DC: US Department of State Counterterrorism Office, 30 April.

US State Department (2020). *Caribbean 2020: A Multi-Year Strategy to Increase the Security, Prosperity, and Well-Being of the People of the United States and the Caribbean.* Washington DC.

Warde, I. (2008). *The Price of Fear: The Truth behind the Financial War on Terror.* Los Angles: University of California Press.

4 The Caribbean making America great again

Introduction

This chapter focuses attention on the CARICOM in the era of US imperialism represented as "make America great again" (MAGA). Bernal (2017) argues however in favor of a Caribbean policy for the Trump Administration which among other things recognizes "a more nuanced appreciation that the economic development of the Caribbean is inextricably linked to other important issues such as democracy, governance, national security, transnational crime, and narcotics trafficking." The MAGA doctrine signifies a form of fascistic capitalism that became the face of US imperialism in the new multipolar world order. It reflects the fact that the US has to share power on the world stage with China, Russia, and the EU. While the MAGA doctrine dismantled neoliberal globalization in the new multipolarity, it negatively impacts the CARICOM states (Charles and Roberts, 2019). It energized the resurgence of the perpetrators of white supremacy in mainstream politics who perceive their racialist origins in the Anglo-Saxon story. The argument is presented in three parts beginning with an assessment of the MAGA phenomenon in terms of its mindset, role in the new multipolarity, and domestic prescriptions and foreign policy. Second, the myth that the US is disengaging from the globe is dispelled; and third the divisions in the CARICOM due to the recent political impasse in Guyana and the current MAGA foreign policy measures concerning Venezuela and China's belt and road initiative are evaluated.

The MAGA mindset

The mindset behind MAGA can be gleaned from Trump's (2016) dark pronouncement: "Look at the state of the world right now. It's a terrible mess, and that's putting it kindly. There has never been a more dangerous time. The so-called insiders within the Washington ruling class are the people who got us into this trouble. So why should we continue to pay attention to them?" McFarland (2020) describes Trumpism in revolutionary terms arguing "the Trump Revolution began before Trump, and it will continue after

DOI: 10.4324/9781003092414-4

he has left the stage." According to McFarland (2020), the dogma will persist because "the main tenets of Trumpism – Make America Great Again, America First, and Peace Through Strength – are driven by the American people themselves." Trump has been "their standard-bearer, the person they have chosen to carry out their mandate" (McFarland, 2020). To let them die from Covid-19 perhaps!

The MAGA doctrine includes the dismantling of Obama-era policies, withdrawing the US from international agreements, dismantling neoliberal globalization, protectionism, nationalism disguised as patriotism, and the promotion of xenophobia. The Trump Administration has embraced an authoritarian leadership style which people are questioning as to whether it can morph into fascism (Mukherjee, 2018; Paxton, 2017). Trumpism's narrative of US decline is bound to the narrative of white and White-Christian decline, reconfiguring "Americanness" in terms of imaginary racial purity (Mukherjee, 2018). The president's appeal among his base is, in part, dependent on his continuous attacks against the free press, penchant for conspiracy theory, and tireless peddling of "alternative facts" (Mukherjee, 2018).

According to Mukherjee (2018), "Trumpism is not a coherent political doctrine but a rhetorical apparatus that can be appropriated by a protean group of political actors." Trump's public speeches "are apocalyptic sermons, warning of the imminent decimation of the West" (Mukherjee, 2018). Mukherjee (2018) noted that "the prophecies of MAGA speak of the coming battle, one not only between civilizations, but between races." It galvanizes the Trump "base around a white theology" and seeks the "re-ethnicization" of America, which may "be a response to a shift in [the] cultural and religious landscape," as the US Census Bureau projected that America will no longer be a white-majority nation in 2043" (Mukherjee, 2018).

The prosperity gospel has resurrected "medieval Christian explanations for the feudal system in affirming that the wealthy are favored by God and the poor, forsaken by him" (Mukherjee, 2018). Many US Christians especially Pentecostals are "convinced that God offers material prosperity," and "the poor have sinned or fallen out of favor with God while the wealthy, despite the tactics employed to acquire their wealth, remain 'blessed'" (Mukherjee, 2018). The prosperity gospel the ideological supplement to late capitalism is a mainstay of Trumpism. It "explains social inequality while also consoling the poor faithful with the promise of God's economic intervention" (Mukherjee, 2018).

It is an explanation of evil, while being "attuned to the deepest needs of Americans in an economic system that is radically unequal" (Mukherjee, 2018). It explains poverty as the result of being spiritually disadvantaged, thus the need to "worship at the altar of Trump" who is rich and therefore blessed. Thus, "Trump Tower is not just his monument. It is seen as God's gift" to him (Mukherjee, 2018). The MAGA dogma does not promote "pluralism, intercultural dialogue, or the reconciliation of cultures," it paints Islam as "intrinsically violent and has rolled back attempts to quell anti-Islamic sentiment in the post-9/11 context" (Mukherjee, 2018). Trump "marshals and mobilizes latent Islamophobic sentiment to cement the base and reproduce the clash of civilizations thesis" (Mukherjee, 2018). Thus, "MAGA gave white anxiety form and legitimated it through recoding it in theological and mythical terms" (Mukherjee, 2018).

MAGA in the new multipolarity

The US must have discovered the uneasiness of sitting at the apex of global power in the neoliberal globalization era, as it eventually succumbed to competition from the EU, China, and Russia. The new reality of America sharing power with its competitors became manifest in the second decade of the twenty-first century. The far-right among the US neoconservatives changed their tune from "new American century" to "MAGA," from globalism to nationalism in a bid to restore America's hegemony. Trumpism became the face of the far-right conservatives that shoulders the responsibility to transpose America's power in a new multipolar world order. The first order of business of Trumpism in reordering US power in the new multipolar world order is to dismantle the institutions of the old unipolar global order.

Trumpism is founded on what is referred to as a "policy of principled realism" which holds the US "will not be held hostage to old dogmas, discredited ideologies, and so-called experts who have been proven wrong over the years" (Kirkey, 2018; Trump, 2018). This is a direct attack on neoliberal globalization, a discredited ideology and old dogma whose experts have been proven wrong about its ability to deliver economic prosperity in developed and developing economies alike. Trumpism's opposition to neoliberal globalization takes the form of US withdrawal and threats of withdrawal from United Nations agencies, and international trade, security, and other agreements.

The global institutions formed at Bretton Woods, New Hampshire and shaped and refashioned to serve US economic and political interests are no longer working for the US due to interventions from the EU, China, and Russia. New institutions that reflect the current multipolar order, will have to be built. The CARICOM will have to align with those institutions, instead of hankering after the institutional arrangements that were built to serve the interest of the US as sole hegemon. Trumpism takes a pragmatic approach to policy that places at the forefront the interest of the ruling elites over those of the US. It engages in great power imperial rivalry, while being anti-communist, anti-terrorist, pro-liberal democracy, and pro-free market.

In the beginning of MAGA

The Trump White House published a Fact Sheet in 2017 that assessed President Trump's first year in office (White House, 2017). The Fact Sheet provides very good insights into the essence of the MAGA dogma. The assessment could be divided into two broad categories, domestic and international, which are sub-divided into 12 sections. The focus of the sub-section headed "jump-starting America's workers and economic engine" is on the US domestic economy. The items emphasized under this category reflect on measures covering taxes, health care, employment, and changes in the national income.

The Fact Sheet mentions President Trump's accomplishments to include a US$5.5 trillion in tax cuts primarily for the wealthy, the nearly doubling of the standard deduction on taxes, the repeal of Obamacare individual mandate in healthcare, the creation of nearly 1.7 million new jobs, lowering the unemployment rate to 4.1 percent, and increasing the GDP growth rate at or above 3 percent for two quarters in a row (White House, 2017). The White House (2017) announced that more than US$5 trillion in wealth was added to the US economy supported by increases in the Dow Jones Industrial Average Index. According to the Fact Sheet, this resulted from President Trump's economic policies to "put American workers and businesses first" (White House, 2017). The Fact Sheet states that President Trump signed an Executive Order expanding apprenticeship, as a "quality alternatives to four-year colleges," and prioritized STEM (Science, Technology, Engineering and Mathematics) education with a focus on computer science. It claimed that the leading private sector technology companies pledged US$300M to amplify computer education, and that approximately US$500M more loans were made to women-owned businesses through the Small Business Administration compared with the previous year under President Obama.

Second, the White House Fact Sheet focused on domestic measures to roll back government regulations of the economy. President Trump signed an Executive Order mandating that two regulations must be terminated for every one created. The administration was so efficient in this matter that it eliminated 22 regulations for every new regulation. It claimed that it saved US$8.1Bn in lifetime regulatory costs, and removed from the books several Obama-era rules and regulations by signing into law 15 congressional review acts resolution (White House, 2017).

This sub-section also focused on the US withdrawal from the Paris Climate Agreement an action deemed necessary to protect the US economy and workers. The Trump Administration estimated that the climate agreement would "cost the United States economy nearly US$3 trillion and 6.5 million industrial sector jobs by 2040" (White House, 2017). It eliminated the Obama's "Stream Protection Rule" because it was assessed to cost the US some US$81M a year. Through an Executive Order President Trump reduced the time to obtain a permit to undertake an infrastructure investment project from up to 10 years to an average of two years (White House, 2017).

The third sub-section had nationalist and internationalist dimensions to put America first in fair and reciprocal trade that according to the Fact Sheet would be advantageous to US workers. In this connection the

US withdrew from the Trans-Pacific Partnership (TPP), and renegotiated trade agreements including the North American Free Trade Agreement (NAFTA), which was estimated to have contributed to the US trade deficit. The Fact Sheet stated that measures were put in place to attract foreign investments to the US, which led South Korean companies to announce that they will invest US$17Bn in the US over four years in 64 projects, and will purchase US$58Bn US goods and services (White House, 2017). Also, the White House (2017) noted that Foxconn announced it would invest US$10Bn to build a factory in Wisconsin, employing up to 22,000 workers indirectly, and that Toyota and Mazda declared a US$1.6Bn investment in a new manufacturing plant in the US creating 4,000 jobs, while Broadcom Limited revealed it was moving its headquarters back to America bringing US$20Bn in revenue.

The White House Fact Sheet stated that by promoting US sales abroad the Trump Administration signed a historic US$400Bn trade deal with Saudi Arabia. President Trump blocked a foreign company from acquiring a US business, and to enforce US trade laws the department of commerce initiated 79 antidumping and countervailing duties (AD/CVD) investigations. According to the White House (2017), investigations were launched into unreasonable or discriminatory practices of Chinese policies, acts, and practices in terms of technology transfer, licensing, and intellectual property, and the Obama Administration's deal with the Cuban regime was rolled back.

The fourth area with serious domestic and international implications concerns the actions taken to advance the US dominance in energy. According to the Fact Sheet, these included revising policies that "locked-up American energy and restricted" US energy sale to other countries. The Trump Administration auctioned off leases for nearly 77 million acres in the Gulf of Mexico for oil and gas drilling, expanded offshore oil and gas drilling, and reissued a leasing program to develop offshore resources. It increased the export of energy resources to the global market, while financing coal and other fossil energy projects, streamlining permits for Liquefied Natural Gas (LNG) terminals including the Lake Charles LNG terminal, and increasing LNG exports to US allies to prevent their dependence on single suppliers, and expanding access to oil and gas development along with infrastructure needed to market the products (White House, 2017).

The Fact Sheet stated that the Keystone XL and Dakota Access Pipelines project, estimated to create 42,000 jobs and US$2Bn in economic benefits was approved. New pipeline approval and production, including the New Burgos Pipeline, to export US gasoline to Mexico was expedited, and oil and gas development on Federal lands was boosted (White House, 2017). The Environmental Protection Agency (EPA) rescinded the Obama Administration's Clean Power Plan (CPP), which in the estimation of the Trump Administration, would have increased electricity rates by as much as 14 percent, costing American households up to US$79Bn (White House,

2017). Also, the EPA planned to reverse an Obama-era rule on methane emissions that in President Trump's estimation would cost American energy developers an approximately US$530M annually.

Immigration laws and alleged concerns with protecting American communities and jobs constituted the fifth set of policies. According to the Fact Sheet, this involved measures to reform the immigration system; fund a wall along the US Southern border; close legal loopholes that enable illegal immigration; end Chain Migration, and eliminate the Visa Lottery program (White House, 2017). The US pulled out of negotiations for a "Global Compact on Migration," a plan for global governance of immigration and refugee policy, with the claim that it had far-reaching implications for US sovereignty (White House, 2017). The Department of Homeland Security (DHS) took steps to abort the Deferred Action for Childhood Arrivals (DACA) program, because in the opinion of the Department of Justice (DOJ) the DACA lacked legal authorization (White House, 2017). In 2020, the US Supreme ruled against the DOJ's assessment that the DACA was illegal.

The Fact Sheet stated that the US DHS launched an office of Victims of Immigration Crime Engagement (VOICE), and that efforts to stem illegal immigration reached new heights with a 40 percent increase or 110,568 arrests by the US Immigration and Customs Enforcement (ICE) in President Trump's first year in office (White House, 2017). According to White House (2017), the arrests resulted in a 37 percent increase in removals of illegal aliens arrested by ICE, and that over 92 percent of ICE arrests had criminal convictions or pending criminal charges, were ICE fugitives, or illegal reentrants (White House, 2017). The Fact Sheet stated that President Trump cracked down on sanctuary cities for illegal immigrants by improving the administration of Federal grants to increase information sharing on such persons, and that local law enforcement entities that delegated authority to ICE to enforce immigration in their jurisdiction, doubled.

The sixth set of policy initiatives under Trumpism concerns protecting America's communities and restoring law and order. The Fact Sheet stated that the DOJ announced a program to provide more than US$98 million in grant funding to hire 802 additional full-time law enforcement officers. It stated that President Trump signed an Executive Order to restore state and local law enforcement's access to surplus Defense Department equipment through the 1,033 program, including safety equipment, and that collaboration between the DOJ and Central American governments led to the arrest and change of about 4,000 MS-13 members, including the alleged leader of organization's East Coast Program (White House, 2017). According to the Fact Sheet, in 2017, the DHS arrested 796 MS-13 members and associates, an 83 percent increase over the previous year, and that measures through Executive Orders cracked down on international criminal organizations. The White House (2017) claimed that the new National Public Safety

Partnership was created as a cooperative initiative with cities to reduce violent crimes.

The seventh set of policy measures surrounds what President Trump refers to as "draining the swamp." In essence, this involved the President's capture of the judicial system by appointing, according to the Fact Sheet, Neil Gorsuch on the United States Supreme Court and nominating 73 Federal judges 22 of whom were confirmed including 12 circuit judges (White House, 2017). It was stated in the White House (2017) that through an Executive Order a five-year ban was placed on lobbying and a lifetime ban on lobbying for foreign countries, and that the President Trump called for a comprehensive plan to reorganize the executive branch and started to do so, while overhauling the digitally delivered government services, and carrying out a full audit of the Pentagon.

Combatting opioids in a fight against drug addiction and opioids abuse is an eighth area in President Trump's MAGA policies. The White House (2017) stated that a Nationwide Public Health Emergency was declared to address the opioids crisis, and that according to research undertaken through the President's Council of Economic Advisers (CEA), there was a 24 percent underreporting of drug overdoses involving opioids (White House, 2017). The Fact Sheet stated that the Department of Health and Human Services (HHS) is combating the opioids abuse crisis through a comprehensive five-point strategy, while the DOJ scheduled fentanyl substances as a drug class under the Controlled Substances Act, criminalizing the possession, import, distribution, or manufacture of illicit fentanyl-related substances similar to other controlled substances (White House, 2017).

The Fact Sheet stated that the first DOJ indictments for distributing fentanyl and other opiate substances were against two Chinese nationals and their North American-based associates, while in excess of 400 people were indicted in an opioids fraud crackdown. The Fact Sheet stated that the individuals charged for prescribing unnecessary opioids that fuel the drug crisis, included doctors and medical facilities, and that the federal government transferred approximately US$500 million to states to prevent and treat opioids abuse in 2017 and 2018 (White House, 2017). Also, it mentions that the National Drug Take Back Day netted a record-breaking 912,305 lbs, or 456 tons of potentially dangerous expired, unused, or unwanted prescription drugs from in excess of 5,300 collection sites.

The ninth set of MAGA policy measures focused on the cultural issue of abortion. According to the Fact Sheet, this involved reinstating and expanding the Mexico City Policy that protects US$9Bn in foreign aid from being used to fund the abortion industry, and withholding US$32.5M funding from the United Nations Population Fund or UN Family Planning Agency (UNFPA) for colluding with China's program of abortion and sterilization. The White House (2017) stated that President Trump signed a bill that overturned the Obama Administration's regulation that prohibited US states from defunding abortion service providers, and that guidelines were published to enforce the Obamacare requirement that taxpayer dollars should not support abortion coverage in exchange plans.

Veteran affairs was covered in the tenth set of MAGA policy measures for which, according to the Fact Sheet, President Trump signed the Veterans Accountability and Whistleblower Protection Act that allows senior officials in the Department of Veterans Affairs (VA) to dismiss inefficient employees and put in place safeguards to protect whistleblowers leading to 1,298 firings, 425 suspensions, and 73 demotions (White House, 2017). The Fact Sheet states that the Veterans Appeals Improvement and Modernization Act was passed to streamline the lengthy process that veterans undergo when appealing disability benefits claims with the VA.

The Fact Sheet stated that the Harry W. Colmery Veterans Educational Assistance Act to fund the Post-9/11 GI Bill was signed into law, and that veterans, service personnel, and their family members are provided with educational benefits including costs for tuition, fees, books, and housing. It stated that an additional US$2.1Bn was authorized for the Veterans Choice Program (VCP) through the VA Choice and Quality Employment Act of 2017 and that a White House-created VA Hotline staffed by veterans and family members announced three initiatives to expand veterans' access to healthcare using telehealth technology. According to the Fact Sheet, these were first the "Anywhere to Anywhere VA Health Care" that allows VA providers to use telehealth technology to serve veterans wherever they are, second, the VA Video Connect allows veterans and providers to connect by video across the country, and third, Veteran Appointment Request (VAR) application allows veterans to schedule appointments at VA facilities on digital devices (White House, 2017).

The policy initiatives that focused on rebuilding the military, defeating terrorist organization, and confronting rogue nations constituted the eleventh area. According to the Fact Sheet, the issues in this area involved constructing a new national defense strategy, comprehensively reviewing US nuclear posture, and fielding state-of-the-art ballistic missile defenses and initiatives. According to the White House (2017), President Trump increased defense spending, fully reverse the defense sequester, expanded US military capacity, and modernize its capabilities. The Fact Sheet stated that Washington stepped back from micromanaging the military empowering the Defense Secretary and US military commanders to make decisions, and that a new national space policy and strategy was developed and implemented by a revived National Space Council, while America's activities in cyberspace was advanced by elevating US Cyber Command into a major warfighting command.

Meanwhile, the White House (2017) stated that ravel restrictions were placed on certain countries that do not have sufficient security or share enough information with the US, and that the Trump Administration took credit for ISIS losing nearly all of its territory, cities, and towns in Iraq and Syria, including Mosul and Raqqa the ISIS-declared capital. The White House (2017) stated that President Trump took action to end North

Korea's aggressive actions and its continued development of nuclear weapons and ballistic missiles, and that the US led the UN Security Council to sanctioned North Korea for its continued rogue actions, while the US sanctioned Chinese financial institutions aiding North Korea, and North Korean trade and financing.

According to the White House (2017), the US strengthened its support for Afghan security forces, and through the new US South Asia strategy, and caused NATO allies and partners to increase their troop contributions to NATO's Resolute Support Mission in Afghanistan. It stated that a new Iran strategy was approved that focuses on neutralizing Iran's regional destabilizing influence, sanctioning Iran's ballistic missile program, and decertifying Iran's compliance with the multilateral nuclear deal.

According to the White House (2017), to prevent further Syrian chemical weapons attacks, US missile strikes were ordered against a Syrian airbase after the Assad regime allegedly used it to launch chemical weapons attacks against civilians. It stated that President Trump imposed new sanctions on the Maduro Administration in Venezuela, targeting the regime and individuals, and that the new financial sanctions prohibit dealings in new Venezuelan debt and its oil company to prevent the regime from using US banks to finance its debt.

The 12th area of policy initiatives focused on restoring confidence in and respect for America through an "America first foreign policy." According to the White House (2017), President Trump often used his personal relationships with world leaders, to secure the release of US citizens held abroad, and personally intervened to secure the release from China of three student athletes from the University of California. The White House (2017) stated that the US and Pakistani forces secured the release of an American, Canadian, and their three children from Taliban custody, and that Otto Warmbier, Sandy Phan-Gill, and Aya Hijazi were released from prison in North Korea, China, and Egypt, respectively.

According to the Fact Sheet, President Trump recognized Jerusalem as the capital of the State of Israel, and toured Asia which resulted in South Korea and Japan pledging to build closer defense relations with the US, and the US committing to provide them with advanced military equipment. The Fact Sheet stated that cooperation was boosted with the Quad States, Japan, India, Australia, and the US, which reaffirmed its commitment to promote prosperity and security in the region, modernizing US development finance institutions, and increasing coordination with Japanese counterparts.

According to the White House (2017), President Trump pushed for greater commitments and cooperation with allies in his travels to the Middle East and Europe, when he visited Mecca, Jerusalem, and Rome, and attended the opening of the Global Center for Combating Extremist Ideology. The Fact Sheet stated that President Trump persuaded NATO leaders to agree to develop national plans to boost defense spending to two percent of GDP by 2024, and for NATO to formally join the defeat-ISIS coalition. It stated that President Trump visited Poland, attended a meeting of the G-20, where he pushed for closer cooperation and "American First" policies, and that the US championed with the G-20 and the World Bank, the establishment of the Women Entrepreneurs Finance Initiative (WeFi), which could leverage in excess of $1 billion in financing to support women entrepreneurs (White House, 2017).

It should be noted that the Trump Administration is known to be notorious for communicating what it calls "alternative facts." The data provided by the Fact Sheet on the achievements of President Trump in his first year in office must be understood in that light. The Fact Sheet is very useful however in terms of providing insights into Trumpian nationalism.

The US disengagement myth

The MAGA and "America first" policies have led to the conjecture that the US is disengaging from the globe. Trumpian nationalism's dismantling neoliberal globalization fuels this view on America's withdrawal from international affairs. The notion of US disengagement however was first leveled at the Obama Administration by the Republicans (Chollet, 2016). According to Chollet (2016), Republican propaganda accused the Obama Administration of being feckless, weak, and illegitimate. Chollet (2016) claims that the Republican Party succumbed "to the forces of nullification, extreme ideology, and alternative reality" and became "a myth-making machine." The Obama Administration was quick to point out however that it was not disengaging from the world supported with evidence provided by Chollet (2016).

Chollet (2016) outlined US engagement in the Asia-Pacific region, Latin America, Africa, Europe, and the Middle East under President Obama. The US employed a "rebalancing" strategy in Asia-Pacific that "delivered far more US diplomatic, military, and economic bandwidth in the region than existed eight years" prior to the Obama Administration (Chollet, 2016). This resulted from strengthened "core alliances with treaty allies like South Korea, Japan, and the Philippines" (Chollet, 2016). The US expanded economic, political, and military partnerships in Vietnam, Laos, and Burma where it has diplomatic relations. It negotiated the Transpacific Partnership, and engaged in managing China's rise by standing firm in the South China Sea, and developing a firm and pragmatic approach toward that country (Chollet, 2016).

The US was in a stronger position in Latin America "in terms of its military, political, diplomatic, and economic relationships, whereas under the Bush Administration the US was a pariah to many" countries in the region (Chollet, 2016). A new context was created "for America's regional leadership by opening up to Cuba" (Chollet, 2016). In Africa, the Obama Administration "expanded significantly counterterrorism operations, military training and assistance," and had a "footprint from Nigeria to Libya to Somalia, and tackled the Ebola outbreaks" (Chollet, 2016). The US was in the "midst of negotiating an ambitious new trade deal with Europe, the Transatlantic Trade and Investment Partnership (TTIP)" (Chollet, 2016). President Obama was "dramatically transforming" America's "defense posture in Europe – reversing a planned drawdown, quadrupling its defense spending there, rotating American ground forces into Central and Eastern Europe to address the Russian threat, implementing missile defense and prepositioning heavy armor and equipment" (Chollet, 2016).

The Middle East constituted the core of the disengagement myth about the Obama Administration, whereas under Obama "the US military footprint in the region [was] greater than before 9/11" (Chollet, 2016). The US had in the region "over 35,000 troops, hundreds of fighter aircraft and ships, and the most sophisticated weaponry on the planet" (Chollet, 2016). The US "security partnerships with Middle Eastern allies" had strengthened, and the US "concluded several of the largest arms sales in history" to the region (Chollet, 2016). The Obama Administration, "worked to bring the military and intelligence partnership with the Gulf Cooperation Council, or GCC, states into the twenty-first century by improving their capabilities against modern threats and ability to fight together" (Chollet, 2016). The Obama Administration engaged the world in terms of broad issues such as from global warming to the threat of the spread of nuclear weapons.

The pretense of US disengagement from the world under the Trump Administration is on a different plain. The impression is given that the US is diminishing its role in the globe because the Trump Administration has withdrawn from a number of global agreements, threatens the North Atlantic Treaty Organization (NATO), the World Health Organization (WHO), and has started a tariff war with China. But, that is only an appearance, the Trump Administration could list in the same way as did the Obama Administration, the various ways in which the US continues to exercise power in Asia-Pacific, Latin America, Africa, Europe, and the Middle East. Old patterns of US militarization of the globe will be deepened and new ones will emerge, especially in terms of the increase and expansion of US military bases and arms sales. Those who express the view that the US is withdrawing from the globe sees that as a bad thing. They believe that US imperialism is necessary among other things to maintain the global order, stability and peace; contain China and Russia; provide aid to poor countries; defeat terrorism; and to be a shining beacon of democracy, freedom, and free trade. For these and other reasons, some sections of the US elites believe that the Trump Administration cannot disengage the US from the world (Kaplan, 2017).

Indeed, under Trumpian nationalism, the US has become even more brazen in its exploitation of the rest of the globe. The proponents of the nationalist doctrine believe that by participating in globalization the US is being asked to give up too much, which is hurting its citizens and threatening instability. Trumpian nationalism returns the US to the days when it was more on a belligerent footing seeking to dominate the entire globe. At that time communism was perceived the only real threat to America. During the

Cold War the US exploited and dominated the capitalist world that came under its leadership. The communist setbacks placed the US in the driver's seat of the globalization train. But, the discontents with globalization have caused the US to change course and to return to the naked promotion of its self-interests.

The CARICOM meets MAGA

Perhaps the most important fact about the CARICOM's encounter with the MAGA doctrine is the division over US policy toward Venezuela amidst US promises of economic support for the region, and the recent political impasse in Guyana. The CARICOM states continue to allow the US to divide them, which is evident under the MAGA doctrine. The CARICOM is divided over support for the US overthrow of the Maduro Administration in Venezuela and to recognize Juan Guaidó as the legitimate interim President of the country. A second source of division is the CARICOM states' approaches to US competitors in the BRICS and the EU – the belt and road initiative with China, and the economic partnership agreement with the EU. The US opposed the Caribbean signing the CARIFORUM-EU EPA, and the Trump Administration is opposed to Caribbean countries signing on to the BRI. A third division concerns the recent political impasse in Guyana, which it would seem has to do with geo-politics and oil.

Division over Venezuela

The Trump Administration claims it wants to be a better partner in trade and investment with the CARICOM but apparently only in exchange for the CARICOM's support of America's policy toward Venezuela. A meagre five out of 15 CARICOM-member states and observer countries – the Bahamas, Dominican Republic, Haiti, Jamaica, and Saint Lucia – met with President Trump at his Mar-a-Lago resort in 2019. The troubling part of the circus meeting was the statement by Jamaican Prime Minister Andrew Holness which was declared on behalf of the Caribbean leaders at the gathering. Prime Minister Holness says, "the message from this meeting was that the United States wants to encourage and promote a stronger relationship with the region," the Caribbean leaders were "very happy with that message," which was "long in coming," and were "satisfied that there will be instrumental action with that message" (Charles, 2019).

The leaders of the five Caribbean countries at the Mar-a-Lago meeting are aligned with the Lima Group in the Organization of American States (OAS) that opposes the Nicolás Maduro regime in Venezuela. They back the OAS resolution "to not recognize the legitimacy of Nicolás Maduro's new term as of the 10th of January of 2019" (Trujillo, 2019). Subsequently, the Bahamas, Haiti, and the Dominican Republic recognized opposition leader Juan Guaidó as Venezuela's interim president (Torres, 2019). The

CARICOM however does not recognize Guaidó and asked the UN to intervene to resolve the issue peacefully.

But, the US claims it had a special relationship with the CARICOM countries invited to meet with President Trump. It wanted to send a strong message to the other Caribbean countries that the US intends to replace Maduro with Guaidó, and that those states needed to come around to that position. President Trump wanted to know what the Caribbean countries were doing to shift from buying Venezuelan oil to buying American oil. The US promoted itself as the largest producer of oil and natural gas with the capacity to accommodate the demands for those products in the entire western hemisphere.

Caribbean leaders remained divided over the activities of the Trump Administration in the region when some of them on principle refused to attend a meeting with US Secretary of State Mike Pompeo in Jamaica in January 2020. The meeting was to discuss the crisis in Venezuela, trade, and national security. The Prime Minster of Barbados Mia Mottley stated that the Pompeo meeting was "an attempt to divide the region." Prime Minister Mottley said: "I am conscious that if this country does not stand for something, then it will fall for anything. As chairman of CARICOM, it is impossible for me to agree that my foreign minister should attend a meeting with anyone to which members of CARICOM are not invited" (*The Guardian*, 2020). Jamaica was joined by the Bahamas, Belize, the Dominican Republic, Haiti, St Kitts and Nevis, and Saint Lucia at the Pompeo meeting.

Threats to the BRI

The US position on the BRI is framed by geo-political concerns viewed as a deliberate attempt to economically marginalize the US (Chance, 2016). Analyzing the situation in Venezuela, and the emergence of China, led MacDonald (2019) to argue that the Cold War has returned to the Caribbean. Donald Tapia the US Ambassador to Jamaica is on record questioning the basis on which China's direct investment and loans injected US$2Bn into Jamaica over the past decade. The Ambassador expressed his concern over China's behavior when countries fail to repay loans. China is said to then control the narrative taking over economic assets in such countries.

The Trump Administration's National Security Strategy states "China seeks to pull the region into its orbit through state-led investments and loans" and expresses concern about China's support for "the dictatorship in Venezuela." Secretary of State Mike Pompeo said in a speech he gave during a visit to Latin America in April 2019 that "when China does business in places like" the Caribbean region "it often injects corrosive capital into the economic bloodstream, giving life to corruption, and eroding good governance" (Sullivan, 2020).

The US Southern Command (SOUTHCOM) has expressed strong concerns about China's activities in the region.

> Its 2020 posture statement maintained that certain Chinese investments in the region have strategic value for future military uses and expressed special concern about China's investments in numerous deep ports and infrastructure on both sides of the Panama Canal. SOUTHCOM also warned about Chinese telecommunications projects in 16 countries in the region that, it argued, could allow China to monitor or intercept official information that the United States shares with its partners.
>
> *(Sullivan, 2020)*

The US' concerns about the activities of China in the Caribbean will definitely have a dampening effect on the regions engagement with China.

Political impasse in Guyana

Since the overthrow of the old People's Progressive Party (PPP) in 1953 under trumped-up communist changes political change in Guyana has always come about with foreign interference. The colonial authorities manipulated a split in the PPP in 1953 along race-lines with the East Indians–Guyanese supporting the original PPP identified as communist, and the African-Guyanese supporting the People's National Congress (PNC) supported by the US. The colonial authorities intervened to rewrite the country's constitution but, despite the constitutional manipulation the PPP won the national elections in 1955 and 1961 because East Indians are a numerical majority in the population.

Political change occurred at the 1964 with US intervention in the midst of the Cold War to pass power to a PNC-United Force (UF) coalition government. The UF left the coalition in the 1968 elections and the PNC as a minority captured power it held until 1992 with the intervention of IFM/World Bank political conditionality and the Carter Center supervising the elections that year. The PPP won the 1992 elections which it contested as the PPPC (PPP plus a Civic component) and held power for 23 years until the Leadership and Democracy Project (LEAD) program supported the by National Endowment for Democracy (NED) and International Republican Institute (IRI) brought political change in 2015.

The APNU+AFC coalition government that won in 2015 power held a one seat majority in the National Assembly. The opposition PPP called for a vote of no confidence in the Coalition government in which a single member of the government voted with the PPP amidst claims that the PPP paid the dissenting APNU+AFC member for his vote. Constitutionally, the APNU+AFC government had to call national election within a given number of days of the no confidence vote. But, due to legal maneuverings the elections were called several months later. The APNU+AFC wanted to conduct house-to-house registration to create a new voters' list. The opposition

PPP pressed and won that the elections be held under the old voter's list it had prepared for the 2015 elections.

The PPP won a majority of the electoral districts, but the Region 4 district which is the largest went to the APNU+AFC in the 2020 elections. The Guyana Election Commission (GEOCOM) was in the process of declaring APNU the winner of the elections but the PPP took legal action to prevent the GEOCOM from proceeding to announce a winner. The PPP claimed it had won the election, and that the APNU was engaged in electoral fraud. The elections observers led by the US, Britain, Canada, and the EU agreed with the PPP's position. The PPP and APNU went outside of the Guyana Laws to agree to a recount of the votes. Initially, the PPP demanded a recount of the Region 4 votes but agreed to a recount of all the votes supervised only by the CARICOM.

At the completion of the recount the CARICOM supervisors declared that the PPP won. The APNU claimed the recount revealed massive voter fraud in the regions won by the PPP and that only the valid votes must be counted. If only the valid votes are counted the APNU says it wins. The legal wrangling which ensued ended-up in the Caribbean Court of Appeal (CCJ). The CCJ instructed among other things that the GEOCOM must declare the winner based on the party that won the majority of votes. The official in the GEOCOM with the responsibility to declare the votes did so based on the valid votes. The claim was that the Guyana Constitution allows only for valid votes to be counted. The election was held on March 2, 2020 and but it was only on August 2, 2020 a new president was sworn in after the APNU conceded.

Both, the Chairman and the Director-General of the CARICOM were accused of being on the take from the PPP. It was a real testing time for the CARICOM, that threatened the organization at its very core. Is there a connection between the political impasse in Guyana and the US geopolitical interests in the Caribbean region? The connection between the two is gradually emerging based on revelations from members of the coalition, the APNU+AFC stance on Abdul Kadir, Venezuela, and the BRI, the actions of the PPP government, and the actions of the Trump Administration.

First, Mr. Tacuma Ogunseye (2020), Secretary of the Working People's Alliance party that formed the APNU, in a letter to the editor of the Stabroek News newspapers in Guyana, said "Reluctantly the APNU+AFC coalition administration revealed to the country and the world that the US government had requested permission to use Guyana's short wave radio frequency for Voice of America to broadcast to Venezuela. That request was correctly denied in the interest of national security by the coalition government."

Second, an interview conducted by the author with a member of the Guyana Election Commission revealed that the US Ambassador to Guyana had invited each commissioner individually to meet with her to discuss the elections. The US Ambassador wanted the GEOCOM commissioners to support the US position on the elections but APNU members refused. The EU representative did the same thing as the US Ambassador and received the same response from the APNU members. Also, the EU requested to attend the GEOCOM meetings. The PPP supported the EU and US attendance at the GEOCOM meetings but the APNU opposed it.

Third, the US convicted Mr. Abdul Kadir, a late former PNC parliamentarian, as a terrorist for his alleged involvement in a plot to blow up the John F Kennedy (JFK) Airport. Kadir died in US prison in 2018 and the APNU+AFC coalition government passed a "sympathy motion" in the parliament in honor of Kadir for his services as a parliamentarian. The motion reads:

> Sympathy On The Death of Mr. Abdul Kadir, Former Member Of Parliament Be It Resolved: That this National Assembly records its deep regret on the death of Mr. Abdul Kadir, on 28th June 2018, and pays tribute to his dedicated service to the Parliament of Guyana as a Member of Parliament where he served in the Eighth Parliament, from 17th April 2001 to 2nd May 2006, and to the people of Guyana; Be It Further Resolved: That the National Assembly directs that an expression of its sympathy be conveyed to his sorrowing widow, children and relatives.

The US Embassy in Guyana condemned the resolution as being "in direct contradiction to the efforts of security cooperation between" America and Guyana (US Embassy Guyana, 2019). The US claimed that the resolution "left a stain" on the legacy of the members of parliament "as representatives of the Guyanese people and on their commitment to the rule of law" (US Embassy Guyana, 2019). The US Embassy stated that the parliament "chose to honor a man who conspired to kill innocent people from across the United States and around the world," and stated that the "resolution is an insensitive and thoughtless act, which demonstrates the National Assembly's disregard for the gravity of Kadir's actions" (US Embassy Guyana, 2019). The Trump Administration however supports the honoring US Confederate officials historically responsible for unleashing terrorist genocide against non-white Americans.

The opposition PPP boycotted the parliament on the day the resolution was passed, but issued a statement in support of the US position against the resolution. The statement said:

> "The People's Progressive Party (PPP), condemns the Motion that was passed in the National Assembly on the 26th day of April 2019, which PPP/C Parliamentarians did not attend...use of the National Assembly, Guyana's highest decision-making body, to honor the People's National Congress (PNC) former Member of Parliament, who was convicted in the United States for plotting to blow up the John F. Kennedy International Airport, is another act of betrayal of democracy and the rule of law as it is clearly not reflective of the will of the people of Guyana...now [there is] an indelible stain on our people and national character that will not easily be forgiven or forgotten by those who have suffered at the hands of international terrorism."

The APNU+AFC coalition government did not withdraw the resolution but issued the following statement on April 29, 2019.

"It is well known that there is a time-honored convention of the National Assembly to observe, in a standard and solemn form, the work of former Members who are deceased. The observance of this tradition has never been selective, and has included, over the decades, persons of all political parties and persuasions who served in the National Assembly.

"The Government of Guyana regrets the interpretation given to the motion passed in the National Assembly on April 26 on the death of Abdul Kadir, a former Member of Parliament.

"The Government of Guyana asserts that it had no intention of conveying the impression that the motion was designed to honor a former MP convicted of terrorism in another jurisdiction. The motion recognizes the member's service as a parliamentarian.

"The Government of Guyana continues to condemn terrorism in the strongest possible way. The Government of Guyana reaffirms its commitment to continue and intensify the fight against terrorism in any form and is proud of its record to date in this regard" Government of Guyana, 2019).

The fourth strike against the APNU+AFC government was its difference with the US over the situation in Venezuela. The Trump Administration is adamant that it is pursuing a policy of regime change in Venezuela and has recognized the opposition leader in that country as its legitimate interim president. The Guyana-government has taken a stance which is consistent with the CARICOM-position on the Bolivarian Republic of Venezuela. This includes calls for dialogue involving all parties and social actors, the preservation of the democratic process, and a return to normalcy in the country. The Government of Guyana remains firmly supportive of efforts to resolve the crisis through peaceful means and with full respect for human rights and the rule of law (Government of Guyana, 2020a).

Guyana's Ministry of Foreign Affairs in a letter to the Stabroek News however corrected the newspapers for printing in an Editorial that the Government of Guyana had recognized the opposition leader in Venezuela as the country's legitimate interim president. The letter read in part that the Ministry was compelled to draw attention to a "glaring error" that the "Government of Guyana had recognized Juan Guaidó as the legitimate Interim President of Venezuela." The statement read that "at no juncture has the Government of Guyana supported or recognized Mr. Juan Guaidó as the Interim President of Venezuela. Suffice to say, that we do not believe that non-recognition of one implies automatic recognition of another (Government of Guyana, 2020b).

Fifth, the Granger Administration entered into agreement through the BRI to secure among other things military support from China. The Chinese donated military equipment to the Guyana Defense Force at a time when the US Southern Commend expressed grave concern about China's projects in the region impacting US communications (Sanchez, 2019). The defense relations between the two countries included the Chinese awarding scholarships to eleven Guyana Defense Force officers to pursue advanced studies in China mainly in scientific, technological, and engineering fields. It involved China's donation of non-lethal military equipment to Guyana including 31 pieces of equipment namely patrol boats, bulldozers, an excavator, water tankers, fuel tankers, tipper trucks, off-road ambulances, and several other vehicles (Sanchez, 2019). The Chinese Minister of Foreign Affairs visited Guyana in September 2018, and President Granger declared the readiness of Guyana to work with China to jointly build the Belt and Road to push forward relations between the two countries (Sanchez, 2019).

Sixth, Guyana, is located on the North Eastern shoulder of the South American mainland next to Venezuela which has the world's largest oil reserves. Guyana is rich in natural resources and is now an oil producing country. Venezuela claims ownership of the lands in Guyana that are endowed with numerous natural resources including oil. The Chinese and Russians are already in Guyana's bauxite industry and China's state-controlled oil company CNOOC Ltd owns a 25 percent stake in the massive Stabroek block as part of a consortium with operator Exxon Mobil Corp and US firm Hess Corp in Guyana's oil sector. It is becoming clearer how much of the political impasse in Guyana after the March 2020 national elections was due to manipulation by foreign forces to secure Venezuelan and Guyana's oil. Undoubtedly, the US is not prepared to allow China, Russia, and the EU to have control over the energy resources in Guyana and Venezuela.

Seventh, since the PPP took over the reins of power the Ali Administration with haste supported the US choice for President of the Inter-American Development Bank (IDB). The Trump Administration's unprecedented picking of a White House official Mr. Mauricio Claver-Carone, Special Assistant to the President and Senior Director of the United States National Security Council's Western Hemisphere Affairs Directorate, to head the IDB is counter to the long-standing principle that Latin America would name to person to head the institution. The Latin Americans have expressed displeasure with the Trump Administration on the matter but Guyana is siding with the US (Saraiva, 2020).

Eight, before the dust was settled after the PPP took power US counterpart to the Chinese Foreign Minister, Secretary of State Mike Pompeo visited Guyana to shore up support for the efforts by the Trump Administration to oust the Venezuelan President Nicolás Maduro and build ties with the booming oil producer (Wilkinson, 2020). The newly sworn in President Irfaan Ali stated at the press availability with Mike Pompeo that his government was "grateful to the United States Government and in particular to Secretary Pompeo for their unwavering support for democracy and constitutional order in Guyana" (US Department of State, 2020). President Ali said: "Secretary Pompeo's visit serves to remind us that the US will continue to be a steadfast partner" of Guyana and "solidifies the bilateral relationship between Guyana and the US and sets the stage for expanding and deepening US cooperation with Guyana" (US Department of State, 2020).

In turn Secretary Pompeo pointed out that he "was proud to publicly support the Guyanese people in their quest to have the results of the election respected. The results certainly took longer than any of us would have wished or hoped, but it was worth fighting for. It was worth fighting to honor the people's sovereign decision. That's indeed – (applause) – that's indeed what democracy is all about" (US Department of State, 2020). Mr. Pompeo does not hold the same position when it comes to the US Presidential elections in 2020. Mr. Pompeo has taken side against democracy by refusing to recognize the will of the American people who have voted to give President-elect Joseph Biden and Vice-President-elect Kamala Harris victory over lame duck President Trump. Mr. Pompeo claims that there will be a smooth transition to a second Trump Administration although the overwhelming evidence is that Mr. Biden has been duly elected as the next US President.

Mr. Pompeo stated that the US was ready to be Guyana's "partner of choice as you face big decisions moving forward, especially on energy and future prosperity in your country" (US Department of State, 2020). Undoubtedly, the "big decisions" that Guyana has to make are in reference to the role of China in the country, and Guyana's position on Venezuela. Mr. Pompeo announced that the USAID had "committed $3 million for a locally led program for citizens' involvement in their government, and a million and a half so that the youth of Guyana will be involved in democracy as well" (US Department of State, 2020). This is virtually an extension of the LEAD program but this time to shore up the PPP in office. The LEAD program that helped to elect the APNU+AFC coalition government had similar objectives to involve citizens especially the youths in politics and government, as a means to build democracy (Canterbury, 2020). The big decisions undoubtedly concerning "energy" is definitely a reference to the dominant role the US intends to play in Guyana's oil sector. Finally, Mr. Pompeo was clear that his discussions with the Guyanese authorities focused on bringing "an end to the illegitimate Maduro regime." Mr. Pompeo announced that the US had "allocated $5 million to help Venezuelans in Guyana who have had to flee from Venezuela to Guyana to escape the horrors and brutality of the Maduro regime" (US Department of State, 2020).

Conclusion

The MAGA doctrine is the current form of US imperialism in the new multipolarity, which is distinguished from the neoconservatives' PNAC doctrine to make the twenty-first century an American century. The MAGA measures seek to maintain America's position not as the sole hegemonic power but as one that has to compete with China, Russia, and the EU to keep its place among rivals. The CARICOM states are at risk of recolonization by America in the great states' competition in the new multipolarity. The US is definitely flexing its muscle openly, in its geopolitical designs for the Caribbean region. This is evident from the MAGA foreign policy toward Venezuela, China, and the BRI. The speculation is that the US wants to control Guyana in order to complete its encirclement of Venezuela which is bordered by Colombia, Brazil, and Guyana. The current regimes in Colombia and Brazil are already supporting the US on Venezuela. But, surprisingly, the APNU+AFC government in Guyana, albeit helping to gain power by the Obama Administration through the LEAD program funded and executed by the NED and IRI, respectively, have ran afoul of the Trump Administration. The CARICOM is slowly falling in line with America's geopolitics in the region.

Secretary of State Pompeo (2020) declared the US and Caribbean are "natural allies." The Secretary of State said it was tempting for the CARICOM states to "accept easy money from places like China," but warned that such money feeds corruption, undermines the rule of law, ruin the environment, and do not create jobs in the region. The Secretary of State proposed what he considers a better alternative to taking money from China. Mr. Pompeo stated: "Western firms, American firms operate according to values proven to produce good deals and quality work, the work that we do in democracies, things like transparent contracts, the respect for the rule of law, honest straightforward accounting practices" (Pompeo, 2020). Pompeo (2020) states that the US has "created a new Development Finance Corporation that works inside of our State Department" to help the Caribbean's "private sector stand on its own." Pompeo (2020) pointed out that American "values are also gaining steam in the energy sector," where collaboration with the Caribbean is expanding. According to Pompeo (2020), the cooperation on energy is significant because "it reduces costs for consumers and for businesses," and PetroCaribe is fading into the sunset, as the Maduro regime itself will do."

America is definitely not going to easily allow extra-regional forces to gain the upper hand in the Caribbean especially given the oil resources in Venezuela, Guyana, Trinidad and Tobago, Barbados, and Suriname.

References

Bernal, R.L. (2017). *A Caribbean Policy for the Trump Administration*. Washington: Center for Strategic and International Studies.

Canterbury, D.C. (2020). *Neoextractivism and Capitalist Development*. London and New York: Routledge (paperback edition).

Chance, A. (2016). *American Perspectives on the Belt and Road Initiative: Sources of Concern, Possibilities for US-China Cooperation*. Washington DC: Institute for China-America Studies, November.

Charles, J. (2019). "Caribbean Leaders Meet With Trump, Says He Promises Renewed US Engagement in Region," *Miami Herald*, March 22.

Charles, C.A.D. and D. Roberts (2019). "The Impact of the Trump Presidency on the Commonwealth Caribbean," *The Round Table: The Commonwealth Journal of International Affairs* 108 (3): 293–305.

Chollet, D. (2016). "The Myth of America's Disengagement," *Defense One*, 20 May.

Government of Guyana (2019). *Statement by the Government of the Cooperative Republic of Guyana*, 29 April.

Government of Guyana (2020a). *Statement by the Government of Guyana on the Situation in Venezuela*. Guyana: Ministry of Foreign Affairs, 24 January.

Government of Guyana (2020b). The Ministry of Foreign Affairs Wishes to Refer to An Editorial Titled "Truth" in Your Publication on Monday March 9, 2020.

Kaplan, R.D. (2017). "Why Trump Can't Disengage America From the World," *The New York Times*, 6 January.

Kirkey, S. (2018). "Is Donald Trump's 'Principled Realism' a Real Doctrine?" *National Post*, 26 September.

MacDonald, S.B. (2019). The Return of the Cold War in the Caribbean, *Global Americans*, 22, April.

McFarland, K.T. (2020). *Revolution: Trump, Washington and "We the People*. New York: Post Hill Press.

Mukherjee, S.R. (2018). "Make America Great Again as White Political Theology," *LISA*, XVI (2). https://doi.org/10.4000/lisa.9887

Ogunseye, T. (2020). Letter to the Editor, Georgetorn, Guyana, *Stabroek News*, 18 August.

Paxton, R.O. (2017). "American Duce: Is Donald Trump a Fascist or a Plutocrat?" *Harper's Magazing*, May.

Pompeo, M.R. (2020). *"Expanding America's Commitment to the Caribbean,"* Kingston, Jamaica, 20 January.

Sanchez, W.A. (2019). *Guyana Matters to China, So It Should Matter to the US*. Washington DC: Providence, 18 November.

Saraiva, A. (2020). "Trump's Pick to Run Latin America's Development Bank Is the Last Thing It Needed," *Foreign Policy News*, 11 August.

Sullivan, M.P. (2020). *China's Engagement with Latin America and the Caribbean*. Washington DC: Congressional Research Service, 1 June.

The Guardian (2020). "Caribbean leaders Boycott Pompeo Talks as Row Grows Over US Relations," 20 January.

Torres, A. (2019). "Here is List of Countries Recognizing Juan Guaidó as Venezuela's Interim President," *Local 10.com*, 13 March.

Trujillo, C. (2019). Remarks by Ambassador Carlos Trujillo US Mission to the OAS (Permanent Council Approves Resolution to Not Recognize the Legitimacy of the Maduro Regime).

Trump, D.J. (2016). *Great Again: How to Fix Our Crippled America*. New York: Threshold Editions.

Trump, D.J. (2018). *"Remarks by President Trump to the 73rd Session of the United Nations General Assembly,"* New York, 25 September.

US Department of State (2020). "Secretary Michael R. Pompeo and Guyana President Mohamed Irfaan Ali at a Press Availability," *Remarks to the Press* Michael R. Pompeo, Secretary of State, State House, Georgetown Guyana, 18 September.

US Embassy Guyana (2019). *"U.S. Embassy Condemns the Resolution by the National Assembly to Honor a Convicted Terrorist,"* Georgetown, Guyana, 29 April.

White House (2017). "President Donald J. Trump: Year One of Making America Great Again, Fact Sheet," White House.gov, 22 December.

Wilkinson, B. (2020). *Pompeo Visits Guyana Hoping to Shore up Support in Venezuela*. Associated Press, Georgetown, Guyana, 18 September.

5 The new multipolar world order

Introduction

The twin purpose here is to explore the dynamic nature of the theoretical debates on the new multipolarity and analyze the characteristic features of the new multipolar world order in which the Caribbean Community states have to formulate economic policies. Never before has the CARICOM states been in a world order where the center of gravity of power is in the East. The central issue for the CARICOM states in the New Multipolar World Order (NMWO) is to have working class interests dominate economic development policy. The chapter is divided into four parts beginning with an outline of the proposition and argument about the NMWO, followed by an analysis of the theoretical debates on the subject. The characteristic features of the NMWO comprising the US power-sharing on the world stage, the European Union's bloc imperialism, the rise of China and its critics, and the Russian pole are analyzed in that order.

Proposition and argument

The principal proposition is the US intended the reversals in Eastern European communism to catapult America into the position of global hegemon in a single global free market economic and liberal democratic political system, but the US dreams were dashed by the emergence of the EU, China, and Russia as counterbalancing forces to its power. On a worldscale a double transformation has simultaneously taken place – the center of gravity of international power has shifted from West to East, concurrently with a shift from a short-lived unipolar global order to a new multipolar world order. There is no general agreement in the emerging literature on the composition of the NMWO. Seemingly, the only agreement is that the US-led unipolar neoliberal global order was replaced by a multipolar one. The new multipolarity as understood in this study comprises four poles of power – the US, EU, China, and Russia. These poles emerged in their own right and the US recognized them as competitors in which the measures of a unipolar global order no longer apply. This is the context in which the US

DOI: 10.4324/9781003092414-5

is dismantling the unipolar neoliberal global order. Capitalist development and class struggle has entered into a new phase – world-wide class action by working people becomes easier through social media and new technologies, as well as capitalist endeavors to accumulate capital.

The NMWO is new because it has replaced the old US-led unipolar neoliberal global order, and because a multipolar world order existed before World War II. The world was multipolar when World War II was fought, whether the poles comprised nation-states or empires (Ferguson, 2006). Each pole engaged in World War II brought their dominions into the conflict. The NMWO is a "world order" and not a "global order" because none of the current poles of power have dominion over the entire globe. A global order exists when a sole superpower imposes its will on all countries on the planet. In a multipolar world order each pole is in its own world interacting with other worlds to gain economic and political advantage.

The US acknowledged that its unipolar global order has ended when it claimed that the world has entered into a new era of great power competition. There has been a transition from a de facto American global sphere to a world order characterized by multiple spheres of influence. The US now shares the global stage with the BRICS (Brazil, Russia, India, China, South Africa) states especially China and Russia, and the EU that are increasingly using their power to assert their interests and values that often conflict with those of America's (Allison, 2020; Saunders, 2020). Undoubtedly, relative economic, political, and military power is shifting away from the West towards Asian regions (Schwarzer, 2017). The rules-based international order and institutional pillars, such as the UN, IMF, and World Bank, founded after World War II, and in place for the past 70 years, are falling apart (Heine, 2020).

This change has resulted from the emergence of Asia and the BRICS that "created a major imbalance in the power distribution and voting arrangements in international organizations (IOs) and international financial institutions (IFIs)" (Heine, 2020). The current institutional structures of the international system are outdated, unrepresentative of the emerging powers, and need upgrading to match the new multipolarity. While "shrinking middle powers like the United Kingdom are among the permanent members of the UN Security Council," there are "emerging giants like Brazil and India" which are not (Heine, 2020). The WTO's appellate body has been inoperative because the US having lost a number of trade disputes brought against it in that organization, blocks the appointments of judges to the body (Heine, 2020). Also, the WTO Director General, and the President of the World Bank have both recently stepped down.

Theoretical debates on the new multipolarity

The literature on the new multipolarity reviewed in the brief survey below does not unravel the nature of class struggle as power is realigned in the international system. There is little or no analysis of the class forces that control state power in the NMWO. The countries and blocs that constitute the poles of power are not stateless or classless. The NMWO is characterized by class struggle within each pole and in the relations between those poles and countries in the global south.

It is believed the idea of polarity goes back to Thucydides' record of the Peloponnesian War which revealed the bipolarity of power between Sparta and Athens (Kratochvíl, 2002). In premodern times polarity existed in different parts of the world (Kegley and Raymond, 1994). Kratochvíl (2002) suggests that in the World War II period Morgenthau (1948) and Waltz (1979) analyzed fundamental theoretical features of polarity. The current debate concerning where, when, and who created the concept (Schulze, 2019), however, seem to point towards post-Soviet Russia. Schulze (2019) noted that the term experienced a rebirth in Russia, China, and the EU as the twentieth century ended and the twenty-first century began. Also, the US Congress and foreign and security communities employed different versions of the term. It is argued that Russia's Prime Minister Yevgeny Primakov conceptualized the term in the mid-1990s to admonish Russian Foreign Minister Andrei Kozyrev for having a romanticized Western orientation in Russia's foreign policy (Schulze, 2019). Buchanan (2019) posits, the multipolar world order is shaped by Primakov's principles of self-sufficiency, independence, openness, and predictability. It is an order in which due to their economic base Russia, China, and India have a greater role in global decision-making (Buchanan, 2019).

The objective of Primakov's multipolarity is an alliance between Russia, China, and India to balance the US hegemonic influence (Schulze, 2019). Turner (2009) argues however multipolarity is an ill-defined concept that Russia and China have repeatedly agreed on and have subsequently included "in or alluded to it in nearly all of their joint declarations, statements, and treaties dating from the mid-1990s." Chebankova (2017) sees Russia's ethical and ideological stance in the international arena to be etched on the notion of multipolarity. Meanwhile, Makarychev (2014) believes that Russian society is understood to be intellectually buttressed by the philosophical tenets of Russia's notions of a multipolar world, a vantage point from which Russia–EU relations are analyzed.

The debate on the future of the world order boils down to two opposite points of view (Timofeev, 2019). First, the world transitioned to a Western rules-based liberal order at the end of the Cold War shored up by the West's military, economic, and moral superiority. Second, the liberal order based on US hegemony is unipolar, unstable, and on the verge of crisis. The unipolar model is seen to have an unlikely chance because it is undermined by emerging centers of power like BRICS. The efficiency of the rules of the game of the liberal model is doubted, and an alternative multipolar or polycentric world was advocated. In this case, the multipolar world comprises a community of equal partners, with the UN and other international institutions ensuring its democratic nature (Timofeev, 2019).

The composition of the poles of power is problematic, although various authors argue that a new multipolar world order has formed. China, Russia, India, Indonesia, Turkey, Brazil, South Africa, the US, EU, G-20, or a combination of these have all been variously identified as current poles of power. Murray and Brown (2013) believe that the new multipolar world order comprises the US, EU, China, Russia, and India. They assessed the development of a multipolar world in the contexts of a US decline or the rise of its putative rivals. Butler (2018) believes that the BRICS states are the most notable rival powers to have emerged simultaneously with the decline in US power.

Freedomlab (2020) presents the view that a new multipolarity is in the making associated with the uneven diffusion of economic, financial, and military power. It will not emerge quickly, so instability will prevail as shadow powers rise and alliances become uncertain (Freedomlab, 2020). Freedomlab (2020) defines multipolarity as "a distribution of power in which more than two states have nearly equal amounts of military, cultural, financial and economic influence." But, historically, there have been considerable instability in multipolar orders because rather than having a balanced equilibrium as multipolarity suggests, there exists greater protectionism and currency wars (Freedomlab, 2020).

States are supposed to balance each other economically, militarily and financially, in a multipolar world, but, the fact is that different countries enjoy different types of power. Thus, if a hegemon loses economic and financial power it might still maintain undisputed military power (Freedomlab, 2020). This situation creates instability because the rising states waiting to supplant a declining hegemon, might not have sufficient power to do so. Meanwhile, the declining hegemon may use its economic, financial or military power to restrain a rising power. This contradiction is destabilizing and could promote aggression by rising powers, while the hegemon may become suspicious and feels threatened by them (Freedomlab, 2020). This situation is unpredictably conflictful, renders alliances ambiguous, and creates the space for the projection of shadow power, by the hegemon and its opponents via digital tools, to manipulate each other (Freedomlab, 2020).

Buchanan (2019) points to the need for the multipolar order to produce a different set of international institutions to those created in the aftermath of World War II on which current international decision-making depends. The current international institutions and structures were not fashioned for a multipolar world. They have to be remodeled and rejuvenated to accommodate the new poles of power in Asia and Africa, to make the mechanisms for decision-making relevant to present realities (Buchanan, 2019). The West has lost its prerogative to shape the international agenda by itself in the new multipolar system. Western ideas on liberal democratic norms that do not consider the interests of non-Western cultures, are the foundation of the current rules-based order (Buchanan, 2019).

Pieterse (2017) argues as power shifts from the West to the East the new multipolarity must reshape and reinforce globalization in a different way not replace it. Oriental globalization preceded occidental globalization, and the orients are making a comeback in various guises as Asia is the driving force in the world economy today (Pieterse, 2017). Petito (2016) investigated multipolarity in terms of trends related to emerging powers and the idea of dialogue of civilizations. In this case, multipolarity is a component of a "broader epoch making process of the transformation of contemporary international society beyond its Western-centric matrix" (Petito, 2016). These broad changes have given rise to "a new multipolar world of civilizational politics and multiple modernities," which have given pause for "reflections on countering the risk inherent in the potential antagonistic logic of multipolarity by critically engaging the normative Huntingtonian construction of a multicivilizational-multipolar world order" (Petito, 2016).

Patriota (2017) understands the new multipolarity in terms of geopolitical changes in the world today. The changes have reinvigorated interest in the international configuration of power exhibited by the rise of China and the BRICS, Brexit, the Arab spring, and the US' relative decline. Levitte (2019) affirms nonetheless that after four decades of a bipolar world order and a decade of a unipolar one we are now living today in a multipolar world where the rules of the game are contested. But, Patriota (2017) believes the primary challenge for the new multipolarity is for it to become a vehicle for sustainable development and durable peace (Patriota, 2017).

Haass (2008) takes a contrary position arguing "the principal characteristic of the twenty-first-century international relations is turning out to be non-polarity: a world dominated not by one or two power or even several states but rather by dozens of actors possessing and exercising various kinds of power." Perhaps the most contradictory idea on the subject is that the US has to create a new multipolar world order by using its influence to identify and help peaceful, prosperous nations to attain major power status (DeYeso, 2006). This newly US created multipolar world will be based on some combinations of the following countries – the US, France, Germany, Britain, Japan, China, or Russia (DeYeso, 2006). But, if the US creates a multipolar world order is it really multipolar or unipolar?

Fabbrini (2010, 2017) takes a different direction in his analysis of the post-globalization world order, arguing for a transition to a post-Western and not a multipolar order. It is contended that the post-global order is a post-Western one which has been in emergence since 9/11 and the financial crash in 2008 (Fabbrini, 2017). The neoconservative approach especially after 9/11 has been a "clear political strategy based on the idea that America comes first" (Fabbrini, 2010, 2017). This stratagem became the official doctrine of the Republican Party after the mid-term election of 2002. Trumpism is a mere continuation of an approach adopted earlier by Republicans (Fabbrini, 2010, 2017). The neoconservatives are still in power, albeit the method used to achieve the "America first" approach is much more brash under the Trump Administration (Fabbrini, 2010, 2017).

The characteristic features of the new multipolar world order

It is articulated in this study that the new multipolar world order comprises four poles of power – the US, EU, China, and Russia. The position taken here on the NMWO is in line with Petras and Veltmeyer (2018) who argue that a major global realignment of economic power from the US and Europe to the BRICS is taking place. The states in the global south are realigning their economies from the US and EU towards the BRICS led by China and Russia.

The US power-sharing on the world stage

Dolan (2018) argues the US has reversed position after 70 years of its hegemony and defending the status quo. The Obama Administration pulled back the US from its role in the world, and the Trump Administration has turned America away from globalization and questions US long-standing alliances. The Obama mantra of "nation-building here at home" gave way to "America First" under Trump but they are quite two similar agendas (Dolan, 2018). The Obama Administration walked back America from the neoconservative idea that America was the world's preeminent power. The evidence of this is President Obama's position on Syria and willingness to play collectively and not have the US be the only global policeman. President Obama engaged in regional negotiations on the Trans-Pacific Partnership (TPP) and Transatlantic Trade and Investment Partnership (TTIP); agreed with China that made the Paris climate accord possible; cooperated with Russia and China and three European countries on the nuclear agreement with Iran (Levitte, 2019), and welcomed China in the Caribbean because China was helping to develop the region.

Trumpian "America first" and "make America great again" nationalism is weakening US ties with its traditional European allies, disrupting the neoliberal globalization rules-based order, and forging stronger links with US adversaries North Korea and Russia. The evidence is President Trump's withdrawal from international agreements supported with the Europeans; attacks on the North Atlantic Treaty Organization; withdrawals from the TTP, the Paris climate agreement, and the nuclear accord with Iran; renegotiation of the North American Free Trade Area (NAFTA); weakening International Organizations (IOs) such as the United Nations, the G7, G20, WTO, and NATO (Levitte, 2019); and recent withdrawal of US financial support for the World Health Organization (WHO) in the midst of the Covid-19 pandemic.

The US has lost its status as the world's preeminent power aiming to shape the globe in its image. America can no longer take military action around the world as it pleases, exemplified by the current situation in the Middle East,

Asia, and Venezuela. In those regions, BRICS countries namely Russia and China are acting as counterbalances to US military power. The US accuses Russia, Iran, and North Korea of electronic interference in its national elections to influence voting patterns in 2016. The Trump Administration is in conflict with China, the EU, and Russia over several issues. America has an ongoing trade war with China, it is withdrawing from international agreements with the EU, and it has imposed trade sanctions on Russia.

The essential feature of the NMWO is its demurring to bringing all countries into a single global economic and political system. There is no such universal objective in the NMWO, albeit all countries seemingly embrace the UN sustainable development goals. In countries where the US is seeking to impose its political will such as Syria and Venezuela it has encountered Russian and Chinese opposition. The colossal change from the unipolar neoliberal global order to the new multipolar world order is on the same scale as the reversals in Eastern European communism with the collapse of the former Soviet Union. The Soviet Union lost power to US-led neoliberal globalization, but now the US has lost power to the new multipolar world order.

The European Union's bloc imperialism

The EU is a bloc with the trappings of a nation-state – parliament, flag, currency, and army, but functions with a different democratic logic characteristic of nation-states (Fabbrini, 2017). It is seen as an "empire of norms" on the world stage, whose rules are necessary because the EU is an integrated market of 500 million Europeans, and an anchor to which the law of the world economy can hitch itself in a globe threatened by the law of the jungle (Levitte, 2019). Levitte (2019) argues that the EU has asserted itself in the legal domain where it exercise its global responsibilities. Seemingly, this assertion is manifested through the European Commission's idea of "global Europe" which is best understood as a grand strategy formulated by the EU to increase and maintain its global economic and political leverage – EU bloc imperialism (Canterbury, 2012). The strategy entails maintaining Europe's competitiveness in world markets, providing opportunities to European companies to operate freely abroad by targeting regulatory frameworks in other countries, and creating a more business-friendly environment in Europe to build strong European companies (Seattle to Brussels Network, 2006).

Its trade policy provides the broad outline of the EU's framework for bilateral free trade agreements with major emerging economies to secure new and profitable markets (European Commission Directorate-General for Trade, 2006). It promotes stronger intellectual property rights, reduced non-tariff barriers by its trading partners, and business friendly reforms in Europe and abroad. The strategy advocates aggressive external competitiveness and policies to pry open world markets for competitive European companies, takes an activist stance in dealing with trading partners initiating bilateral trade agreements, and forces prior consultation with businesses in the design of new regulations (Maisano and Rondinella, 2006).

It indorses private access to dispute settlement for EU companies, restricts entrée to government procurement contracts in the EU for countries that do not reciprocate, and encourages full parity in bilateral negotiations (Canterbury, 2012). The strategy seeks to expunge all barriers to trade, and to have the EU's domestic and foreign agendas ensure all regulations only have minimal distortion of trade (Canterbury, 2012). It breaks down the regulatory environment in other countries, to give the EU greater leverage in its external relations with the global south. The strategy is founded on free competition, flexibility, deregulation, and dismantling the European social model (Maisano and Rondinella, 2006).

The global Europe strategy has fostered a new generation of bilateral agreements identified for target countries based on market potential – size, growth and profit prospects, the level of protection against EU export interests, and the number of bilateral agreements countries already have with other trading partners (Maisano and Rondinella, 2006). The Association of South East Asian Nations (ASEAN) group, South Korea, Mercosur (Argentina, Brazil, Paraguay, Uruguay, Venezuela), India, Russia, and the Gulf Cooperation Council are identified as priority targets for EU bilateral agreements. The EU divided the Organization of Africa, Pacific and Caribbean (OACP) group of countries into various sub-regions – Central Africa, Eastern and Southern Africa, East African Community, Southern African Development Community, West Africa, Caribbean, and Pacific – with which it negotiated Economic Partnership Agreements (EPAs) as mechanisms for its bloc imperialism.

The rise of China

The Belt and Road and Made in China (MIC) 2025 initiatives are cases in point about the meteoric rise of China to global prominence. The BRI launched by President Xi in 2013 (Office of the Leading Group for the Belt and Road Initiative, 2017), aims to boost economic integration and connectivity in infrastructure, trade, and investment with China's neighbors and various trading partners in Asia, Africa, Europe, and beyond by land and sea (Lawrence et al., 2019; Morrison, 2019; Xi, 2017). The BRI recognizes and embraces the "trend towards a multipolar world, economic globalization, cultural diversity and greater IT application" (PRC, 2015). It was "designed to uphold the global free trade regime and the open world economy in the spirit of open regional cooperation" (PRC, 2015).

The BRI aims to promote the orderly and free flow of economic factors, efficient resource allocation, and deep market integration. Countries along the Belt and Road are encouraged to coordinate their economic policies while engaging in higher standards, detailed, and more comprehensive regional cooperation (PRC, 2015). According to PRC (2015), the architecture advocated for regional economic cooperation is one that is open, inclusive, and balanced. The BRI is in search of new ways to promote international cooperation and global governance, while connecting the Asian, European, and African continents and their adjacent seas, with the aim to establish and strengthen partnerships among participating countries (PRC, 2015). It proposes to establish "all-dimensional, multitiered and composite connectivity networks, and realize diversified, independent, balanced and sustainable development" in BRI countries (PRC, 2015). The purpose of the connectivity projects is to align and coordinate development strategies, exploit market potential, "promote investment and consumption, create demands and job opportunities, [and] enhance people-to-people and cultural exchanges," in the BRI region (PRC, 2015).

China is obligated through the BRI to stay committed to the global economy; pursue policies to open-up its own economy; build new patterns of all-round openness to integrate itself deeper into the world economic system; expanding, deepening, strengthening, and open-up cooperation in Asia, Europe, and Africa and the rest of the world; and specifically bringing together China, Central Asia, Russia and Europe (the Baltic), the Persian Gulf and the Mediterranean Sea, Southeast Asia, and South Asia and the Indian Ocean (PRC, 2015). The BRI has two principal considerations for economic activities on land and sea – to build "a new Eurasian Land Bridge" and develop the "China–Mongolia–Russia, China–Central Asia-West Asia and China–Indochina Peninsula" economic corridors; and to build "secure and efficient transport routes connecting major sea ports along the Belt and Road" (PRC, 2015). China–Pakistan, and Bangladesh–China–India–Myanmar are two other economic corridors earmarked for further cooperation. The BRI is funded through a number of sources including the Agricultural Bank of China, China Development Bank, Export–Import Bank of China, China Investment Corporation, and the Industrial and Commercial Bank of China. The Asian Development Bank, Asian Infrastructure Investment Bank, and the New Development Bank are also funding agencies of the BRI.

The State Council of the People's Republic of China (PRC) through Premier Li Keqiang announced the MIC 2025 initiative in May 2015. Premier Li announced that China had intended to upgrade its industrial structure to a medium-high level through its MIC 2025 initiative (Keqiang, 2015). This involves seeking innovation-driven development, the application of smart technologies, the strengthening of foundations, pursuit of green development, and redoubling China's efforts to upgrade itself from a manufacture of quantity to quality (Keqiang, 2015). The MIC 2025 entails the provision of subsidies and acceleration of equipment depreciation to push forward the upgrading of traditional industries (Keqiang, 2015). It is a deliberate strategy to restrict the growth of some industries, promote expansion in others, cut overcapacity, support business acquisition and restructure, and allow market competition to determine the survival of businesses (Keqiang, 2015).

The extensive application of information technologies in industrialization, the development and utilization of networking, digitalization and smart technologies, and the emphasis on making key breakthroughs in those areas are key components of MIC 2025 (Keqiang, 2015).

With respect to emerging industries and new types of businesses, major projects will be launched through MIC 2025 to develop high-end equipment, information networks, integrated circuits, new energy, new materials, biomedicines, aero engines, and gas turbines to transform the emerging industries into leading ones (Keqiang, 2015). China intends to develop its "Internet Plus" action plan to integrate the mobile Internet, cloud computing, big data, and the Internet of Things with modern manufacturing, "to encourage the healthy development of e-commerce, industrial networks, and Internet banking, and to guide Internet-based companies to increase their presence in the international market" (Keqiang, 2015).

The services sector is seen as being able to provide employment opportunities because of its vast potential for development (Keqiang, 2015). Based on the premise that it is people who make innovations and create things China plans to "speed up the reform to manage the use and commoditization of and distribution of profit from scientific and technological advances of public institutions and allow coverage of policies which allow for incentive mechanisms for innovation based on shares and dividends" (Keqiang, 2015). Legislation on commercialization of research and development deliverables, policies to encourage the flow of researchers and engineers, reform in the system of their appraisal, the conferring of professional titles and national awards, reform research institutions, and the attraction of high-caliber foreign professionals and the employment of other experts from overseas are integral components of the plan.

China intends to "implement and improve preferential policies, such as extra tax deductions for research and development costs" and implement "policies that support new- and high-technology enterprises, so as to encourage enterprises to increase their spending on innovation" (Keqiang, 2015). The MIC 2025 program entails encouraging "enterprise involvement in implementing major science and technology projects and building research platforms," and the promotion of "collaborative innovation by bringing together enterprise, academia, and research institutes, with enterprises playing a leading role" (Keqiang, 2015).

The 10-year MIC plan aims to close the high-tech gap with Western powers, lessen China's dependence on foreign technology, while specifying ten areas in which China should take the lead over all countries (Tse and Wu, 2018). The MIC 2025 is being implemented in three phases beginning with the 2015–2025 period when China proposes to become one of the world's strongest manufacturing power. In the second phase between 2026 and 2035 China proposes to rise to the intermediate level among the world's manufacturing powers. China anticipates to become the world's leading manufacturer in the final phase between 2035 and 2049 (Tse and Wu, 2018).

Critics of the BRI

The foregoing descriptive analysis of the BRI and MIC 2025 provides China's bona fides as a world power in a post-neoliberal globalization NMWO. The argument is that BRI and MIC 2025 are only possible because of the economic power and corresponding military strength China possesses. Currently, no other country is really in a position to undertake such ambitious economic ventures. The scope and nature of the BRI and MIC 2025 provide the evidence of China's arrival as a global power. Although they both have internal and external impacts MIC 2025 focuses on building China's internal economic and military capabilities, while the BRI focuses on spreading Chinese influence overseas. This latter has the potential to shut the door on US economic relations with the largest portion of humanity located in Africa, Asia, and Europe.

US analysts are therefore skeptical about the BRI viewing it with much suspicion and trepidation (Chatzky and McBride, 2020). It is regarded as serving China's vision for hegemony (Rolland, 2018); "debt diplomacy" (Lawrence et al., 2019); and unfair competition (Tse and Wu, 2018). The Trump Administration launched a trade war with China implementing tariffs that target inter alia energy equipment, parts for offshore oil and natural gas, drilling, and production platforms. The tariffs impact Chinese companies engaged in the industrial robotics industry, the new generation information technology sector namely machines and apparatus to manufacture semiconductor devices or electronic, integrated circuits, and maritime equipment (Tse and Wu, 2018). Also impacted are the aviation and aerospace equipment industries that produce communication satellites, spacecraft including satellite (other than communication satellites), and suborbital and spacecraft launch vehicles (Tse and Wu, 2018).

The maritime equipment and hi-tech ships industry that produces steam turbines for marine propulsion, ship or boat propellers, and blades are also impacted by the tariffs (Tse and Wu, 2018). The tariffs affect railway or tramway track fixtures and fittings, mechanical signaling, and safety or traffic control equipment of all kinds (Tse and Wu, 2018). Also affected are the new energy and energy-saving vehicles industry in terms of storage batteries used as the primary source of power for electric vehicles. US tariffs in the agricultural equipment industry will impact parts of agricultural, horticultural, or forestry machinery for soil preparation or cultivation, and parts of lawn or sports ground rollers. In the biopharma and hi-tech medical devices sector the tariffs will affect apparatus based on the use of X-rays other than for medical, surgical, dental, or veterinary use (Tse and Wu, 2018).

Critics argue that democracies are turning against the BRI due to corruption, debt, and backlash (Balding, 2018). Balding (2018) observed that the BRI faces backlash at home, as many Chinese claim the initiative is wasteful spending abroad as countries grow wary of China's growing influence.

China's no-strings attached approach does not require its partners to meet any conditionalities related to corruption, human rights, or financial sustainability. Critics argue the result is China's investment approach has fueled corruption, increase debt, and stimulate anger among local populations that is making itself felt at national elections (Balding, 2018).

Chaudhury (2019) stated the BRI has led to neglect of China's domestic consequences including corruption, financial deficiency, and the rise of xenophobia. It appears that ordinary Chinese are not benefiting from the expansionist role of the Chinese state (Chaudhury, 2019). In Zambia, China is taking over an International Airport after a debt installment default, and Congo is highly indebted to China due to China-funded projects (Chaudhury, 2019). The BRI is used to launder money, and secretly transfer national wealth abroad (Chaudhury, 2019). China's expansionary stance means that the state will have to spend more on the military to protect its overseas interests (Chaudhury, 2019). Increased military spending would translate into cuts to education, social welfare, or other public spending (Chaudhury, 2019). African students who travel on scholarship to China under the BRI are accused of having higher scholarship payments than Chinese students, and of being the cause of an increase in AIDS in China (Chaudhury, 2019).

Russia has embraced the BRI although there was some reservation that the BRI would outshine Moscow's vision for a Eurasian Economic Union and impinge on its traditional sphere of influence (Chatzky and McBride, 2020). The economic opportunities presented by the BRI have caused some EU states to be torn between traditional ties with the US and China. Several Central and Eastern Europe states have been funding their infrastructure shortfalls through BRI financing. President Macron of France however has urged prudence in dealing with the BRI since it could convert partner countries into "vassal states". US Vice President Mike Pence claims the BRI is constricting and a one-way road (Chatzky and McBride, 2020).

The Trump Administration has pursued a confrontational approach towards China. It has rejected the multilateral TPP agreement in favor of bilateral agreements. It counters the BRI with the Better Utilization of Investment Leading to Development (BUILD) Act, which created a separate agency that consolidated the Overseas Private Investment Corporation (OPIC), that has responsibility for development finance, with components of the US Agency for International Development (USAID) (Chatzky and McBride, 2020). The new agency was given a budget of $60M to counteract the more than $1 trillion that China was expected to spend on the BRI. Advocates of this US initiative claimed that the idea is to crowd in a large pool of private investment by underwriting risk (Chatzky and McBride, 2020). In addition, there is an argument that the US could use China by having the BRI pay for infrastructure projects in Central Asia that are also in the US interest (Chatzky and McBride, 2020).

72 *The new multipolar world order*

The Russian Pole

There is general agreement that Russia has been expanding its global influence since the return of Vladimir Putin to power in 2012 (Stronski and Sokolsky, 2017). This can be gleaned from the accusations leveled by the US and EU that Russia is pursuing "objectives, such as tarnishing democracy and undermining the US-led liberal international order, especially in places of traditional US influence; dividing Western political and security institutions; demonstrating Russia's return as a global superpower; bolstering Vladimir Putin's domestic legitimacy; and promoting Russian commercial, military, and energy interests" (Stronski and Sokolsky, 2017).

Russia aims to "create a multipolar world in which it plays a more prominent role" (Stronski and Sokolsky, 2017). To "wield influence and expand its global footprint," Russia "has relied on relatively inexpensive diplomatic, military, intelligence, cyber, trade, energy, and financial tools" to "influence political systems, public attitudes, and elite decisionmakers in Europe, the Middle East, Africa, Asia, and Latin America (Stronski and Sokolsky, 2017). It has "capitalized on Western missteps and growing anti-establishment sentiments in Europe and North America" (Stronski and Sokolsky, 2017). Undoubtedly, "Russia will likely continue trying to fill global power vacuums resulting from US President Donald Trump's 'America First' foreign policy" (Stronski and Sokolsky, 2017).

Arguably, the Kremlin launched its global Russia campaign in retaliation to Western democracy promotion initiatives to instigate mass protests to destabilize the country and promote regime change in 2012. With the annexation of Crimea and conflict in Ukraine in 2014 the global Russia counteroffensive intensified and took on new qualities (Stronski and Sokolsky, 2017). Hitherto, Russia focused its attention in the post-Cold War period on its sphere of influence around its periphery. But, the global Russia campaign "has sought to damage the international image of Western democracy, exacerbate the internal tensions within Western political and security institutions, and expand Russia's global reach at the expense of Washington and its allies by playing on Western missteps in different parts of the world (Stronski and Sokolsky, 2017). For the first time since the dissolution of the Soviet Union, Russia is projecting power well beyond its periphery.

The dynamics of the new multipolar world order with respect to Russia are such that while the US and Europe "are increasingly focused on their own domestic challenges and regional crises in Asia and the Middle East," the Kremlin "is keen to exploit increased opportunities in the resulting vacuum, using both hard and soft power, to expand its influence and presence and to take advantage of Donald Trump's presidency (Stronski and Sokolsky, 2017). Stronski and Sokolsky (2017) have divided Russia's global activism into four geographic regions the first being "efforts to retain its influence or counter Western influence in the states of the former Soviet Union." The goal here is "to prevent additional countries from aligning too closely with the West, and to preserve a buffer zone of pro-Russian or, at least, neutral states around it" (Stronski and Sokolsky, 2017). The countries that are aligned with the West – Georgia, Moldova, and Ukraine, are finding that their political transitions are being undermined, publics courted, and their integration with Western political, economic, or security structures stymied by Russia (Stronski and Sokolsky, 2017). The Kremlin is also bolstering its influence in the Central Asia region that China is increasingly dominating, economically (Stronski and Sokolsky, 2017).

The second geographic region in which Russia is projecting its influence concerns efforts "to undermine the Western and transatlantic institutions it considers its principal adversaries – the United States, the European Union (EU), and the North Atlantic Treaty Organization (NATO)" (Stronski and Sokolsky, 2017). The internal divisions and challenges in the US, EU, and NATO, and the "uncertainty about Washington's commitment to its allies and partners since President Donald Trump's embrace of the 'America First' agenda" are exploited by Russia to its benefit (Stronski and Sokolsky, 2017). The administrations of former Presidents Obama and Bush, Jr. have "actively sought to weaken Russia domestically, undermine its influence internationally, increase its isolation, and carry out regime change around Russia's periphery and even in the country itself" (Stronski and Sokolsky, 2017). Russia is now doing to the West what the West has been doing to Russia.

In the third instance, the Kremlin is actively seeking to "gain or regain influence in other places where the Soviet Union once held sway" (Stronski and Sokolsky, 2017). Moscow "plays the nationalist and Christian Orthodox cards" in the Balkans "to complicate Western efforts to integrate these countries into European structures" (Stronski and Sokolsky, 2017). Meanwhile "Russia seeks to protect its longstanding equities in Syria," convey its "great power status to domestic and international audiences," and demonstrate "its capacity to act beyond its immediate neighborhood and gain a foothold in what is seen as a traditionally US sphere of influence (Stronski and Sokolsky, 2017).

The Kremlin's "efforts to gain influence in parts of Asia, Africa, and Latin America represents the fourth category (Stronski and Sokolsky, 2017). Here Russia forms coalitions with "rising powers willing to challenge the Western-dominated international system," as it "cultivates authoritarian leaders and take advantage of frictions between the United States and some of its traditional allies or partners" (Stronski and Sokolsky, 2017). The US views Russia as siding with Venezuela to challenge US power in Latin American and the Caribbean.

Russia's growing Caribbean interests include re-engagement with Cuba, promoting Russian tourism in the region, improved relations with the Anglophone Caribbean with investments in Guyana's and Jamaica's natural resources sector, and proposal in explore the Caribbean sea for natural resources. Russia's state-owned oil company Rosneft has been accepting

Venezuelan oil as a form of loan payment counteracting the US sanction against that country. Also, Russian troops have embedded themselves in garrisons around Venezuela according to the head of US Southern Command (Berg, 2019).

Conclusion

The significance of the NMWO for the CARICOM states is that they can deliberately address the class interest of working people as they reorient their economies from European and American domination. The CARICOM states must demonstrate the will to ensure that workers exercises ownership and control over production and that the right to work are properly enshrined in new agreements. They must strive to overcome the authoritarian traditions evident in the region, and ensure that work, politics and social organizations are democratic. Fundamental rights, freedom of expression and organization, privacy of the individual, and the abolition of repression and torture must be enshrined in the new model. The realignment must address working people's interests in terms of the preservation of the environment, and sustainability in accordance with the UN's sustainable development goals, with the state leading the way.

References

Allison, G. (2020). "The New Spheres of Influence: Sharing the Globe with Other Great Powers," *Foreign Affairs* March/April: 30–40.
Balding, C. (2018). "Why Democracies are Turning against Belt and Road: Corruption, Debt and Backlash," *Foreign Affairs*, 24 October.
Berg, R. (2019). "Russia is Gearing Up for a Conflict with the United States in the Caribbean," *Foreign Policy*, Washington DC, 9 October.
Buchanan, E. (2019). "What Russia Wants in a Multipolar World," *The Interpreter*, Lowy Institute, 31 October.
Butler, S. (2018). "Visions of World Order: Multipolarity and the Global 'Constitutional' Framework," *European Society of International Law*, 2018 Research Forum (Jerusalem), September.
Canterbury, D.C. (2012). *European Bloc Imperialism*. Chicago, IL: Haymarket Publishers.
Chatzky, A. and J. McBride (2020). *China's Massive Belt and Road Initiative*. Washington: Council on Foreign Relations, 28 January.
Chaudhury, D. R. (2019). China's BRI Comes Under Severe Criticism on its Fifth Anniversary, *The Economic Times*, 4 January.
Chebankova, E. (2017). "Russia's Idea of the Multipolar World Order: Origins and Main Dimensions," *Post-Soviet Affairs* 33 (3): 217–234, DOI: 10.1080/1060586X.2017.1293394.
DeYeso, R.L. Jr. (2006). "A Newer World Order - The Return to a Multipolar Era. Paper Submitted in Partial Fulfillment of the Requirements of the Master of Strategic Studies Degree," U.S. Army War College, Carlisle Barracks, Carlisle, PA, 17013-5050, 15 March.

Dolan, C.J. (2018). *Obama and the Emergence of a Multipolar World Order: Redefining U.S. Foreign Policy*. New York: Lexington Books.

European Commission Directorate-General for Trade (2006). *Global Europe: Competing in the World*. Brussels: Commission of the European Communities, Ref. 318/06.

Fabbrini, S. (2010). "After Globalization: Western Power in a Post-Western World," *Global Policy*, 18 September.

Fabbrini, S. (2017). "Which Democracy for a Union of States? A Comparative Perspective of the European Union," pp. 14–22 in Held, D. and R. Schütze (eds.) *Global Policy Special Issue: Democracy Beyond Borders*, vol. 8 (S6), DOI.org/10.1111/1758-5899.12486.

Ferguson, N. (2006). *The War of the World: Twentieth-Century Conflict and the Descent of the West*. New York: The Penguin Press.

Freedomlab. (2020). "Towards a Multipolar World Order," Amsterdam, Netherlands, 20 January.

Haass, R.N. (2008). "The Age of Nonpolarity: What Will Follow U.S. Dominance," *Foreign Affairs*, May/June.

Heine, J. (2020). "World Trade, From Bad to Worse?" *Global Times*, 26 May.

Kegley, C.W. Jr. and G.A. Raymond (1994). *A Multipolar Peace?* New York: St. Martin Press.

Keqiang, L. (2015). *Report on the Work of the Government*. The People's Republic of China, Beijing, China: The State Council.

Kratochvíl, P. (2002). "Multipolarity: American Theory and Russian Practice," paper presented at *Annual CEEISA Convention*, Moscow, Russia.

Lawrence, S.V., C. Campbell, R.F. Fefer, J.A. Leggett, T. Lum, M.F. Martin, and A.B. Schwarzenberg (2019). *US-China Relations*. Washington: US Congressional Research, Report, 3 September.

Levitte, J.-D. (2019). "With the End of Four Centuries of Western Dominance, What Will the World Order Be in the 21st Century?" Speech before the Academy of Moral and Political Sciences in France, 7 January.

Makarychev, A. (2014). *Russia and the EU in a Multipolar World: Discourses, Identities, Norms*. Stuttgart, Germany: ibidem-Verlag/ibidem Press.

Morgenthau, H.J. (1948). *Politics among Nations*. New York: Alfred A. Knopf.

Morrison, W.M. (2019). *China's Economic Rise: History, Trends, Challenges, and Implications for the United States*. Washington: US Congressional Research, Report, 25 June.

Murray, D. and D. Brown (eds.) (2013). *Multipolarity in the 21st Century: A New World Order*. London and New York: Routledge.

Patriota, A.A. (2017). Is the World Ready for Cooperative Multipolarity? *Rising Powers Quarterly* 2 (2): 15–29.

People's Republic of China (PRC) (2015). *Vision and Actions on Jointly Building Silk Road Economic Belt and 21st-Century Maritime Silk Road*. Beijing, China, 28 March.

Petito, F. (2016). Dialogue of Civilizations in a Multipolar World: Toward a Multicivilizational-Multiplex World Order, *International Studies Review*, 18 (1): 78–91, DOI.org/10.1093/isr/viv030.

Petras, J. and H. Veltmeyer (2018). *Imperialism and Capitalism in the Twenty-First Century: A System N Crisis*. London and New York: Routledge.

Pieterse, J.N. (2017). *Multipolar Globalization: Emerging Economies and Development*. London and New York: Routledge.

Rolland, N. (2018). "China's Belt and Road Initiative: Five Years Later," *The National Bureau of Asian Research*, 25 January.

Saunders, P. (2020). "US Embrace of Great Power Competition Also Means Contending With Spheres of Influence," *Russia Matters*, Harvard Kennedy School, Belfer Center for Science and International Affairs, 13 February.

Schulze, P.W. (2019). *Multipolarity and Multilateralism: Cooperative or Rival Cornerstones of a New World Order?* Berlin: DOC Research Institute.

Schwarzer, D. (2017). "Europe, the End of the West and Global Power Shifts," *Global Policy* 8 (S4): 18–26.

Seattle to Brussels Network (2006). "The New 'Global Europe' Strategy of the EU: Serving Corporations Worldwide and at Home," pp. 173–179 in Maisano, T. and T. Rondinella (eds.) *Budgeting for the Future: Building another Europe European Economic Policies from a Civil Society Perspective*. Amsterdam, The Netherlands: Transnational Institute.

Stronski, P. and R. Sokolsky (2017). *The Return of Global Russia: An Analytical Framework*. Washington DC: Carnegie Endowment for International Peace, 14 December.

Timofeev, I. (2019). "A New Anarchy? Scenarios for World Order Dynamics," *Russian International Affairs Council*, 6 August.

Tse, A. and J. Wu. (2018). "Why 'Made in China 2025' Triggered the Wrath of President Trump," *South China Morning Post*, 11 September.

Turner, S. (2009). "Russia, China and a Multipolar World Order: The Danger in the Undefined," *Asian Perspective* 33 (1): 159–184.

Waltz, K.N. (1979). *Theory of International Politics*. Reading: Addison-Wesley.

Xi, J. (2017). "Full Text of Chinese President Xi's Address at APEC CEO Summit," *Xinhuanet*, 11 November.

6 Theoretical advances with Caribbean capitalist development

Introduction

This chapter serves the purpose of analyzing the theoretical frameworks that accompanied capitalist development in the Caribbean. The argument is that capitalist development in the Caribbean and corresponding policy prescriptions evolved through three historical periods with matching theoretical trajectories. The three broad directions of theory that impacted economic policy first began in the era of conquest, plunder and settlement were consistent with mercantilism, classical political economy, Marxism, neo-classicism, and Keynesianism. Marxism, was a critique of classical political economy and helped to stimulate the development of neo-classicism, but was not itself instrumental in impacting policy in that era. The second consisted of challenges to those standard theories of capitalist development that informed colonial economic policy and which coincided with the historical period marked by a bipolar world order. The contestations included Lewis' theory of industrialization, import substitution industrialization (ISI), plantation dependence economy model, and searches for "another development" influenced by Marxism. The third was based on the neoliberal counter-revolution which generated new thinking on development that derailed Keynesianism and the Marxist search for development alternatives in a neoliberal unipolar world order.

Capitalist development in the Caribbean commenced under mercantilism an economic system in which founding the region was integral. The Caribbean has been a part of every twist and turn in the evolution of theory and policy concerning the development of capitalism. The problem is that although the Caribbean has been on a rollercoaster ride with capitalism, the region is not as well off as its counterparts in Europe. Why is that so? What is the cause that capitalist development in the Caribbean did not bring about the same quality of life in the region as it did in England even though the two areas entered the process together? Evidently the Caribbean and Europe did not enter the process as equals. The former was merely the footstool as the system got created by the Europeans. Thus, the benefits of capitalist development were distributed in an uneven manner, with fewer gains accruing to

DOI: 10.4324/9781003092414-6

78 *Theoretical advances*

the region. The principal theoretical and policy frameworks that formed the bases for capitalist development in the Caribbean are analyzed below.

Mercantilism

The economic doctrine that Smith (2008) labeled "mercantilism" supported the feudal agrarian economy from the sixteenth to the nineteenth centuries (Bulmer-Thomas, 2012). It was a system of economic organization of commerce that placed European powers and their colonies in trade boxes. England and its Caribbean colonies formed a single trade box, as did France and its colonies. It was founded on laws that restricted the carrying of trade to subjects of the imperial power and based on a set of specific ideas. The imperial power was the single buyer for the exports of the colonies and the single seller for the imports into the colonies. This fulfilled the development objective to accumulate specie, money in the form of gold and silver coins rather than notes, through a balance of trade surplus.

Mercantilism was manifested through a series of Navigation Acts that were in place for nearly 200 years to promote and regulate British ships, shipping, trade, and commerce with foreign countries and British colonies. The goal was to keep the benefits of trade inside the British Empire, minimize losses in gold and silver, maximized profit from trade with foreigners, guarantee markets in England for the produce of colonies, and assured markets for British goods in the British colonies.

The Navigation Acts were dismantled in the nineteenth century in four stages beginning with the "freedom of trade" but not "free trade" (Bulmer-Thomas, 2012). The freedom of trade meant certain cities were designated as free ports, and laws that restricted the transport of goods to imperial subjects, were abrogated. The second stage involved the reduction of tariffs from the very high levels in force at the end of the Napoleonic Wars. Third, imperial preferences were abolished so that the tariff structure no longer favored colonial imports (Bulmer-Thomas, 2012). The final stage was the altogether elimination of tariffs a goal that is still to be accomplished.

Britain was the leader in industrial production and did not require tariff protection for the development of its manufacturing sector, so it entered into an era of zero or low tariffs which lasted until the First World War (Bulmer-Thomas, 2012). Industrialist interests had gained ascendancy over agricultural interests in Britain and the fiscal system in England no longer depended on taxes on trade. The growing competition in manufactures from France, Germany, and the US however evoked calls by British industrialist for the reintroduction of tariff protection which were taken up from the 1890s onwards (Bulmer-Thomas, 2012).

British trade policy in the nineteenth century nonetheless did not mean the abolition of tariffs in the Caribbean. Tariffs comprised 90 percent of colonial revenue at the time (Bulmer-Thomas, 2012). England ensured that the colonies did not become a burden by draining the imperial coffers.

Therefore, the abolition of tariffs in the Caribbean was never an option. Subject to these constraints the Caribbean colonies were generally free to buy from cheap sources and sell to whomever.

Four points can be gleaned on capitalist development in the Caribbean, from the foregoing discussion. First, the colonies were an organic part of mercantilism, integral to its founding and functioning, as England was the sole buyer of their product and seller for their imports but derived a higher quality of benefits from the trade arrangements. Importantly, however, the colonies were extensions of European empires at the center of the triangular trade, and were not in a system of dependence or core-periphery relations. The Caribbean only became a periphery after the reform of the colonial slave mode of production which began in the nineteenth century.

Second, a serious tension existed between free trade and competition that can be described as the free trade enigma. The British industrialists advocated free trade when they had a monopoly on manufacturing, but called for state protection when competition arrived from the French, German, and the US. Free trade is only good for countries that have a monopoly on the product or service traded. On the other hand, countries that want to break a monopoly call for free trade but when they arrive in a monopoly position they restrict trade. An example of the latter is the British and French in their push for free trade to break the Portuguese monopoly in Africa. The latter laid claim to Africa after the Treaty of Tordesillas in 1494 that divided the non-Christian world between Spain and Portugal. But, then once they out competed the Portuguese and Spanish the British and French established protectionist trade arrangements.

Third, Britain reduced tariffs in England to facilitate trade, while simultaneously maintaining tariffs in the colonies to generate revenue in a "one Empire two systems" type policy. This was similar to China's one country two systems policy – Hong Kong being capitalist and mainland China communist. Britain began to separate itself from its Caribbean colonies although the colonies supplied ninety percent of colonial revenue. The Caribbean financed itself through the revenue it supplied to England, which went back to the region. But, undoubtedly, much of the revenue did not return to the Caribbean given the disjuncture in economic development of the two geographic spaces.

Fourth, as the colonies began to take decisions on their own and trade with whomever, albeit constrained by English law, center-periphery dependency relations began to emerge. The dismantling of the mercantilist colonial slave mode especially from the 1840s, stimulated this development. England and the colonies began to part ways as England established its Asian empire in India, and the colonies pushed for freedom from British imperialism.

Classical political economy critique

The mercantile system was protectionist, inefficient, wasteful, and could not adequately improve the conditions of the European poor. Free trade was advocated as a means to bring progress to the growing working class as the transition from feudal agricultural to industrial production gained momentum. The classical political economists supplied the ideas which became the central currents that informed economic policy in contradistinction to the mercantile economic doctrine. The economic and social transformation as industrialization took root in England, necessitated a reorganization of the economic system to further industrialists interests.

The industrial revolution induced rural depopulation due to demographic transitions from rural–urban migration. It stimulated concerns inter alia with population growth, instability, poverty, the growing working class, the causes of economic growth, the role of money in the economy, and the source of value. The classical political economists rejected the mercantilist idea that the wealth of a nation was determined by the amount of gold and silver monarchs held in their coffers. Gold and silver in the hands of the monarch did not translate into food, housing, social protection, and improved living conditions for the poor.

The classical economist's belief was that the best way to create wealth was to produce commodities and sell them for a profit in free markets. The free-market economy was regarded as a natural phenomenon founded on freedom of the individual and private property. The classical political economist's approach was presented as one that would lift the poor out of their wretchedness by creating jobs for them through the division of labor. This in turn would lead to mass production of commodities for trade and consumption. The capitalists engaged in commodity production and trade, would gain a bonanza in profits thereby increasing the process of capital accumulation. Free trade capitalism was regarded as superior to the protectionist mercantile capitalism, because it would improve economic welfare and combat inequality and poverty. But, although the classical economists favored the free market they were not adverse to state intervention to correct economic intransigences such as unemployment and economic downturns.

The classical political economists focused attention on how value was determined and distributed among the economic classes they identified. They assumed that land, labor, and capital were three factors involved in the production of a commodity and that each factor earned a separate income in the process. The owners of land or landlords earned rent, while the owners of capital or the capitalist earned profit and interest, and laborers or working people earned wages. The assumption was that labor produced the value of all commodities and so the classical political economists formulated a "labor theory of value." This theory says that the value of a commodity is determined by the socially necessary labor taken up in its production (Ricardo, 2012; Smith, 2008).

Marx's critique of political economy

Marx (1986, 1993, 2011) embraced the classical labor theory of value but altered it in a significant way. Marx reasoned that value was not determined by labor, since labor is the embodiment of the laborer's entire life-long capacity to work. Instead, value is determined by the socially necessary labor-time the laborer expends on the production of a commodity. Whereas the labor of the slave, his life-long ability to work, was the property of the slave's owner, the capitalist who hires a worker purchases his labor-power and not his labor. The capitalist does not own the worker's life-long ability to work, but only owns the worker, who works for him, for the duration of time in a day the worker is on the job. The capitalist pays the worker for the time of the day he works. Thus, labor-power is a commodity that the laborer owns which he sells to the capitalist for wages. Marxian economic theory is organized around the idea that labor-power is a commodity owned by working people. But, the capitalist pays the laborer less than the value of the commodity the worker produces with his labor-power.

The Marxist critique of capitalism and its corresponding socialist agenda took hold in the Caribbean during the nationalist struggles in the twentieth century. These views found expression in labor organizations which focused on broad issues of national political and economic import, rather than merely concerning themselves with wages and conditions of service. The labor unions did not confine themselves to negotiating for improved wages and conditions of service, they raised the stake to concern themselves with poverty reduction, injustice, adult suffrage, improving the standard of living, and the defeat of colonialism. The manifesto of the British Guiana Labor Union (BGLU) for example one of the earliest trade unions in the Caribbean, formed in 1919 and recognized in 1921, explicitly stated its objective was to build a socialist Guyana (Canterbury, 2019). A Marxist tradition emerged in Caribbean politics and scholarship but has ebbed and flowed in accordance with the changing power dynamics of the bipolar and unipolar orders – the cold war and neoliberal globalization.

The neoclassical critique

The theoretical reform from classical to neoclassical ideas provided a different bourgeois understanding about the organization of capitalist development in the Caribbean. The latter half of the nineteenth century was mostly associated with economic theory and policy supposedly that made a break with the classical political economy system and the embrace of neoclassical economics, whose theorems came to dominate economic policy. This was an intra-class struggle between two strata of the ruling elites to produce the dominant ideas for the construction and organization of capitalist development. The break was founded on what was described as the marginal revolution in the evolution of economic thought during the pivotal decade of the 1860s. In the same manner that mercantile economic policy was adjusted in the wake of the new bourgeoisie championing classical political economy thinking, the principles of classical political economy were adjusted to accommodate the newer ideas on economics espoused by the neoclassical economists.

The neoclassical economists represented the class forces that opposed the labor theory of value, for its potential to stimulate social unrest. The neoclassicals focused their attack on the determination of value in the classical system in order to steer economic theory away from socialism (Mandel, 1968). This was the case because the labor theory of value became the basis for Marxist socialist economic theory which advocated revolutionary change. The labor theory of value was used to explain the origins of profit from the exploitation of wage-labor. The marginal revolution was keen to reverse the perceived socialist threat especially in the light of the revolution in 1848 and the Paris Commune in 1871 (Mandel, 1968).

The new ideas that came to be identified with the marginal revolution were developed simultaneously and independently by Menger (1981), Jevons (2013), and Walras (2014). The works of these scholars supported the central argument that the price of a commodity does not reflect the value of labor that produced it. Instead, the value of a commodity reflected the marginal usefulness to the consumer of the last purchase. Thus, it was people's preferences that determined equilibrium price. The price of labor only determined the value of a commodity, indirectly. First, the idea that value was determined by the general equilibrium of supply and demand provided the primary challenge to the labor theory of value. The three leading traditions in the marginal revolution were the theories of general equilibrium and optimality developed by Pareto et al. (2014) and Walras (2014); the theories of partial equilibrium developed by Jevons (2013), Marshall (1910), and Pigou (1932); and the theory of capital developed by the Vienna school comprising Böhm-Bawerk (2017), Friedrich von Wieser (2018), and Menger (1981).

European trade policy was transformed amidst the theoretical wrangling between classical and neoclassical schools. There were various mechanisms, institutions, and theories of modern trade policy that took shape during that period. Indeed, the growth in foreign trade exceeded the growth in production (Bairoch, 1972). The nineteenth century represented a thriving liberalism in international trade theory, simultaneously with the emergence of new forms of protectionism (Bairoch, 1972).

The Caribbean was directly impacted by the neoclassical revolution. The region depended on preferential markets in Europe and had to contend with being ruled from abroad, until the great pushback that led to political independence in the twentieth century. The Caribbean had to endure another period of economic reform as capitalism was hit by severe economic depression in the late 1800s due to a decline in the local sugar industry. The big idea of the resulting 1897 British Royal Commission of Inquiry into the economic situation was for the widespread establishment of smallholders in the agricultural sector. That justified the presence of smallholders in a sector hitherto dominated by large-scale sugar plantations (Richardson, 2007).

The Keynesianism revolution

The Keynesian revolution shifted the debate from the determination of value to the identification of the factors that determined the employment level. The neoclassical economists had a similar concern but they reasoned that supply was the determining factor in the level of employment. This supply side economics places the responsibility on producers to create employment. Government policy must be unashamedly pro-business promoting free market efficiency, competitiveness, privatization, deregulation, lower income tax rates, and rolling back the power of labor unions.

Keynes (1936) argued that demand determined the employment level – demand had to be created to stimulate employment. Thus in a crisis such as the Great Depression, financial crash in 2008, or the Covid-19 pandemic where workers lose their jobs in the millions, the government has to take steps to put money in the pockets of working people to create demand. With more money in the pockets of working people aggregate demand will increased because the workers will spend to purchase their daily needs. The higher level of demand places pressure on producers to increase price to meet the new demand, and then to expand production thereby employing more workers. Thus, an increase in demand, initially raises price and profit, and eventually amplifies supply and employment. This demand side economics is also referred to as interventionist to overcome market failure.

The foregoing theoretical frameworks were evident in the development of capitalism in the Caribbean. They shaped economic policy since the advent of capitalism in the region, even as the international political economy became bipolar between the end of World War II and the end of the cold war.

Challenges to colonial policy

Colonial policy in the Caribbean during the war years and immediate aftermath fully embraced Ricardian comparative advantage, although by the time of the war neoclassical theory had ascended to displace classical political economy, but had fallen into disrepute due to its role in, and failure to end, the Great Depression which Keynesian policies did. Furthermore, comparative advantage whether driven by technology or factor endowment was also at the core of neoclassical trade theory (Costinot, 2009).

The Moyne Commission Report in the aftermath of World War II embodied the essence of colonial policy in the Caribbean. It reinforced the idea that the Caribbean needed to specialize in agriculture production, because of its endowment with land. Efficient agricultural production was determined to be necessary to promote both economic and social development. The increase in income from agricultural production would be used to finance social development. But, the agricultural sector suffered from a variety of problems including poor technology, finance, and infrastructure, while social development was constrained by poor housing, education, health, water, electrification, sanitation, etc. The colonial idea was that there can be no economic development without improved social services, and that there can be no proper permanent standard of social services without economic development (Stanley, 1943: 1076).

Lewis on industrialization and development

Lewis (1950, 1954) wanted to put people to work in industry to complement the development of agriculture and improve society by raising the standard of living. This view was premised on the evidence that industrial production paid higher wages, and that industrialized countries had a higher standard of living compared with agricultural economies. The conditions that generated the need for Caribbean industrialization included the retreat of women from the workforce, endemic unemployment, growth in unproductive jobs, increasing population, mechanization of plantation agriculture, unproductive labor, and scarcity of land except in Guyana and Belize to employ surplus labor (Lewis, 1950).

The development puzzle Caribbean states needed to solve was presented as follows – due to population growth agriculture was incapable of absorbing all employable labor. But agriculture needed to become efficient by reducing its workforce without decreasing total agricultural output. This would raise the standard of living of the employed and generate the demand for manufactures where the surplus labor would be absorbed (Lewis, 1950). The survival of the manufacturing sector depended however on its satisfaction of domestic demand and exports given the small size of the Caribbean market. Industrialization was critical not merely in its own right, but also for the development of agriculture. It is not an alternative to agriculture but a complement since the two sectors stimulate the development of each other (Lewis, 1950).

The success of an industrialization development strategy depended on the right economic policies, resources, and markets. The assumption was that industrialization should not be based on *laissez faire* which was a stumbling block in the way of the Caribbean becoming industrialized. This is because *laissez faire* was considered the domain of the private sector which was supposed to lead the industrialization process. The colonial authorities advocated that Caribbean governments leave industrialization to the private sector. The belief was that if an economic venture was profitable, then private individuals would undertake it, and that if the state undertakes an economic venture that private individuals are loath to start then the government is working against the public interest. The colonials forbad the state from promoting industrialization and was restricted to providing the economic, political, and social frameworks for the private sector to freely operate (Lewis, 1950: 35). This was essentially the *laissez-faire* line of reasoning, which obstructed the industrialization of the Caribbean.

There are numerous reasons why the private sector in the Caribbean cannot be left to itself to stimulate industrialization or development. The domestic capitalist class in the Caribbean was inexperienced with industrialization and hesitant to embrace the associated investment risks. It had expertise mainly in agriculture and commerce and focuses its attention on import and export rather than production. In such circumstances the state has to take the lead on industrialization, which once commenced would gain momentum on its own. But, the appropriate state agencies must be created to deliberately advance the industrialization of the Caribbean.

The role of the state was not limited to leading and creating the agencies in support of industrialization. It included taking action to foster the free movement of labor, encourage foreign direct investment, and even invite successful foreign transnationals to invest in the region. Foreign capital nonetheless should not be left to do whatever it pleased, state regulations must be imposed to protect the legitimate interest of the country (Lewis, 1950). In this approach, foreign private capital, state capital, protectionist measures, government regulation, and inward- and outward-looking policies, co-exist with one aim in mind – to create employment in industry and agriculture and raise the standard of living through industrial production.

Lewis' (1954) approach to economic development was based on the assumption that the advanced capitalist states had a limited supply of labor but that the developing countries such as the former British colonies in the Caribbean had an unlimited supply of labor. The economic development or industrialization of the latter countries required them to resolve their surplus labor problem. This demanded policies to absorb the labor surplus, including the reinvestment of profit in the capitalist sector in combination with measures to attract foreign direct investment, and market protection. Expanding the capitalist sector will provide surplus agricultural labor with gainful employment at higher wages.

It could be surmised from Lewis' postulations on economic development that the demand for labor in the capitalist sector in the closed single-economy expands continuously in the short-term. When the economy opens up to international trade the demand for labor must constantly expand since capital will seek outlets in countries with surplus labor. This is definitely Lewis' theory of capitalist globalization on a world scale, or an economic theory of imperialism. Economic development, therefore, depends on an ever-expanding demand for surplus labor. But, it could also be argued that this theory of globalization and economic imperialism will lead to the stagnation of capitalism, when it reaches a point where all labor is gainfully employed – no place is left to reinvest profit to absorb surplus labor and economic contraction will occur.

Import substitution industrialization

Import substitution industrialization (ISI) had its origins in Latin American structuralism pioneered by the Economic Commission for Latin America and the Caribbean (ECLAC) School. This approach replaces foreign imports with domestically produced substitutes. A country will reduce its economic dependence, stimulate self-sufficiency and development, if it engages in the domestic industrial production of substitutes for foreign imports. Lewis' (1950, 1954) theory of industrialization which emphasizes export promotion as a significant component is not considered to be in accord with the ISI approach executed in the Caribbean (ECLAC, 2001). The latter has the specific objectives to reduce manufactured imports, replace them with substitutes produced domestically, and increase employment. To stimulate domestic industrial production, a slew of incentives were initiated such as providing industries with tax holidays, the development of industrial estates, tariff protection for local companies, and the introduction of Industrial Development Corporations (IDCs) and credit schemes (ECLAC, 2001). These policies combined with those advocated by Lewis (1950, 1954), led to the emergence of budding manufacturing sectors in Trinidad and Tobago, Jamaica and Barbados that helped to ease unemployment due to the long-term declining trend of employment in agriculture.

Nationalization of the commanding heights of the economies through expropriation of foreign companies and/or government majority shares in Jamaica, and mortgage-finance-type purchases in Guyana, complemented ISI. Nationalizations included state take-over of foreign-owned banks and commercial, agricultural, and industrial enterprises. Through nationalization the state sector led the economies in Guyana and Jamaica, while the government of Trinidad and Tobago utilized the country's oil and natural gas earnings to build the largest state sector of these three of the English-speaking Caribbean's more developed countries (MDC).

Plantation dependence economy model

The plantation dependence economy model in large measure was a reaction to Lewis' (1950, 1954) theory on the industrialization of the British West Indies. It classifies Lewis' model as "industrialization by invitation" and argues that it is not beneficial to the region because of the plantation dependent characteristics of Caribbean economies. A plantation economy is considered a high-cost satellite export propelled economy, specializing in the production of raw materials for industry in the metropolis and importation of all their consumption goods. The central theses of the plantation dependence economy school (Best, 1968; Best and Levitt, 2009; Girvan, 1973) is that "the Caribbean economy has undergone little structural change since the establishment of the slave plantation" (Best and Polanyi Levitt, 2009: 13). There was no significant alteration to the character of the economic process in the Caribbean since the sugar plantation was built there in the seventeenth century. The economy remains "passively responsive to external demand and external investment, almost exclusively from metropolitan sources" (Best and Polanyi Levitt, 2009: 13). Thus, "the frustrations of the industrialization program in the Caribbean can only be understood in the light of the legacy the territories have inherited from their common plantation history" (Best and Polanyi Levitt, 2009). The plantation economy does not conduct business in accordance with the theory of international trade since it does not export to increase domestic supply of imports. Comparative advantage does not apply to these economies (Best and Polanyi Levitt, 2009).

The original authors of the plantation dependence economy model argue that the concrete economic conditions that led to the development of their theory was "the failure of post-war industrialization policies to reduce unemployment" (Best and Polanyi Levitt, 2009). This failure was due to the "basic weaknesses in the theoretical approach to policy making" since neither the "Keynesian growth models" nor the Lewis (1950 and 1954) model were "appropriate to the analysis of the type of economy prevailing in the Caribbean" (Best and Polanyi Levitt, 2009). Puerto Rico, Jamaica, Trinidad and Tobago, Suriname, Barbados, and Cuba pursued the model of "industrialization by invitation," which paid little attention "to the geographic, historical and cultural differences of these diverse societies emerging from colonialism" (Best and Polanyi Levitt, 2009).

Critiquing plantation dependence economy theory Thomas (1974, 1984) argues that the plantation in the Caribbean was the main means of global capitalist commodity production. It was the most efficient way to organize the capitalist labor process, and provide the capitalist with a hierarchy of power that enabled a few individuals to maintain control over a large number of forced laborers. The plantation was therefore an institutional mechanism for commodity production and not the economy as a whole as advanced in plantation dependence economy theory.

The search for "another development"

The search for "another development" is geared toward meeting human needs, including endogenous, self-reliant, ecologically sound development based on structural transformation (Nerfin, 1977). Thomas (1988) was the foremost advocate for "another development" in the Caribbean. Thomas (1988) diagnosed that the Caribbean needed to undertake three specific tasks in its pursuit of another development. The identification of "the essential rhythms of underdevelopment in the region" was necessary before "strategic choices can be made about how these rhythms should be altered" to help to determine by way of deduction the development of the appropriate "lines of production, consumption and social organization" (Thomas 1988). Thomas (1988) argues the principal problems of Caribbean development are first "the pattern of consumption in the region fails to satisfy the basic needs of the broad mass of the population" reflecting "the unequal distribution of wealth and income, disparities in urban and rural development and the poverty and dispossession of large social groups, particularly the peasants and urban poor" (Thomas 1988). Second, "the pattern of resource use and resource endowment" do not reconcile because the "imperatives for bringing resources into production in the past derived largely from the needs of international capitalist expansion" (Thomas 1988). Third, this improper reconciliation produced a "pattern of property ownership and the social relations" that "show sharp and worsening inequalities both at the national/international level within each national territory" (Thomas 1988).

Thomas (1988) outlined an alternative conception of development to tackle those three principal problems by identifying eight points on the meaning of development in a Caribbean context. First, development requires a system of ownership, control, and production oriented toward satisfying the basic needs of the masses. Second, there can only be real development if these basic needs are satisfied through planned and effective implementation of the right to work. Third, reversing the region's authoritarian tradition means the material conditions of life should be reproduced within a self-reliant and endogenous pattern of growth. Fourth, development implies that work, politics, and social organization are based on democratizing power in society and on the effective (as opposed to nominal) exercise of fundamental rights, such as those to free expression and organization, respect for an individual's privacy and the abolition of repression and torture. Fifth, development implies preserving the stability of the environment and putting an end to the degradation it has suffered through the growth of national production in Caribbean societies. Sixth, it is important to recognize that because of the polarity between the state and the private sector, the state would have to play an important part in the development of the region, but only within the context of a participatory political process in which the ordinary West Indian's status as a citizen, producer and consumer of wealth was enhanced. Seventh, a realistic approach to development must begin by recognizing the stark reality of the hostile environment created by living in imperialism's backyard. Eight, the external context is relevant to the region's development (Thomas, 1988: 356–362).

Thomas' (1988) diagnosis and prescriptions for possible solutions to the Caribbean's development dilemma hold today and must form the basis for economic policy in the new multipolar world order.

The neoliberal era

This section focuses on theoretical developments in the Caribbean as the transformation occurred from a bipolar world order when independent thought flourished to a unipolar neoliberal global order dominated by structural adjustment theory that stifled critical thinking. The primary change has been the centering of "radical social analysis" on "critiques, that is, the deconstruction of the neoliberal paradigm" rather than on "constructing alternatives" (Thomas, 2001: 498). The deconstruction of neoliberalism in the Caribbean "have been considerably influenced by postmodernist ideas – a situation that is common to scholarship in many other parts of the world"

(Thomas, 2001: 499). A "noticeable consequence of this has been while several of the 'alternative' models of political economy has embraced a 'class' approach .... the influence of postmodernist literature has led to a retreat from" class analysis (Thomas, 2001: 499). Class was seen as an antiquated concept with little or no usefulness in the analysis of Caribbean political economy. Thomas (2001) observed however that "the radically changed circumstances" in the social life of the region at "the start of the twenty-first century" compared with those of the 1960s and 1970s have produced "a pressing need once more to embark on sustained scholarship focusing on reconstructing and developing alternative models of political economy for the region and less on deconstruction" (Thomas. 2001: 501). The models for Caribbean alternative development in the current period have to build on those hitherto existing (Thomas, 2001).

Theoretical premises of neoliberalism

Neoliberal structural adjustment represented an ideological swing from state interventionist, back to free market economic theories (Kotz, 2002). It has three dimensions – the first was a set of economic measures to evict the state from the economy and to confine its duties to merely providing the framework for private capital to accumulate, the stabilization of macroeconomic imbalances, and the political conditionality of "free and fair" national elections under the watchful eyes of international observes. The policies included the devaluation of currencies to reduce balance of payments deficits; cutting public sector employment, subsidies, and other spending to reduce budget deficits, privatizing state-owned enterprises and deregulating state-controlled industries; easing regulations to attract foreign direct investment; and closing tax loopholes and improving tax collection domestically. Structural adjustment and stabilization policies were introduced in the late 1970s but became full-fledged in the Caribbean during the 1980s. Their implementation closely overlapped with the ascendancy of the US to the position of sole superpower after the collapse of the former Soviet Union, 1989.

The neoliberal counter-revolution in economics, the crisis of overproduction in the 1970s, and a weakening Soviet Union were some of the factors that consolidated structural adjustment in the World Bank and IMF. The economic functions of structural adjustment included the recouping of debt owed to US and European banks by countries in the global south (Bienefeld, 2000), and the replacement of state interventionist policies with free market measures. The political functions included the goal to erase socialism from the economic and political agendas in the global south, with the declaration that western capitalism and liberal democracy had triumphed over communism and Soviet-democracy.

The IMF and World Bank were converted from their respective functions, to stabilize domestic and international macroeconomic imbalances, and provide long-term low-interest loans to finance infrastructure development projects, to that of collecting debt on behalf of US and European banks (Bienefeld, 2000). This resulted in a net flow of capital from the poor to the rich capitalist countries. State interventionist policies included government direct participation in economic activity through public ownership of business ventures, and regulation of the economy and private sector through state legislation. Structural adjustment removed government regulations and divested state-owned public enterprises to private investors.

The neoliberal counter-revolution vilified well-established pro-capitalist approaches because they encouraged state intervention in the economy. The Lewis two-sector model for the development of capitalism in labor surplus economies, was relegated to the scrap heap merely because of its dependence on the state. The Keynesian model which saved capitalism in the great depression came in for ridicule because it had a role for government action to stimulate economy recovery. Import substitutional industrialization and Marxist socialist and welfare socialist models were also dismantled.

The neoliberals declared that there was only one economics with universally applicable theories (Lal, 1983). It did not matter whether a country was rich and developed like the US or poor and underdeveloped as Somalia the same economic theory would apply to them both. Economic theories were believed to be universal like laws of nature such as Newtonian gravity or Darwinian natural selection. Development economics was pronounced unscientific because its theories were said to be devoid of universal applicability, only tailored to the economic needs of developing countries (Lal, 1983). Lal (1983) described the dominant paradigm in development economics as dirigiste dogma – a form of direct state rule over the economy as opposed to merely regulating it. The principal elements of dirigiste dogma were identified as the replacement of markets with direct state control, the substitution of microeconomic concerns with macroeconomic aggregates such as savings, investments, and balance-of-payments, restrictions on free trade, and government intervention to redistribute resources and control prices to diminish poverty and improve income distribution. Structural adjustment countered such ideas and left no room for innovative thinking about how to resolve the economic problems in poor countries.

Neoliberal economic theory and policy stance (Kotz, 2002) existed in the academy before the emergence of the neoliberal counter revolution. It adjoined with its theoretical predecessors that sought to defeat protectionism and establish a global economic system that was truly based on free trade. The neoliberal counter-revolution pointed fingers at protectionism and state interventionism as the causes for the economic crisis in the 1970. The merger of neoliberal economic theory with economic policy in England under Prime Minister Thatcher and the US under President Regan set a new standard to achieve the neoclassical aspiration of a global economy founded on free trade. This dream required a political agenda under the auspices of the European- and US-controlled Bretton Woods institutions to spread the merger of neoliberal economics and economic policy to the rest of the globe. Neoliberal economics was merely a development in economic theory before it became a political project under the leadership of US and British imperialisms. This transformation accompanied the collapse of the former USSR at a historical conjuncture in which the US-led unipolar neoliberal global order came into existence.

That was the context in which globalization as a political and economic exercise and subject for academic study emerged. Globalization was then understood as the spread of the merger of neoliberal economic theory and economic policy around the world which was now being described as a globe because all countries would implement the same economic policies. There was no need for the US to support authoritarian states in the global south as buffer zones to socialism/communism. The political dimension of democratization was therefore added to complement neoliberal economic theories, although initially, it was believed these policies were best implemented by strong governments. The particular definition of globalization embraced in this book is that it is the historical processes through which capitalism and liberal democracy are dispersed from Europe to other countries around the world beginning with mercantile capitalism. The spread of capitalism has been an imperialist process which includes inter alia colonization, Westernization, Americanization, financialization, and neoliberalism. US-led neoliberal globalization is a narrower concept confined to the historical period when the US was the sole superpower.

New thinking on development

Several broad themes have appeared in the Caribbean political economy literature including ideas about rethinking (Wedderburn, 1991) and reinterpreting Caribbean development (Girvan, 2007). The rethinking brought ideas on development in line with neoliberal economics or deconstructed neoliberal economics. There were some elements of despair and fear associated with the rethinking as concerns were expressed about the relevance and professional survival of Caribbean scholars if they failed to pivot their scholarship toward neoliberal globalization. The usefulness of the very taxonomy of developmental social science to provide understanding of contemporary trends came into question (Meier, 1991). Categories such as state, class, race, occupation, employment, economy, GDP, per capita income, and economic growth were seen to reflect a prior state of conceptualization and contained a degree of implicit theorizing that implied specific normative criteria of progress (Meier, 1991). The rethinking of development was encouraged to emphasize a departure from the tyranny of the materialist idea of progress (Meier, 1991). Reinterpreting Caribbean development involved seeing the Caribbean in its entirety and not merely in terms of colonial and linguistic terms.

Much of the new thinking on Caribbean development can be found in Hall (2001), Hall and Benn (2000), and Meeks and Lindahl (2001). Hall and Benn (2000) focus on the Caribbean in the twenty-first century. The concerns are with strategic perspectives for the future where the focus is on reconfiguring Caribbean development, human resources in support of development, economic policy options, and the challenge of change. Other concerns are with geography, culture, history, and identity; economic policy options for the twenty-first century; science, technology, and sustainable development; social integration/disintegration; thought and the political process of the Caribbean in the international system; and the creative imagination. Hall (2001) is concerned with the survival of the Caribbean community. Its focus is on questions, ideology, mechanisms, and diplomacy for Caribbean survival, and beyond.

Meeks and Lindahl (2001) focus on the context, conjunctures, critiques, and construction of new Caribbean thought. Meanwhile, more recent work by Levitt (2005) seeks to reclaim development and promotes Caribbean independent thought. Sprague (2019) is concerned with globalizing the Caribbean with respect to political economy, social change, and the transnational capitalist class, while Khan (2020) focuses on globalizing the Muslim Caribbean.

Conclusion

Undoubtedly, the Caribbean embarked simultaneously with the European powers on the process of capitalist development and its theoretical machinations. The colonial policies spawned for the Caribbean were spurned by regional scholars who utilized those very theoretical frameworks to formulate development alternatives. The neoliberal counter-revolution brought about a hiatus in experimentation with development alternatives while in the main confining economic thinking to capitalist free market ideology. The collapse of neoliberal globalization and rise of a new multipolar world order has opened up the way for a return to experimentation with development alternatives for the Caribbean.

References

Bairoch, P. (1972). "Free Trade and European Economic Development in the 19th Century," *European Economic Review* 3 (3): 211–245.

Best, L. (1968). "Outline of a Mode of Pure Plantation Economy," *Social and Economic Studies* 17 (3): 283–326.

Best, L. and K. Polanyi Levitt (2009). *Essays on the Theory of Plantation Economy: A Historical and Institutional Approach to Caribbean Economic Development.* Jamaica, Barbados and Trinidad and Tobago: The University of West Indies Press.

Bienefeld, M.A. (2000). "Structural Adjustment: Debt Collection Device or Development Policy?" *Review* 23 (4): 533–582.

Böhm-Bawerk, E. (2017). *Capital and Interest: A Critical History of Economic Theory* (Translated by William A. Smart). Germany: Jazzybee Verlag.

Bulmer-Thomas, V. (2012). *The Economic History of the Caribbean Since the Napoleonic Wars*. Cambridge: Cambridge University Press and Kingston Jamaica: Ian Randle Publishers.

Canterbury, D.C. (2016). "Natural Resources Extraction and Politics in Guyana," *The Extractive Industries and Society* 3 (3): 609–702.

Canterbury, D.C. (2019). *Neoliberal Democratization and New Authoritarianism*. London and New York: Routledge.

Costinot, A. (2009), "An Elementary Theory of Comparative Advantage," NBRE Working Paper No. 14645.

ECLAC (2001). *The Impact of Privatization on the Banking Sector in the Caribbean*. Sub-Regional Headquarters for the Caribbean, Port of Spain, Trinidad and Tobago: Caribbean Development and Cooperation Committee, LC/CAR/G.671.

Girvan, N. (1973). "The Development of Dependency Economics in the Caribbean and Latin America," *Social and Economic Studies* 22 (1): 1–33.

Girvan, N. (2007). "Reinterpreting Caribbean Development," pp. 16–53 in The Eastern Caribbean Central Bank, *Economic Development and Development Options for the Caribbean: The Sir Arthur Lewis Memorial Lectures 1996-2005*, Jamaica and Miami: Ian Randle.

Hall, K.O. (2001). *The Caribbean Community: Beyond Survival*. Kingston Jamaica: Ian Randle.

Hall, K.O. and D. Benn (eds.) (2000). *Contending With Destiny: The Caribbean in the 21st Century*. Kingston Jamaica: Ian Randle.

Keynes, J.M. (1936). *The General Theory of Employment, Interest, and Money*. London: Macmillan.

Mandel, E. (1968). *Marxist Economic Theory*. London: Merlin Press.

Marshall, A. (1910). *Principles of Economics: An Introductory Volume*, Sixth Edition. London: Macmillan and Co. Ltd.

Marx, K. (1986). *Capital Volume II: A Critique of Political Economy*. New York: Lawrence and Wishart.

Marx, K. (1993). *Capital Volume III: A Critique of Political Economy*. New York: Penguin Classics.

Marx, K. (2011). *Capital Volume I: A Critique of Political Economy*. New York: Dover Publications.

Menger, C. (1981). *Principles of Economics* (Translated by J. Dingwall and B.F. Hoselitz). New York: New York University Press.

Nerfin, M. (1977). *Another Development: Approaches and Strategies*. Uppsala Sweden: Dag Hammarskjöld Foundation.

Jevons, W.S. (2013). *The Theory of Political Economy*. London: Palgrave Macmillan and Co. Ltd.

Khan, A. (2020). *Far From Mecca: Globalizing the Muslim Caribbean*. New Brunswick: Rutgers University Press.

Kotz, D.M. (2002). "Globalization and Neoliberalism," *Rethinking Marxism* 12 (2): 64–79.

Lal, D. (1983). *The Poverty of "Development Economics"*. London: Institute of Economic Affairs.

Levitt, K. (2005). *Reclaiming Development: Independent Thought and Caribbean Community*. Kingston Jamaica: Ian Randle.

Lewis, W.A. (1950). "Industrialization of the British West Indies," *Caribbean Economic Review* 2 (1): 1–61.

Lewis, W.A. (1954). "Economic Development with Unlimited Supplies of Labor," *The Manchester School* 22 (2): 139–191.

Meeks, B. and F. Lindahl (eds.) (2001). *New Caribbean Thought: A Reader*. Jamaica, Barbados Trinidad and Tobago: The University of the West Indies Press.

Meier, G.M. (1991). "Reviewed Work(s): Rethinking Development by Norman P. Girvan and Judith Wedderburn," *Social and Economic Studies* 4 (1): 242–247.

Pareto, V., A. Zanni, L. Bruni, and M. McLure (2014). *Manual of Political Economy: A Critical and Variorum Edition*. Oxford: Oxford University Press.

Pigou, A.C. (1932). *The Economics of Welfare*, Fourth Edition. London: Macmillan and Co. Ltd.

Ricardo, D. (2012). *The Principles of Political Economy and Taxation*. New York: Dover Publications.

Richardson, B.C. (2007). "The Importance of the 1897 British Royal Commission," pp. 17–28 in Besson, J. and J. Momsen (eds.) *Caribbean Land and Development Revisited*. New York: Palgrave Macmillan.

Smith, A. (2008). *An Inquiry into the Nature and Causes of the Wealth of Nations*. Chicago: University of Chicago Press.

Sprague, J. (2019). *Globalizing the Caribbean: Political Economy, Social Change, and the Transnational Capitalist Class*. Philadelphia: Temple University Press.

Stanley, O. (1943). HANSASRD HC Deb 16 March 1943, vol. 387, cc1044-142.

Thomas, C.Y. (1974). *Dependency and Transformation: The Economics of the Transition to Socialism*. New York: Monthly Review Press.

Thomas, C.Y. (1984). *Plantations, Peasants, and State: A Study of the Mode of Sugar Production in Guyana*. University of California: Center for Afro-American Studies.

Thomas, C.Y. (1988). *The Poor and the Powerless: Economic Policy and Change in the Caribbean*. New York: Monthly Review Press.

Thomas, C.Y. (2001). "On Reconstructing a Political Economy of the Caribbean," pp. 498–520 in Meeks, B. and F. Lindahl (eds.) *New Caribbean Thought: A Reader*. Jamaica, Barbados Trinidad and Tobago: The University of the West Indies Press.

Walras, L. (2014). *Elements of Pure Economics: Or the Theory of Social Wealth* (Translated by D. A. Walker and J. van Daal). Cambridge: Cambridge University Press.

Wedderburn, J. (1991). *Rethinking Development*. Mona, Jamaica: Consortium Graduate School.

Wieser, F. (2018). *Natural Value*. London: Franklin Classics.

7 The CARIFORUM-EU EPA and Brexit

Introduction

This chapter analyses the Caribbean Forum–European Union Economic Partnership Agreement (CARIFORUM–EU EPA) and Brexit. It is argued that the CARIFORUM–EU EPA was undemocratically formulated and should be dismantled. The principal decision-makers in the EU are not democratically elected by the European electorate, while the Caribbean Regional Negotiating Machinery (CRNM) usurped the power of the elected Heads of Government of the Caribbean to sign the EPA which was foisted on the region. Brexit has changed the dynamics of how the Caribbean Community (CARICOM) is represented in the EU, as England was the main spokesperson for the region in the union. Given the undemocratic manner in which the CARIFORUM–EU EPA was formulated, Brexit provides an excellent opportunity for the CARICOM to renegotiate the agreement, and formulate alternative international economic relations with the BRICS (Brazil, Russia, India, China and South Africa), Africa Union (AU), and Latin America in the new multipolar world order.

The purpose here is to provide a descriptive analysis of the social, economic, and political circumstances that stimulated the formation of the EU, CARIFORUM, EPA, and the emergence of Brexit. Why were the EU and CARIFORUM formed? Why was the CARIFORUM–EU EPA negotiated and implemented? Why did Brexit emerge? These questions will be answered in turn to present the analyses in support of the argument for the CARICOM states to dismantle the CARIFORUM–EU EPA and pursue another development that does not tie the region's economic relations primarily to Europe but which allows the community to develop firmer economic ties with the BRICS including China and Russia, and Latin America, AU, and the Eurasian Economic Community.

The argument is presented in four parts beginning with a discussion on the EU's birth trajectory, through a brief descriptive analysis of the origins and development of that agency. Second, there is an analysis on the genesis of the Caribbean Forum through the divide and conquer tactics of the EU. This is followed by a brief analysis of the objectives and key

DOI: 10.4324/9781003092414-7

provisions of the CARIFORUM–EU EPA. Fourth Brexit is analyzed in its class dimensions accompanied by a discussion on the Caribbean's reactions to the Brexit vote. The conclusion presents some of the main advantages for the CARICOM if the community was to pursue economic realignment in the new multipolar world order.

The birth trajectory of the EU

The EU did not come into existence all at one stroke it was a process that commenced after World War II ended. The European colonial empires were dismantled and the US and USSR assumed leadership of two blocs, Western and Eastern, respectively, each with a distinct ideology – capitalism and socialism/communism, and political and economic organizations. Now, relegated from the apex of world power after their devastation from the war, and having to be content with US and USSR leadership in a bipolar world order, the former European empires began to take steps to transform Europe into a single economic and political bloc. As early as 1946 Winston Churchill had called for the building of a United States of Europe and the Council of Europe the first pan-European institution was launched in 1949. Subsequently, the French government proposed that Europe integrated its coal and steel industries. Through the Treaty of Paris in 1951, the European Coal and Steel Community (ECSC) was created by France, Italy, Belgium, Netherlands, Luxembourg, and West Germany in 1952. Thereafter there was a stead push toward the establishment of what became known as the European Union. The stated reasons for the initial actions that led to the emergence of the EU had to do with the curtailment of Germany, the maintenance of peace in Europe, and the control of coal and steel the main elements of war weaponry at the time (Canterbury, 2012).

The European Economic Community (EEC) and the European Atomic Energy Community (EURATOM) were created by the Treaty of Roam in 1957. The three separate communities, ECSC, EEC, and EURATOM were brought together into a single body, the European Communities (EC) by the Merger Treaty of 1967. The EC was expanded thereafter to incorporate more European states, and since the collapse of the USSR in the 1990s a number of former communist states in Eastern Europe became members of the EC. The EU which currently comprises 27 countries, now with the exit of the England, was created by the Maastricht Treaty in 1993. It is considered as the most advanced regional integration arrangement in the world (Dent, 1997). The EU has a politically independent executive arm known as the European Commission that has the responsibility for new legislation, and implementing the decisions of the European Parliament and Council of the EU. The European Council defines the priorities and political direction of the EU and sets its policy agenda, while the Council of EU comprises national ministers of each EU country and has the responsibility to adopt laws and coordinate policies.

There is a European Parliament elected by universal adult suffrage, a European Flag, currency, and central bank. The unification of Europe however constitutes more of a challenge to US global hegemony and the restoration of Europe as a global imperialist force not as single states but as a single bloc (Canterbury, 2012). The EU has even incorporated states that were in the former Eastern European socialist/communist bloc. It would seem that Europe is leading the way in the dismantling of individual nation-states in favor of a larger bloc that would become something other than a nation-state. It is an entity that behaves like a nation-state with all of its trappings, but which is not in itself a nation-state. The EU had the world's third largest population with 446 million inhabitants, covering 4 million km^2 behind China 1.393 billion and India 1.353 billion in 2018. It is apposite to note just for comparative purposes that in 2016 the populations of Asia was 4.463 billion, the African continent 1.216 billion, North America 579 million, and South America 422.5 million. The population of AU was 1,068,444,000 billion in 2013, and in 2019 that of the US was 328.2 million, and the Caribbean 44.42 million, the CARICOM 18,472,860, and the BRICS (Brazil, Russia, India, China, South Africa) 3.08 billion. With a combined population of 5.769 billion it is understandable why Asia and Africa should have a greater say in world affairs than merely follow the lead of the EU and North America that has a combined population of only 1.025 billion.

The emergence of the Caribbean Forum

The context for the emergence of the CARIFORUM was the attempt by US-led globalization to liberalize the trade relations between the EU and the Organization of Africa, Caribbean, and Pacific (OACP) states. The CARIFORUM emerged as a part of the process to liberalize the Lomé Conventions. The US banana multinationals and ruling elites used the World Trade Organization (WTO) to pry open the EU banana market to their "dollar" bananas. The Lomé Conventions I to IV were a set of agreements on trade as development assistance that the EC signed with 48 former colonies beginning in 1975 and lasting until 2000 (Babarinde, 1994; Moss, 2019). These agreements covered inter alia trade, industrial, finance and technical cooperation, services, capital movements, mineral exports, development of mining and energy, agricultural cooperation, food security, drought, desertification, fisheries, industrial development, transportation and communication, and cultural and social cooperation. Lomé IV had a special role, it was namely a system of support for the hitherto conventions to embrace neoliberal structural adjustment policies (Canterbury, 2012).

On the basis of the Lomé Conventions almost all exports from the OACP states had free access without reciprocity to European markets. The provisions of the agreements were particularly favorable to OACP states' products such as sugar, rum, bananas, rice, beef, and veal. The conventions operated on the principle that the EU and OACP states, accepted their economic and political differences, and subscribed to mutual respect for each other's sovereignty, cultural identity, and the type of development to which each aspires. The Lomé Conventions nonetheless helped to deepen neocolonial relations in the OACP states, and with the restructuring of global capitalism they took on the garb of neoliberal structural adjustment through the EU–OACP Cotonou Partnership Agreement (CPA) in 2000 (Canterbury, 2012).

That agreement represented a step toward the market liberalization of the Lomé Conventions. The CPA sought to promote and expedite the economic, cultural, and social development of the OACP states, as well as peace, security, and a stable, democratic political environment. Its objectives were poverty reduction and eradication, sustainable development, and the integration of the OACP states into the world economy. It was a step along the way to the formulation and implementation of the EU's economic partnership agreement. The EU broke down to the relentless pressure by the US banana multinationals and political elites reaching a settlement with them in 2001. The then EU commenced EPA discussions with the OACP, termed the all-OACP–EU phase of EPA negotiations in September 2002 (Canterbury, 2012). These discussions divided the EPA negotiations into two components – an all-OACP–EU part and the other regional concentrations.

The first phase negotiations agreed that the CPA provided the basic principles and objectives of EPAs, namely sustainable development of the OACP states, their smooth and gradual integration into the global economy, and poverty eradication. Specifically, the EPA would promotion sustained growth, increase the production and supply capacity of the OACP states, and bring about structural transformation and diversification of OACP economies, and support for regional integration. The OACP group of countries was divided into different regional groups under Article 37(5) of the CPA in order to facilitate the negotiation of regional concentrations of EPAs. These regions are the Pacific OACP (POACP), the Caribbean Forum (CARIFORUM), Central African, West African, Southern African Development Community (SADC), and Eastern and Southern African (ESA) (Canterbury, 2012).

The EPAs had a divisive effect on existing regional integration initiatives in EPA regions. In the Caribbean for example, the CARICOM countries did not negotiate the EPA as the CARICOM or the Organization of Eastern Caribbean States (OECS). The CARIFORUM which included the Dominican Republic, was created as a separate entity specifically to negotiate the EPA. The integration movements in Africa had similar experiences, and in some cases, a country might be in a particular economic integration community, but it was placed in a different EPA negotiation region (Hurt, 2016). The CARIFORUM–EU EPA fractured the Caribbean at several levels as regional governments, civil society, rank-and-file, and academics were in disaccord with it.

The origins of the OACP can be traced back to the World War II, which dismantled European empires and had the effect of bringing into existence independent states in the former European colonies in Africa, Asia, and the Caribbean. The former colonies organized the Africa-Asia Bandung Conference in 1955 that laid the foundation for the Belgrade conference in 1961 from which emerged the non-aligned movement (NAM) (Köchler, 1982). The Association of African and Malagasy States (AAMS), comprising former French African colonies was created in that same year (Cosgrove and Twitchett, 1970; El-Agraa, 2011). They entered into the Yaoundé Conventions 1 and 2 with the EEC in 1963 and 1969, respectively (Cosgrove and Twitchett, 1970; European Community Information Service, 1966). The Yaoundé Conventions created the avenue for cooperation between the signatory countries – Germany, Belgium, France, Italy, Luxembourg, and Holland, and their Overseas Countries and Territories (OCTs), essentially the West and Central African countries with ties to France.

The Yaoundé Conventions allowed the African and Malagasy member-states to export their manufactured goods duty free into the EEC but with much less preference for exports of agricultural products that had the potential to undermine the Common Agricultural Policy (CAP) of high food prices that protected EEC farmers. In return, for EEC preferential treatment for their limited industrial exports the AASM countries would accept comparable exports from EEC countries (Cosgrove and Twitchett, 1970; European Community Information Service, 1966).

The accession of Britain to the EEC in 1973 gave the UK's Commonwealth territories greater access to the Yaoundé Conventions. It paved the way for the extension of the Europe–Africa cooperation agreement to the British Commonwealth countries in Africa, the Caribbean, and the Pacific. This expansion in economic collaboration transformed the relationship between Europe and its former colonies. It resulted in the creation of the OACP Group of States by the Georgetown Agreement in 1975, and the replacement of the Yaoundé Conventions with the Lomé Conventions in that same year (Canterbury, 2012).

In essence, while the EU was created to consolidated Europe in a changing bipolar world dynamic, the OACP emerged as a counter force to have the former colonies speak with one voice in their dealings with Europe. The EPAs squashed any such outcome on the part of the OACP states by dividing them into separate regions.

The CARIFORUM–EU EPA

The CARIFORUM was the first region to complete negotiating a comprehensive EPA with the EU in October 2008. The CARIFORUM–EU EPA includes a WTO-compatible trade-in-goods agreement, an agreement on trade in services, rules on trade-related areas, as well as provisions for development cooperation. The EU is the CARIFORUM's second largest trading partner after the US. The main exports from the Caribbean to the EU are fuel and mining products, notably petroleum gas and oils, bananas, sugar and rum, minerals (notably gold, corundum, aluminum oxide, and hydroxide), iron ore products, and fertilizers. The main imports into the Caribbean from the EU are boats, ships, cars, constructions vehicles and engine parts, phone equipment, milk and cream, and spirit drinks. In 2018, CARIFORUM goods exports were valued at €4.28 billion and imports at €7.55 billion, giving the EU a surplus of €3.27 billion (Morgan, 2019). The main CARIFORUM exporters are the Dominican Republic and Trinidad and Tobago, while Jamaica moved from having a trade surplus with the EU to a deficit (Morgan, 2019).

The CARIFORUM agreed to the EC's Most Favored Nation (MFN) clause, although some member governments expressed concerns over the provision. Agreeing to the MFN clause means that if a CARIFORUM country through a trade agreement grants any concession, privilege, or immunity to another country then it must do so for all WTO member-states. The CARIFORUM-EU declaration on development stipulated that both sides were committed to channel EPA support through a CARICOM Development Fund.

The CARIFORUM-EU has six objectives the first being to contribute to the reduction and eventual eradication of poverty through the establishment of a trade partnership consistent with the objective of sustainable development, the Millennium Development Goals, and the Cotonou Agreement. Second, the EPA seeks to promote regional integration, economic cooperation, and good governance to establish and implement an effective, predictable, and transparent regulatory framework for trade and investment between the EU and the CARIFORUM and, within the CARIFORUM region (Canterbury, 2012).

The third objective is to promote the gradual integration of the CARIFORUM States into the world economy, in conformity with their political choices and development priorities. Fourth, the EPA seeks to improve the CARIFORUM states' capacity in trade policy and trade-related issues. The fifth objective is to support the conditions for increasing investment and private sector initiative and enhancing supply capacity, competitiveness, and economic growth in the CARIFORUM region. Finally, the EPA is supposed to strengthen the existing relations between the EU and CARIFORUM states on the basis of solidarity and mutual interest.

The EPA promises to take into account the respective levels of development of the EU and CARIFORUM states, and in line with WTO obligations enhances commercial and economic relations, support a new trading dynamic between the EU and CARIFORUM through progressive, asymmetrical liberalization of trade between the two sides, and reinforces, broadens and deepens cooperation in all areas relevant to trade and investment (Canterbury, 2012). But, after the hasty negotiation of the CARIFORUM–EU EPA with the foregoing objectives, the Chief Caribbean negotiator Bernal (2013) argued that the EPA was not a panacea for development but has the potential to make a contribution to Caribbean development.

The reality is that in the absence of an appropriate clause in the agreement, the CARIFORIUM–EU EPA ties Caribbean trade indefinitely to the EU in a new-styled mercantile arrangement. It grants EU products unhindered access into the CARIFORUM countries guaranteeing markets for the goods produced by European multinational corporations. It secures for the EU multinational corporations unhindered access to raw materials from the CARIFORUM states, guaranteeing them necessary productive inputs that came from the Caribbean. The EPA is an instrument of political control in that it has mechanisms for CARIFORUM states to police themselves to ensure that they do not renege on the agreement. Thus, the EU does not have to resort to military or colonial occupation of any country in the Caribbean community, as European powers did in their relationship with their colonies in the past (Canterbury, 2012).

With the support of the ruling elites in the CARIFORUM states, the EU exercises political control by erecting institutional mechanisms such as the supranational CARIFORUM Council which has political oversight over the implementation of the EPA. Through the EPA new bodies were created such as the ministerial level Joint CARIFORUM–EC Council that deals with all policy and related decisions concerning Caribbean trade. This Council is incompatible with the Treaty that established the Caribbean Community and Common Market. The CARIFORUM–EU Trade and Development Committee (TDC) is an implementing agency at the level of officials. Then, there is a joint CARICOM–EU Parliamentary Committee for political debate on relevant issues, and a CARIFORUM–EC Consultative Committee that aims to involve the private sector and other social partners in the EPA process. These institutional structures have bypassed the CARICOM and the CSME two existing institutions that promote Caribbean integration as a regional development strategy. The mandate to coordinate Caribbean Member States' implementation of the EPA was given to the CARICOM Secretary General by the CARICOM Heads of Government in March 2009. This has created further problems for the governance structure of the EPA (Canterbury, 2012).

Eleven years after the CARIFORUM-EU EPA was signed in 2008, the Caribbean remains the only OACP region which concluded a comprehensive EPA with the EU (Morgan, 2019). The second five-year review of the EPA was due in 2019 and is supposed to be presented in 2020. The first five-year review of the CARIFORUM-EU EPA assessed the degree to which the EPA's provisions were implemented on both sides, the impact the agreement has had on major trade and development trends within CARIFORUM, and the major issues that both sides should focus on in the context of the Five-Year Review (Silva, 2014). The study found with respect to the implementation of the EPA that there were important deficits in some basic institutional and strategic foundations of implementation (Silva, 2014). Also, concerning development cooperation it was found that most of the EU's support only came on stream in the latter half of the review. There was still much work to be done in implementing obligations and activating key provisions regarding trade in goods. The same was true for trade in services and investment, both in terms of implementation of obligations and the use of innovative provisions under the Agreement (Silva, 2014).

Trade-related issues varied significantly across CARIFORUM jurisdictions, while the EPA was hampered by the global recession in 2008 (Silva, 2014). CARIFORUM goods imports from the EU differed dramatically from predictions, while with respect to CARIFORUM goods exports to the EU, there were a few impacts linked to the agreement, but a number of the effects cannot be so connected (Silva, 2014). The global recession also overwhelmed any EPA impact on government revenues. The EPA had little impact on either intra-CARIFORUM or CARICOM–French Outermost Region (FCOR) trade. According to Silva (2014), there have not been significant changes in terms of trends in FDI or trade in key sectors that could be traced back to the agreement. There were no measurable EPA effects on sustainable development in terms of poverty, labor, and the environment or the data was insufficient. According to Silva (2014), the EPA did not address many policies that directly affect CARIFORUM's attractiveness for investment and export, showing the limitations of its potential impact. However, the EPA did have some impact on certain policy orientation within the region for example, it stimulated private sector interest between the Dominican Republic and the CARICOM states in part through EU trade missions funded under the agreement (Silva, 2014).

The key conclusions of the first five-year review were that the trade agreement at best can act as a signal for investors and governments far beyond the technical details of commitments and implementation (Silva, 2014). According to Silva (2014), the implementation work still needed to be done on the big ticket items concerning commitment to the agreement comprised ratification by all CARIFORUM and EU states including support to bring Haiti back as an active member of the EPA process. Also, there is need to begin substantive discussion on the regional development fund to channel resources for implementation, and for continued efforts to engage the private and public sector on the agreement and to combat misconceptions about its provisions. The establishment of a sub-committee on Development in the TDC, the convening of the Consultative Committee, and continued discussion on a joint monitoring mechanism were other concerns (Silva, 2014).

The study found shortfalls under specific areas of the agreement that required priority attention (Silva, 2014). According to Silva (2014), these areas included a renewed effort to widen compliance with the agreement's provisions on tariff reduction, based on a speedy resolution of the differences over modification of harmonized systems (HS) convention of the goods schedules. The HS conventions harmonize the description, classification, and coding of goods in international trade as a means to collect external trade statistics, implement customs tariffs, and facilitate trade and information exchange. There was the need for renewed and detailed discussions on strengthening market access in services, including the clear recognition of special benefits accorded under the EPA, particularly for short-term business visitors (Silva, 2014).

Other priorities included widening and strengthening efforts to negotiate agreements on mutual recognition; activating the provisions of the Protocol on Cultural Cooperation; and continued and stronger support to CARIFORUM services suppliers, particularly in the tourism sector (Silva, 2014). There was need to fast-tract and strengthen competition and investment frameworks in terms of legislation and institutions, including amendments to existing laws given the numerous regulatory provisions under the agreement that refer to competitive practices (Silva, 2014). Priorities existed for a strong push to conclude negotiations on geographical indications, backed by EU support; and for the establishment of an online portal or notification mechanism on measures that could affect goods and services trade to act as an early warning signal of factors that could impede the EPA's effectiveness and simplify the task of monitoring the agreement (Silva, 2014).

According to Silva (2014), another priority was for there to be continued engagement with the FCORs in the discussion on the EPA implementation, backed by a renewed push for a practical resolution of CARIFORUM concerns on trade barriers, including the *octroi de mer* or dock dues that are a type of tax imposed on products imported into or produced in France's regions of Guadeloupe, Martinique, French Guiana, and La Réunion. The study concluded by emphasizing the importance of agreeing on a joint mechanism that is manageable for both sides, and which yields usable information on the compliance, use, and impact of the agreement (Silva, 2014).

Brexit and Caribbean reactions

This section provides a class analysis perspective of Brexit and the Caribbean's reactions to Britain leaving the EU. Brexit presented the CARIFORUM a signatory to an EU EPA, with a dilemma unlike the problem it posed for EPA negotiation regions in Africa that did not sign on to the agreement. Those African states had the choice to use the uncertainties surrounding Brexit to refuse to sign the EPA (Mwilima, 2019).

A class analysis of Brexit

Brexit, the withdrawal of the UK from the EU, was an intra-class power struggle over whether the British ruling elites or those located in Brussels would exercise control over the UK economy. According to Coles (2016), "the bureaucratic nature of the EU slowed the workings of neoliberalism. That's why a powerful sector of the UK's policy-making elite" wanted out. It was the people in Britain and the US advancing the global policy of neoliberalism who wanted out. "They wanted more deregulation, more privatization, and more internationalism at the expense of domestic investment and production" (Coles, 2016). But, working people who voted for Brexit wanted less neoliberalism. The pro-Brexit wealthy funders made it look like they shared the interests of working people. Hedge funds gained by betting on the financial volatility caused by the shock outcome of the referendum, as well as mega-market players who bet on the rise and fall of currencies (Coles, 2016).

The conservative government of Edward Heath forced Britain into the European Economic Commission without a vote in 1973 (Coles, 2016). The Harold Wilson's Labor government held a referendum in which the British public had a say whether or not the country should remain in the EEC in 1975. According to Coles (2016), Brexit serves the financial and geopolitical interests of US corporations. The Heritage Foundation initially saw America's interest in a United Europe as a buffer against the Soviet Union, but as the Soviet Union collapsed there is no need for a United Europe. Furthermore, a regulated EU that erects barriers to US products is bad for US corporate profits. Europe started regulating financial markets after the 2008 crash, but the US had used Britain as a Trojan Horse to push through deregulation in Europe (Coles, 2016).

Also, a small number of London-based hedge fund CEOs decided to get revenge on Brussels, which implemented some regulations after the financial crash in 2008. These financial services institutions make money betting on the rise and fall of prices, performances, currencies, etc. London is the most deregulated city in Europe hosting 66 percent of Europe's 1,400 hedge fund companies in 2006. The CEOs in these companies worth US$4.8 trillion in 2018 did not like Brussels dictating policy and regulation to them and so they backed the Leave Camp (Coles, 2016).

There were several reports commissioned by the Tories evaluating Britain's role in Europe. It was decided in balance that Britain should remain in the EU, but simultaneously distance itself from Brussels. This was to be achieved by the Britain investing more in emerging markets – Brazil, China, India, Mexico, South Korea, and in resource-rich countries, America, Australia, Canada, and New Zealand. Although the UK trade with these countries, European regulation prevents the UK from making trade and investment deals which lower trade barriers and reduce tariffs, i.e., the EU stops the UK from forming a customs union. This is because the European countries would see an additional customs union as unfair competition (Coles, 2016).

The ruling elite in the UK favored a neoliberal agenda while the rest of Europe was more reluctant to embrace the nineteenth-century free-trade economic model. The theory is that by deregulating, the wealth acquired from trade, investments, mergers, and acquisitions, will trickle down to the working classes and spread. The reality is that neoliberalism is a form of socialism for the rich and capitalism for the poor. A prime example of this was when taxpayers had to step in to bailout the financial institutions that caused the crash in 2008. This is known as corporate socialism as the gap between the rich and poor widens. The EEC was infected with the ideology of neoliberalism in the 1980s and 1990s (Coles, 2016).

The British working class who voted for Brexit did so because they wanted less neoliberalism, while the mega-rich who voted for Brexit did so because they wanted more neoliberalism. The mega-rich succeeded in turning working people against their self-interest by blaming immigrants and technocrats in Brussels for the consequences of neoliberalism – economic downturn, job insecurity, and declining life quality (Coles, 2016). Leaving the EU would solve these problems. While most businesses wanted Britain to remain in the EU, we should note that big business is not a monolith pursuing the exact goals. Although these businesses have common goals such as cost minimization and profit maximization. While hedge funds thrive on market instability and volatility, banks prefer stability and consider hedge funds as rivals (Coles, 2016).

The Brexit yes vote must also be analyzed against the backdrop of class politics that emerged after World War II. There are three broad push and pull factors that must be taken into consideration the first being the push by the European ruling elite for European unity after the devastation of the war. The second was the ruling elite in the former European colonies wanted to secure better trade deals with Europe. The third was the division of the world into capitalist and socialist/communist ideological camps, after the war ended. The Europeans elite wanted to unite to prevent any future war among themselves and the US ruling elite wanted Europe to unite as a buffer to Soviet communism. A united Europe meant that the OACP countries would no longer be dealing with their former masters in separate empires. They will be dealing with Europe as an imperialist bloc (Canterbury, 2012).

Caribbean reactions to Brexit

Reactions in the Caribbean to Brexit were superficial, lacking in-depth analysis of the class dynamics behind the "yes" vote. There was no attempt to understand the class dynamics of Brexit including the determination of class forces in the region who represented the same interests as those of the British mega-rich who voted for Brexit. Instead, there was a rush in typical fashion to conjecture about the different ways the region will be negatively impacted by Brexit. Caribbean scholars and policymakers began speculating about what can be done to cushion and avert the perceived impacts of Brexit on the region. Their thinking clearly reflected the English-speaking CARICOM states' continued dependence on England despite their claims to political independence. The region is still holding on to Britain when there are other options for the Caribbean to simultaneously pursue in the new multipolar world order.

Caribbean scholars and policymakers were concerned about what will happen to Caribbean–EU relations when the region's principal advocate in the EU was no longer a member of that institution. The impression conveyed was that if Britain was no longer in the EU then the Caribbean was doomed in its negotiations with the EU and ability to secure favorable trade deals with Europe. It would seem that the Caribbean countries still regarded Britain as a parent who would defend the economic, social, political, and security interests of its children who are now politically independent states. The Caribbean secured preferential deals from the EU on trade and tourism through British representation. The fear was that when England leaves the EU the Caribbean would lose the perceived advantage of having an insider representing the region.

The anticipated fallout from Caribbean–EU trade and tourism was projected to have major negative impacts on the community. British trade and tourism in the Caribbean was projected to decline. The number of Britons holidaying in the region was predicted to fall simultaneously that they will have less money to spend because of the projected decline in value of the pound sterling when Brexit happened. Approximately 1.5 million British tours visited the Caribbean in 2015, and British nationals have significant foreign direct investments in real estate in the region especially in Barbados (*Trinidad and Tobago Guardian*, 2016). But, funny how things work no one foresaw the Covid-19 pandemic and the havoc it has visited on British–Caribbean trade and tourism.

There was fear of the erosion of the special trade and commerce deals Britain secured for the region through the CARIFORUM–EU EPA. But, the CARIFORUM–EU EPA merely represented the class interest of the European and Caribbean ruling elite. The benefits of the EPA are supposed to trickle down to Caribbean working people, who are still awaiting for these gains along with those of neoliberal capitalism to filter down to them. Indeed, the CARIFORUM–EU EPA is founded on the principles of neoliberal economics. The British exit from the EU, it was surmised, will leave the English-speaking Caribbean with virtually no relationship with the EU. This view stimulated ideas that the Caribbean needs to reorganize its relationship with Britain, in the moment seeing that the latter will no longer be an EU member. Bold and proactive measures were encouraged to recalibrate the Caribbean's relationship with the UK. In turn it was suggested that the UK will have to engage in a series of difficult bilateral trade negotiations with Caribbean states. The anticipated problem the Caribbean will face in these talks is that regional negotiators do no possess the skills in the art of negotiations. This lack of skills heightens the relevance of the Diplomatic Academy of the Caribbean which must ensure that it properly trains the region's chief negotiators (*Trinidad and Tobago Guardian*, 2016).

A major concern was over the bigotry and xenophobia promoted in the Brexit campaign by Conservative Party members. The apprehension was about its negative impact on Caribbean immigrants in Britain and Caribbean immigration to Britain. It was predicted that the xenophobic and bigoted Donald Trump campaign would have gained energy from the Brexit yes vote. The anti-establishment sentiments in both Britain and the US were seen to be similar. There was uneasiness that Brexit could stimulate a copycat domino effect that will be a blow to regionalization and globalization. The speculation was that the CARICOM member countries could even follow the British example, and leave the Caribbean Single Market Economy (CSME) and the Caribbean Community. It was believed that "Brexit will cause countries that have more or less succumbed to the conclusion that 'there is no alternative' to globalization to begin to question that premise" (*Trinidad and Tobago Guardian*, 2016).

The 12 English-speaking independent countries in the CARICOM were called on to formulate a plan to counteract the exit of Britain from the EU because the Caribbean will have no structured trade relationship with a post-Brexit Britain (Sanders, 2016). When Britain joined the EEC in 1973 it transferred all authority for its trade arrangements to the EEC. From that moment the formal trade, aid and investment relations between the 12 Caribbean countries has been with the EU and not Britain. These trade relations among others were formalized successively in the Lomé Conventions, the CPA, and the EPA. But, the Caribbean entered into these agreements through Britain, since prior to the UK joining the EEC, its trade with the 12 Caribbean countries was conducted under the Commonwealth preference scheme (Sanders, 2016). Once Britain joined the EEC and negotiated the extension of some of those preferences to the English-speaking Caribbean through the EEC, the Commonwealth preference scheme became inoperable (Sanders, 2016).

The small size of the 12 Caribbean countries with only about seven million people may not be a priority for Britain as it renegotiates trade agreements with all countries. Britain remains the major trade partner in the EU with the Caribbean, and the EPA does not cover trade with Britain as a separate entity. The envisioned dilemma for the Caribbean was that when Britain leaves the EU the region will lose its principal trade partner in Europe, but at the same time the Caribbean will not have a trade agreement with Britain. Meanwhile, simultaneously that the Caribbean loses its market in Europe, the British contribution to official aid and investment in the region through the EU will cease to exist. Also, the 27 EU states that have no real historical relationship or colonial responsibility to the English-speaking Caribbean may not want to maintain the level of official aid and investment to which Britain is committed. The CARIFORUM–EU EPA is the only formal comprehensive arrangement that Caribbean countries have with any other country or region of the world (Sanders, 2016).

Jessop (2016) argue that possible effects of Brexit on the Caribbean would include uncertainty and a possible negative impact on trade and development flows. Also, Brexit would have a diminution in the region's ability to influence thinking on its policy concerns in Europe. The UK's overseas territories in the Caribbean will be affected by a range of problems, and a long period of uncertainty as Britain's foreign, trade, and development policy is reoriented (Jessop, 2016). Brexit could have wider consequences for Europe's future relationship with the OACP, and accelerate the general trend toward dialogue with Latin America and the Caribbean as an undifferentiated whole (Jessop, 2016).

An alternative view

The foregoing represented just some of the thinking on the impact of Brexit as it concerned the Caribbean. But, an alternative view is that Brexit provides the CARICOM with an excellent opportunity to withdraw from the CARIFORUM–EU EPA. The CARICOM states must now reevaluate their economic ties with the EU, UK, and US, with a view to expanding their economic relations with the OACP group of countries, AU, Latin America, China, India, and Russia. The CARICOM can hit the reset button on its international economic relations and trade agenda in the new multipolar world order. It is therefore advantageous that the CARICOM has no other such comprehensive agreement with any other country or region.

The CARICOM must renegotiate its trade arrangements with England, and the EU outside of the EU EPA, as an alternative to the CARIFORUM–EU EPA. It must expand its economic relations with the US, AU, Latin America, China, India, the Eurasian Economic Union (EEU), in particular Russia, and the OACP group of countries. The principal advantages of this realignment in CARICOM economic relations will be as follows.

First, the CARICOM will put itself in a position to exercise greater independence in its trade negotiations, without being subjected to undemocratic neoliberal ideological conditions, as is the case with the CARIFORUM–EU EPA. Second, the CARICOM could reduce its dependence on former colonial masters and create new vistas of economic survival and prosperity by looking toward other regions of the globe. The Caribbean was created by European mercantile powers but the region does not have to remain under the cloud or within the light rays of European colonialism. It must look elsewhere to secure for itself the best trade deals. Third, by negotiating trade arrangements in its self-interest the CARICOM could set itself on a path to sustainable development and achieve the UN Sustainable Development Goals.

Finally, Brexit has created a high degree of uncertainty in the global capitalist system. But, for the Caribbean, it should be a time of certainty and clarity – the CARIFORUM–EU EPA founded on the neoliberal globalization financialization model is undemocratic and must be dismantled. It would seem that democratically elected governments in the region are no longer making the economic decisions for their countries. There are unelected bureaucrats in agencies such as the IMF, World Bank, IDB, and in Brussels who are making these decisions, which must be implemented by elected officials in the nation-states. The critics of neoliberal globalization have been making this point for several years, but the neoliberal ideologues have responded that there is no alternative to globalization. Now that neoliberal globalization is being dismantled, a new multipolar world order has emerged as a clear alternative in which China and the BRICS play a prominent role.

Conclusion

The CRNM did not have the mandate of the Caribbean electorates to negotiate the EPA, and neither did the Council of the European Union. The Council of the EU, the principal decision-making authority of that body, is a political structure that is superimposed on European states. It negotiates and adopts EU laws, coordinates EU countries' policies, develops the EU's foreign and security policy, conclude agreements between the EU and other countries or international organizations, and adopts the annual EU budget. It is not an elected body like the European Parliament with which it closely works. It comprises government ministers from each EU country whose decisions are binding on all countries.

The Caribbean governments created the CRNM in 1997 to streamline the region's negotiating structure with the responsibility to coordinate the external negotiations of the CARICOM. The governance structure of the CRNM was such that it reported to the CARICOM Council for Trade and Economic Development (COTED). The COTED was supposed to provide the CRNM with guidance and its negotiation mandate. The Director-General of the CRNM was responsible to the Caribbean Heads of Government through the Prime Ministerial Committee on External Negotiations. The CRNM's finance committee was responsible for the financial governance of the CRNM. The finance committee comprised representatives from some member states, a representative of the CARICOM Secretariat, and the CRNM Director General and Directors.

The CRNM usurped the powers of Caribbean governments to negotiate the CARIFORUM–EU EPA without appropriately consulting with the elected CARICOM Heads of Government that created the agency to ensure that the different regional constituencies understood what it was doing. The outcry against the CARIFORUM–EU EPA came from various sections of the Caribbean Community including governments, civil society, labor unions, and academics. The business sector was the principal supporter of the CARIFORUM–EU EPA. It shared the class interests that the Caribbean and European negotiators of the agreement represented. In the end the Principal Negotiator resigned, the CARICOM Heads of Government disbanded the CRNM and created in its place the Office of Trade Negotiators as a department of the CARICOM Secretariat, but the damage was already done (Canterbury, 2012). The CARIFORUM–EU EPA is therefore a creature of an undemocratic process, and must be dismantled.

References

Babarinde, O.A. (1994). *The Lomé Conventions and Development: An Empirical Assessment.* Aldershot: Ashgate.

Bernal, R.L. (2013). *Globalization, Trade, and Economic Development: The CARIFORUM-EU Economic Partnership Agreement.* New York: Palgrave Macmillan.

Canterbury, D.C. (2012). *European Bloc Imperialism.* Chicago, IL: Haymarket Publishers.

Coles, T.J. (2016). *The Great Brexit Swindle: Why the Mega-rich and Free Market Fanatics Conspired to Force Britain from the European Union.* Great Britain, Clairview Books.

Cosgrove, C.A. and K.J. Twitchett (1970). "The Second Yaoundé Convention in Perspective: An Examination of the Association of Eighteen African and Malagasy States with the EEC," *International Relations* 3 (9): 679–689.

Dent, C.M. (1997). *The European Economy: The Global Context.* London: Routledge.

El-Agraa, A.M. (2011). *The European Union: Economics and Policies,* Ninth Edition. New York: Cambridge University Press.

European Community Information Service (1966). "Partnership in Africa: The Yaoundé Association," *Community Topics,* vol. 26, London, England.

Hurt, S.R. (2016). "Why African Countries Are Refusing to Sign On to EU Trade Deals?" *World Politics Review,* 9 November.

Jessop, D. (2016). "Brexit: An Unwelcome Divorce," *The Caribbean Council,* 14 February.

Köchler, H. (ed.) (1982). *The Principles of Non-Alignment VII.* Vienna and London: International Progress Organization and Third World Centre.

Morgan, E. (2019). "CARIFORUM/EU EPA: Implementation Review" CARICOM Today, 4 December.

Moss, J. (2019). *The Lomé Conventions and Their Implications for the United States.* London: Routledge.

Mwilima, H.K. (2019). "Brexit Linkage in Trade Negotiations: A Strategy for Rejecting the European Union – East African Community Economic Partnership Agreement?" *L'Europe en Formation* 1 (388): 69–80.

Trinidad and Tobago Guardian. (2016). Brexit Fallout: Problems for Trade, *Tourism in the Caribbean*, 26 June.

Sanders, R. (2016). "Brexit Creates EU–Britain Nightmare for the Caribbean," *Jamaican Observer*, 25 June.

Silva, S. (2014). *Monitoring the Implementation and Results of the CARIFORUM-EU-EPA: Final Report*. Luxembourg: Publications Office of the European Union.

8 Neoliberal financialization in the Caribbean

Introduction

The CARICOM has constructed a subservient financial architecture in accordance with neoliberal financialization, whereas the community is better served by engaging alternative financing provided by the New Development Bank (NDB) and China's Belt and Road Initiative (BRI). The argument is constructed around some relevant theoretical discussions on financialization, and colonial finance and financial self-determination focusing on colonial financial arrangements, and the struggle for financial self-determination. The dynamics of financialization in the Caribbean comes into vogue with analyses on the financial sector in Caribbean development, financial sector growth and the region's economy, non-banks and financial instruments, and the emerging financial architecture. Finally, the alternative financial arrangements developed by the BRICS (Brazil, Russia, India, China, South Africa) and China through which the region could strive for financial self-sufficiency are discussed.

In conclusion, the recommendation is for the rekindling of their ideas on financial independence to further industrialization as a central means of Caribbean development. This can be achieved through alternative financing provided by BRICS Bank and China's BRI.

Some relevant theoretical considerations

Theoretical discussions on financialization goes back to the early debates on finance capital commencing with Marx's (2011) notion of capital as a process of circulation of money. Hilferding's (1981) treaties on finance capital and the literature it spawned including the works of Kautsky (1911), Lenin (1963), and Luxemburg (1951), address the subject in a more direct manner. Some of the relevant takeaways from that literature are first finance capital is unpaid labor – it is the accumulation of a portion of the total value produced by the worker that the capitalist appropriates as profit (Marx, 2011). Second, finance capital is bank capital – monies from unpaid labor stored in banks – capital in money form that industrialists borrow and convert

DOI: 10.4324/9781003092414-8

into industrial capital – factories, etc. (Hilferding, 1981). Third, domination by finance capital is imperialism (Lenin, 1963). It is finance capital that spearheads the conquest of non-capitalist regions to bring them within the orbit of the capitalist world system. But, there is controversy concerning the role, causes, and future of imperialism and hence over the question of finance capital. Fourth, imperialism is merely a specific method of capital accumulation and not finance capital (Luxemburg, 1951). Finally, money is not the real measure of value of the commodity, but the commodity is the real measure of the value of money (Kautsky, 1911).

Goldstein (2009) observed that the term "financialization" was less than a decade old dating to 2000. Various social sciences disciplines utilized the concept albeit with no precise singular definition. Lapavitsas (2013) argues financialization today is characterized by the "unprecedented expansion of financial activities, rapid growth of financial profits, permeation of economy and society by financial relations, and domination of economic policy by the concerns of the financial sector." Three tendencies that characterized financialization are the financialization of monopoly capitals, the restructuring of banks to partly reflect the "altered conduct of non-financial enterprises," and the financialization of the personal revenue of workers and households across social classes (Lapavitsas, 2013). The debate has therefore shifted from seeking to understand finance capital as imperialism or as a method of capital accumulation, to trying to shed light on how the society and economy work to accommodate finance capital thereby reinforcing its dominance.

Polanyi-Levitt (2013) sources financialization to the end of the three decades of prosperity following World War II. There has been unprecedented investments in production and improvements in the material conditions of life. But, since the 1980s there has been a return to accumulation by dispossession "and the increasing contribution of finance, distribution and business services to GDP" (Polanyi-Levitt, 2013). Polanyi-Levitt (2013) claims finance has been "decoupled from production" and "the capital market has lost its useful function of judging the long-term productive capabilities of different firms." The capital market "has become a gigantic casino where people attempted to guess the market with confidence that it would maintain a secular rising trend" (Polanyi-Levitt, 2013).

Amin (2013) believes that financialization is driven by the imbalance between monopolistic and imperialistic rent-maximization in which "a growing proportion of the surplus can no longer be invested in broadening and deepening production systems." According to Amin (2013), the result is "*financial* investment of the surplus is the only viable outlet available to monopoly-driven accumulation." Financialization is facilitated by certain institutional change such as shifts in management focus from "long-term profitability in the real economy to the short-term objective of maximum shareholder value" (Amin, 2013). Other changes include the replacement of "pay-as-you-go arrangements by funded pensions systems," the adoption of a system of flexible exchange rates, and market rather than central bank determination of interest rates (Amin, 2013).

Petras (2007) holds the view that finance capital does not operate in isolation and therefore cannot be "counter-posed to the productive economy except in the most marginal local activity." The many faces of finance capital can only be understood in the contexts of specific sectors – investment banking, pension funds, hedge funds saving and loan banks, and investment funds. Power and wealth are structured such that workers, peasants, and salaried employees produce value that become the foundation of lucrative financial instruments. The financial elites are the most parasitical component of the ruling class, which is divided into three sub-groups – private equity bankers and hedge fund managers, Wall Street chief executives, and senior associates or vice presidents of big private equity funds (Petras, 2007).

Financialization is also understood to mean the expansion of the activities of the financial sector to bring under its jurisdiction monetary transactions from migration processes (Canterbury, 2013). Here, financialization concerns the entrapment by the financial sector of capital emanating from migrants. This capital includes remittances, fees charged by banks and non-banks for money transfers, and the charges by telephone companies for the use of their technologies such as smart telephones and satellites to remit monies electronically. The relevant institutional mechanisms and regulations are created and implemented to bring all monies remitted under the control of banks and non-bank financial intermediaries. The more monies remitted are brought under the financial sector and the higher the volume of those transactions, the more billions are accumulated from fees and charges by banks, non-banks intermediaries, and the information communication technology sector to move migrant's money around. This is an important source of financial accumulation worth billions of dollars in the current period of financialization. But, it is not only monetary transactions form migration that the financial sector entraps, it does so in other areas including the sex and drugs trade, trafficking in persons, money laundering, and other such social pathologies. This dimension of financialization – the accumulation of capital from monetary flows from migration, the sex and drugs trade, trafficking in persons, money laundering, etc. needs further investigation.

Colonial finance and financial self-determination

The Caribbean first encountered finance capital when colonial capital was exported from Europe to spearheaded the imperialist penetration in the region. Colonial finance served the interests of imperial powers not those of the region. The conditions were thus laid for a struggle for financial self-determination to emerge in the nationalist period after the collapse of the colonial slave mode of production. This struggle which in essence is to alter the structures of power in Caribbean relations with the mature capitalist economies, continues until today as the region encounters the NMWO.

The Caribbean can alter the power relations it has with European and US capital to achieve financial independence by embracing the alternative sources of finance provided by the NDB and BRI.

Colonial financial arrangements

The structure of capitalist production, distribution, exchange (circulation), and consumption produce the need for finance capital. There was no real distinction between the European mercantile imperial state and the investors in economic ventures in the Caribbean. The economic activities of mercantile capital were essentially an extension of the European medieval state which commissioned private individuals to engage in Caribbean trade and production. The financial arrangements put in place to fund the activities of those private-state companies marked the earliest beginnings of finance capital in the Caribbean.

The emergence of industrial capitalism shifted the Caribbean's economic structure to resource-based large-scale plantation agricultural production, and the extraction of natural resources including, forestry products, minerals, oil, and natural gas. Finance capital was refocused and geared toward funding those activities in the emergent colonial economic structure founded on plantation agriculture, natural resources extraction, and commerce. The firms that dominated the economy were all foreign owned, and their requirements for finance capital had a particular dynamic. They assembled finance capital in their home countries and the Caribbean, to finance the production and sale of raw materials. The profit was retained by the colonial powers, not reinvested to finance Caribbean economic development. The goal of finance capital was to further the colonial interests of the transnational companies rather than the development needs of the Caribbean.

Public policy formulated for the financial sector reinforced the colonial financial status quo. The colonial powers assumed the Caribbean could achieve economic development by importing foreign capital, skills, and technology (Thomas, 1972). Thus, a framework of laws and institutions were created to minimize the risks of independent national economic policies, and maximize capital and other resource flows between the Caribbean and the European powers (Thomas, 1972). This was the context for the framework of laws and regulations and organization, which governed the operations of companies, foreign exchange, the national budget, labor, money, banking, and finance (Thomas, 1972). These laws and regulations reduced "the scope for national discretionary control of the monetary system," and maximized the "unfettered action of foreign private investors" (Thomas, 1972).

The colonial state erected laws that rigorously "tied the operations of all major local financial institutions to the metropolitan money and capital markets" (Thomas, 1972). This was the basis for the almost exclusive foreign ownership of local financial institutions. The end result of these colonial financial relations was that "the processes of creating and making available local financial claims" were dominated by foreign securities holdings. Also, "the granting of domestic credit has been geared to the servicing of branch-plant exporting firms" (Thomas, 1972). Foreign banks such as Barclays and the Royal Bank of Canada provided very basic services including loans, lines of credit, export credit, and overdraft facilities.

International banks operating in the Caribbean viewed the region as a small part of their global operations (ECLAC, 2001; Thomas, 1972). Their main goal was to maximize "profits, market share and shareholder returns," and export capital. Banks operated with the economic cycles increasing investment and lending with an export boom and improved terms of trade, and reducing investment in the local economy in a recession or when there was poor profitability due to declines in commodity prices. The banks operated in an oligopolistic market structure in which they captured rent in the midst of significant "inefficiencies in the intermediation process." Contributing to this situation were inadequate government regulation and control, the small number of players in the market, and the "substantial pre-emptive competitive advantages" banks enjoyed. Furthermore, the banks operated as cartels, colluding to set interest rates and other terms of credit. This resulted in the banks making significant profits on account of the large interest rate spreads and the payment of relatively low wages and salaries (ECLAC, 2001; Thomas, 1972).

The local ruling elites who inherited those colonial financial arrangements aimed to reform existing, and establish new, institutions to stimulate economic development. It seemed the idea at the time of Caribbean independence was to build in the region the identical economic institutions found in Europe and the US. The financial system served an economic structure founded on the production of primary products for export, thus investment funds were needed primarily to finance expansion in output of those commodities. But, as Caribbean countries struggled for and obtained their political independence economic nationalism began to spread to the arena of money and finance. The Caribbean nationals wanted to create monetary and financial institutions that would function to benefit the region rather than the colonial powers. The main thrust was to craft institutions to raise money domestically and responsibly from abroad to finance economic development. Finance capital had to serve the interest of Caribbean industrialization the perceived foundation of economic development.

The struggle for financial self-determination

The early attempt to obtain financial independence was an integral part of the struggle to bolster the Caribbean's political and economic sovereignty. The colonial view that the Caribbean was not suited for industrialization was already challenged by Lewis (1950). Financial self-determination would mean that the industrialization of the Caribbean is financed through institutional mechanisms of the region's own doing, rather than those established by the colonial authorities. The struggle for financial self-determination is therefore not the same as financialization. The former bolsters the Caribbean's economic independence, while the latter deepens the linkages between the region's financial sector and the capitalist global financial grid. The linkages strip the Caribbean of financial independence and security and reinforces its financial dependence. The neoliberal argument is that financial and economic independence are anachronisms in the light of the globalization of financial markets.

In reality, global financial markets operated on the long-established principle of the strong overpowering the weak (Petras and Veltmeyer, 2001). There are participants in neoliberal global financial markets who have and exercise greater political and economic power than others. Participation in global financial markets is not a recipe to reduce global inequality or transform the power structure in those markets. The poorer countries still need to fight for their financial independence. Thus, ECLAC (1996) argues the development needs of the Caribbean cannot be adequately addressed by the extant underdeveloped financial system. A market for long-term finance was absent and the financial sector was in a rudimentary state of formation. The Caribbean governments intervened in domestic financial sectors to address these problems to ensure priority projects identified in their development plans were adequately funded, resources redistributed, and attention paid to low-income sections of the population such as farmers (ECLAC, 1996).

The Central Banks of the Caribbean Community and the University of the West Indies established the Regional Program for Monetary Studies (RPMS) in 1968, as the region's premier research institution on monetary and financial policy. In May 1995 the RPMS was renamed the Caribbean Center for Monetary Studies (CCMS) and August 1995 Caribbean Center for Money and Finance (CCMF) to make monetary and financial research in the region a creature of neoliberal financialization. The CCMF undertakes studies and provides information for monetary and financial policy issues. The Institute of Social and Economic Research (ISER) at the University of the West Indies, now the Sir Arthur Lewis Institute for Social and Economic Studies (SALISES) plays a similar role and at times in collaboration with the CCMF.

Sampling some key publications by the RPMS and CCMF leads to the conclusion that these institutions are not the same today as when they were first established. The same is true of the ISER and SALISES. Arguably, while the RPMS and ISER tended to focus more on financial self-determination, the CCMF and SALESES are more concerned with integrating the Caribbean and global financial markets. The RPMS and ISER had a more nationalist focus, with their published works on money and finance concentrating on reinforcing national independence. This tendency is present in some of the earliest studies under their aegis such as the works by Thomas (1965b, 1972). The works by Odle (1972, 1974) exhibit a similar tendency (Canterbury, 2016).

The ideas of Odle (1972, 1974) and Thomas (1965a, 1972) are presented here to show the thinking at the time on financial self-determination. Thomas (1972) proposed counterpoints to the colonial monetary and financial arrangements. The region must devise its own monetary and financial strategy from the shortcomings of the colonial measures. Emphasis is placed *inter alia* on greater regional co-operation on day-to-day financial and monetary practices, a more interventionist role for central banks, and regional contribution to decisions to reform the global framework of monetary arrangements that impinge on Caribbean economies.

Thomas (1972) argues the short- and long-term goal of the regional approach to money and finance is "to overcome the chronic pattern of developing monetary arrangements either in defense or in imitation of overseas monetary developments in the United Kingdom" (Thomas, 1972). A regional approach must give primacy to Caribbean needs, while recognizing the limitations of the institutional arrangements in the absence of fundamental changes in the real structure of the Caribbean economy. Change in the real economic structure in the Caribbean is a necessary condition for the region to break its cycle of dependent monetary and financial arrangements (Thomas, 1972).

The economic structure of the Caribbean is characterized by a heavy specialization in the production of primary commodities for sale in overseas markets. Foreign transnational corporations control the specialized production in the region, and the consumption pattern in the Caribbean maintains a high import coefficient. The export-oriented production of primary commodities is serviced by institutional structures that govern banking, foreign exchange legislation and policies, and other financial arrangements, which facilitates the flow of goods and investment funds for expansion of output. With such structural characteristics Thomas (1972) argues the "integration of capital markets naturally favors a high degree of capital mobility between the dependent and metropolitan economies" (Thomas, 1972).

Odle (1972) recognized that non-bank financial intermediaries were in a better position than banks to provide long-term finance. Non-banks were therefore identified as having to play an increasing role in the transformation of the Caribbean economy. The argument was presented that people have preference for long-term rather than short-term saving as their incomes increase, and that since non-banks were good at long-term finance, there could be less of a dependence on foreign banks to finance Caribbean development. Appropriate policies must be put in place to facilitate domestic savings in non-bank financial intermediaries.

Odle (1974) on pension funds in labor surplus economies expresses the idea that accumulated pension funds could be compensating if "invested in employment creating and structurally transforming activities." But, rather than investing pension funds regionally, they were exported to the headquarters of the multinational pension schemes. The situation is made worse due to the inefficient investment of both the public sector funds and the national insurance fund. The result of the export of private pension funds and the inefficient investment of national insurance and public sector funds is that a great deal of the economic benefits that could accrue to the region is lost (Odle, 1974). These funds could be a huge source of financing for Caribbean economic development if they are retained in the region.

Odle's (1974) emphasis on the use of non-bank financial institutions must be understood in a different context to Lapavitsas' (2013). The latter recognizes non-banks as major sources of finance, taking on banking functions, and constituting a central plank of neoliberal financialization, along with the participation of households in the financial sector through the operations of their pension schemes. Odle (1974) is arguing a case for non-banks financing as a means of financial liberation – to break the stranglehold of foreign financial institutions on the Caribbean. Lapavitsas (2013) is merely highlighting a characteristic feature of financialization in the current era.

Dynamics of financialization in the Caribbean

What are the mechanisms through which the Caribbean is being financialized? The World Bank and CCMS helped to set the tone for financialization in their review of the Caribbean's financial sector (World Bank and CCMS, 1998). The review demonstrated "the common characteristics and constraints of the financial markets and institutions throughout the wider Caribbean," and identified "factors which might improve the availability and security of capital needed to find productive investment in the region" (World Bank and CCMS, 1998). Financial sector development was seen as dependent on macroeconomic stability, strengthened supervision of banks and non-banks, and public debt management (World Bank and CCMS, 1998). The Caribbean economies were constrained by the absence of well developed, flexible, and liquid financial markets. But, the solution was not to pursue a single country approach, but a more common financial space across the region to avoid fragmentation, and market inefficiencies (World Bank and CCMS, 1998).

The Revised Treaty of Chaguaramas, the Draft CARICOM Investment Code and the CARICOM Financial Services Agreement are part of the blueprint to achieve financialization whose advocates seek to position the financial sector as the engine of economic growth and development. The advocates of financialization seek to bring households, non-banks and firms into the realm of financial accumulation through trading in stocks and bonds and engaging in various forms of speculative activity. The state, domestic and regional institutions are called upon to play a stronger role in facilitating this process. The state must be prepared to bail out the banks in crisis and provide appropriate security mechanisms to prevent a crash. Thus, when CL Financial Limited crashed due to its reckless financial activities the Trinidad and Tobago government bailed it out. The financial crash in 2008 also forced the state to react with prescriptions to buttress financial security in the Caribbean.

The financial sector in Caribbean development

Bennett (2008) advocated financial reform to increase the role of finance capital in economic development with the caveat that country-specific factors may prevent funds mobilized for development from going to productive investment. This can be counteracted by gearing financial reforms toward positioning the financial sector in a central role to contribute to a more dynamic entrepreneurial environment (Bennett, 2008). Progress along this line is undeniable as evidenced by the emergence of genuine regional financial corporations like Sagicor, Guardian Holdings, Grace, AIC, Republic Bank and the recently collapsed CLICO (Farrell, 2010). These are important additions to the several international banks operating in the region for over 100 years (Farrell, 2010).

The development of equity markets are encouraged as engines of economic growth for the Caribbean Single Market Economy (CSME), but appropriate public policy and international aid must be directed toward their development in an "institutional framework that is free of corruption and excessive government control" (Jones, 2006). This will increase long-term growth rates and economic wellbeing in the CSME. The notable problem however is economic growth spurred by equity does not favor production and employment, but is more based on speculation.

The development dilemma the Caribbean faces is the inadequacy of strategic planning of capital markets, and the state of underdevelopment of the three CARICOM stock markets in Jamaica, Trinidad and Tobago, and Barbados (Cozier, 2010). Many of the indicators such as market capitalization ratios, market turnover ratios, volume and value of shares traded, fees for insurance, etc., in these markets are "well below those of the more advanced emerging markets such as Singapore" (Cozier, 2010). Economic growth depends on advances in the region's capital markets. Barriers to financial development and inclusion include small size and scale, depth and breadth of the financial sector, prolonged low growth, high debt, vulnerability to external factors, natural disasters, the loss of correspondent banking relations, and "how widespread is the access to and use of financial services by firms and individuals" (Li and Wong, 2018).

The development of capital markets is tied to building confidence in the financial sector's role in development. Regulators are concerned with stimulating greater public confidence in the effective role of the financial sector in national and regional development. The outdated and inadequate regulatory framework to cope with the changing global financial environment and new emerging issues such as banks taking on non-bank functions, non-banks taking on banking functions, excessively risky lending and investment, large interest rate spreads, capital adequacy, the control of financial institutions by commercial and industrial companies, and linkages between various types of financial institutions, required regulators to revamp the system (Ramsaran, 2013). Also, the increasing expansion of cross-border activities of financial institutions requires effective regulatory and supervisory arrangements, to reduce risks to savers and investors (Ramsaran, 2013).

The Revised Treaty of Chaguaramas removed restrictions on banking, insurance, and other financial services to build confidence in the financial sector. The revisions prohibit the introduction of new restrictions, and encourage the removal of existing limitations on the movement of capital and currency transactions within the community, sets the framework for the coordination of foreign exchange policies, and promote the exchange of information (Shridath Ramphal Center, 2010; CARICOM Secretariat Economic Intelligence and Policy Unit (CARICOM-EIPU, 2011). The CARICOM's EIPU identified the beneficiaries of these changes as financial institutions, consumers, business organizations, and the economy.

The benefits to financial institutions include greater opportunity for product innovation; lower transactions costs; greater global competitiveness; lower liquidity risk; larger market for high-risk capital, such as venture capital; increased market depth; increased competition; and access to a larger pool of potential investors (CARICOM-EIPU, 2011). Consumer-benefits include a wider range of financial products; lower transactions costs; increased choice, and overall improvement in service quality, while businesses have easier access to financing capital; increased investment opportunities, and lower cost of capital. The economy benefits from larger and more efficient financial institutions; increased investment and production; increase in employment, and positive impact on the level and growth of GDP. The overall benefits to the economy and society include a predictable environment for financial markets, which is fair, efficient, and transparent. Pooling liquidity, and allowing supply and demand for financial instruments to interact on a CARICOM-wide basis are key overall benefits (CARICOM-EIPU, 2011).

The Revised Treaty of Chaguaramas provisions to build confidence in the financial sector take effect through the CARICOM Investment Code and the CARICOM Financial Services Agreement. The movement of capital is tied to the provision of financial services and Article 38 removes all discriminatory restrictions on banking, insurance, and other financial services. The CARICOM Financial Services Agreement establishes a regional framework for the supervision and regulation of financial entities, which operate cross-border in the regional economic space while the Intra-CARICOM Double Taxation Agreement was amended to incorporate provisions for the application of the global standard for the exchange of tax information among CARICOM Tax Administrations (CARICOM, 2013).

The responsibilities of CARICOM's Council for Finance and Planning (COFAP) are economic policy coordination and financial and monetary integration of the community. Its objectives are to streamline and facilitate the cross border operations of financial institutions; create the environment for enhancing competitiveness of the Single Market in financial services; reduce explicit or hidden barriers to cross border financial flows while ensuring transparency with respect to the rules of the game; reduce payments system and portfolio risks, while ensuring stability and soundness of the financial system and the integrity of financial markets in the CSME; provide for the harmonization of essential definitions of principles in order to avoid loopholes and different approaches, thereby, minimizing regulatory arbitrage; provide a mechanism for ongoing consultation and review to assess the implementation of the financial integration and to resolve problems affecting the delivery of cross border financial services; and strengthen the process of capital market integration (CARICOM, 2013).

COFAP functions to establish and promote measures for the co-ordination and convergence of national macro-economic policies of the Member States and for the execution of a harmonized policy on foreign investment (CARICOM, 2001). It promotes and facilitate the adoption of measures for fiscal and monetary co-operation among the Member States, including the establishment of mechanisms for payment arrangements (CARICOM, 2001). It recommends measures to achieve and maintain fiscal discipline by the Governments of the Member States (CARICOM, 2001). Also, pending the establishment of a monetary union in the Community, it recommends arrangements for the free convertibility of the currencies of the Member States on a reciprocal basis (CARICOM, 2001). In addition, it promotes the establishment and integration of capital markets in the Community (CARICOM, 2001). The Committee of Central Bank Governors under the direction of COFAP, assists in the performance of these functions.

Continuity in overseeing the development of capital and financial markets are made possible by the revolving door between Caribbean academics, public sector officials, the IMF, and the CCMF. The directors of the CCMF have either been academics or central bank or Caribbean Development Bank (CDB) governors, or senior staff personnel at the IMF. These Caribbean elites who collaborate, albeit from a subservient position, with their counterparts in the US and EU controlled IFIs, help to set the region's financial development agendas.

Financial sector growth and the region's economy

The financial sector comprises bank and non-bank institutions, which according to available data contributed between 5 and 15 percent to regional GDP in 2009 (Ramsaran, 2013). In Trinidad and Tobago, the Caribbean's financial hub, the financial sector accounted for about 12 percent of GDP in 2015 (Bhagoo-Ramrattan, 2015). The institutions provide critical services to the region's development. The stock markets have not performed to expectation raising capital for investment. The commercial banks still possess the largest share of financial assets (Ramsaran, 2013). This is because consumers prefer bank credit, the family ownership of businesses, and the general population's unfamiliarity with the stock exchanges (Ramsaran, 2013).

Non-bank financial institutions have experienced significant growth and restructuring since the mid-1990, due to closures, mergers, acquisitions, and rebranding (Ramsaran, 2013). Between 1996 and 2007 the non-bank financial institutions increased their assets almost fivefold with the insurance companies accounting for about 30 percent of the sector's assets (Ramsaran, 2013). But, the dilemma is the financial sector may be highly liquid simultaneously "with low investment, zero or negative growth rates, increasing public debt and high levels of unemployment" (Ramsaran, 2013). The characterization of the financial landscape by systemic excess liquidity had a negative effect on interest rate spreads. The accumulation of excess liquidity was a major concern for central banks and commercial banks, as countries reported increases in total deposits. The reported slowing in the pace of accumulation resulted from central banks efforts to mop up excess liquidity.

Non-Banks and financial instruments

The Caribbean's ruling elites believe a well-developed capital market exerts considerable influence on economic growth, poverty alleviation, and the distribution of income. Thus, the CARICOM Heads of Government agreed to establish a CARICOM Regional Stock Exchange (CRSE) to bring together the stock exchanges in Jamaica, Trinidad and Tobago, and Barbados (CARICOM, 2011; Witter, 2010). Today there are as many as twelve stock exchanges in the region (Cassell, 2015). There are mixed views that a single CARICOM regional stock exchange is best suited for the region. The JSE, TTSE, and BSE began cross-listing their stocks after an agreement in 1991, and companies are currently listed on all three exchanges which stimulated a move toward the formation of a Caribbean Exchange Network (CXN) to harmonize the three stock markets via a common trading platform. The CXN is to facilitate the inter-regional movement of capital, and to attract foreign capital to buy stocks in Caribbean companies (Shridath Ramphal Center, 2010).

The failure to launch a regional stock exchange except for the Eastern Caribbean Securities Exchange (ECSE) in the Organization of Eastern Caribbean States (OECS) sub-region, did not prevented a proliferation of national stock exchanges, with more than a dozen of them on the records (Witter, 2010), while Cozier (2010) noted the existence of seven bond markets.

Financialization is moving a pace based on the number of financial institutions, including banks, trusts, and insurance companies of different varieties, international or off-shore banks, credit unions, and pension funds. Non-bank institutions were the greatest number of financial institutions in the region. Several other indicators point to the increasing importance of finance capital alongside the intensification of monetization of various economies. These were the growth in banks assets; the ratio of broad money to GDP; the spread of banking habits; technological innovations; and an increasing range of services and instruments (Ramsaran, 2013). Also, the spread of financial instruments, products and securitization is evident since the 1990s (Zephirin and Seerattan, 1997). These financial instruments include "bankers' acceptance, commercial paper, convertible bonds, foreign currency options, forward contracts, mutual funds, options, participating forwards, principal exchange-rate-linked securities, repurchase agreement (Repos), secondary mortgage institution, securitization, short-term investment pools, stripped bonds, swaps, syndicated, synthetic securities, universal life product and warrants" (Zephirin and Seerattan, 1997). Zephirin and Seerattan (1997) examined the specific contents and environments through which these various financial instruments emerged or have been innovated in the Caribbean.

Collister (2007) pointed to a number of new financial products in Jamaica including syndicated lending or co-financing, securitization and structured finance, mortgage securitization, short-term financing, factoring, and Exim bank lending. Williams (2004) argues Caribbean companies could fulfill their financial needs directly through capital markets, but that this is not "normal in the development of financial systems, and not as a circumvention of the banking system." Indeed, "capital markets are not substitutes for a well-functioning banking system but are complementary to traditional financial intermediaries" (Williams, 2004). According to Williams (2004), as capital markets deepen the result is bank securitization of existing loan assets. It will be normal and expected for the banks "to provide advisory and underwriting services for the issue of securities" (Williams, 2004). The advantage of securitization is its allowance for "comparatively riskier firms to access to capital markets, and lowers financing costs by segregating higher quality receivables or assets from the risky firms" (Williams, 2004). It is argued however that securitization must be undertaken in conjunction with derivatives since "it can facilitate the transfer of risks of commodities, foreign exchange and interest rates, to investors willing to accept these risks for a fee or profit" (Williams, 2004).

The belief is that as capital markets mature the structure of regional stock exchanges would change dramatically. Thus, Williams (2004) argues, "derivative transactions, which isolate risks intrinsic to underlying assets and enable trading in these risks separately are now becoming the norm in other exchanges and will become the norm in the region as well." Domestic savings are seen to be a more stable and important source of investment funding for the region than international capital flows. These are the funds identified for trade in stocks and bonds and derivatives. The new developments in capital markets and the crisis they engender have produced a newly emerging financial architecture in the Caribbean.

Emerging regional financial architecture

The CARICOM Secretariat has identified the emerging financial architecture as being characterized by four sets of agencies in development finance and resource pooling, financial standards support and facilitation, financial industry associations, and regulatory financial organizations

(CARICOM, 2010). The CDB, CARICOM Development Fund (CDF), Caribbean Catastrophe Risk Insurance Facility (CCRIF), Sub-Regional Stock Exchange Mechanisms, and Caribbean Association of Investment Promotion Agencies (CAIPA) are in the first category. The Regional Credit Rating Agency (CariCris), Regional Credit Bureau (a Trinidad and Tobago headquartered organization that is yet to become truly regional), Caribbean Financial Action Task Force (CFATF), and CCMF constitute the second category. The third set of agencies are the Caribbean Association of Indigenous Banks (CAIB), Insurance Association of the Caribbean (IAC), and Caribbean Confederation of Credit Unions (CCCU). The regulatory financial organizations are the Committee of Central Bank Governors (CCBG), Eastern Caribbean Central Bank (ECCB), Caribbean Group of Bank Supervisors (CGBS), Caribbean Association of Insurance Regulators (CAIR), CARICOM Association of Pension Supervisors (CAPS), Caribbean Group of Securities Regulators (CGSR), and CARICOM College(s) of Regulators (CARICOM, 2010).

The effective implementation of the Financial Action Task Force (FATF) 40+9 recommendations to fight money laundering and the financing of terrorism (AML/CFT) was identified as of utmost importance to the Caribbean. Money laundering and terrorism are indeed serious issues, but they are really the agenda items and interests of the developed capitalist countries. Forcing these issues on the front burner of financial policy in the Caribbean is a clear indication of the region's continued inability to set its own financial agenda. The other concerns are the "undercapitalization of banks, insurance companies and other financial institutions," as well as "poor risk management practices and distorted incentives, contaminated balance sheets, striking the appropriate balance between better regulation and supervision and over-intrusive public intervention, and forestalling the disruptive effects of derivative transactions and aggressive action by hedge funds" (Cox, 2011).

The 2008 financial crash produced intense concentration on regulations, the emergence of complex financial structures and instruments, and less hindrance on the movement of capital. The Heads of Government of the CARICOM issued the Liliendaal Declaration on the Financial Sector that recognized the need for financial sector policy and regional financial architecture reform focusing on regulatory and supervisory systems (CARICOM, 2010). The CARICOM (2010) identified nine specific proposals to protect the regions' financial sector. However, the key point about the financial architecture and the response to insulate the region from financial crises is the prominence of the affairs of finance capital in the economy and society. The Caribbean is completely subordinate to the system of global capitalist finance through the harmonization of laws and regulations in which all CARICOM member countries participate. Further evidence of this is "de-risking" in the Caribbean which is forcing Caribbean states to become even more subservient to the rules of US and European global financial arrangements (MacDonald, 2019; CFATF, 2019).

Alternative sources of finance

The CARICOM states do not have to continue to depend on the IFIs controlled by the US and the EU to finance their economic development. Through the CDB, the NDB, and the BRI's financing, the CARICOM can finally break the chains that historically tied the region to the imperialist monetary and financial arrangements. Finance is needed for investment projects and historically these projects were dictated by imperialist interests that did not utilize Caribbean resources to satisfy consumption in the region. The Caribbean states can now pick development projects that use Caribbean resources to satisfy regional demand and finance them through the BRICS Bank and the BRI without having to go to the capitalist international capital markets to do so. The BRICS Bank and BRI are alternative forms of finance despite criticisms that the BRI is "debt-trap diplomacy." The Trump Administration argues that China provides infrastructure loans to developing countries under opaque loan terms with a view to strategically leverage the recipient country's indebtedness for its own economic, military or political ends or the seize its assets (Furness, 2020).

Capital flows from China to the Caribbean come in "the form of loans to governments to finance infrastructure projects and to expand production of oil and other raw materials," and from "Chinese enterprises and entrepreneurs" (Bernal, 2016). However, whether Chinese capital flows to the state or private enterprises, it is the independent CARICOM institutions which negotiate the terms and conditions including oversight, with Chinese agencies. The onus is on the CARICOM institutions to negotiate the best deals for the region. The CARICOM cannot negotiate deals and then say the Chinese want to entrap them in debt in order to seize their assets. The Caribbean countries did not have a say in the creation of the imperial monetary and financial arrangements in which they are currently entangled. But, they definitely have a say in fashioning any new monetary financial arrangements with the BRICS Bank and China. The alternative monetary and financial arrangements with the BRICS and China are the counterpoints to the foregoing descriptive analysis of neoliberal financialization in the Caribbean.

The New Development Bank and BRI

The NDB or BRICS Bank is a financial counterpoint to the multilateral development banks (MDB) controlled by the EU and US. The NDB is a MDB controlled by BRICS. The mission, objectives and activities of the NDB allows participating developing countries to secure investment finance for their sustainable development. The NDB values are egalitarian, transparent, inclusive, and democratic which are different to those of the typical capitalist multilateral bank. As a partner it goes beyond the conventional codes of capitalist multilateral banks. The NDB is open and approachable, operates on the basis of mutual respect, collaboration, the needs of developing countries, transformative values that link need and finance for holistic development, and brings about structural transformation by financing sustainably driven infrastructure projects. The NDB deliberately focuses on the projects it does because of the skewedness, insufficiency, and often environmentally unfriendliness of development in the current century.

The NDB seeks to change the face of development finance, make the value chain efficient and fast, take bold decisions, implement groundbreaking process innovation, and apply technology for global development. The bank employs flexible processes and approaches favorable to customers, and adapts systems to quicken loan disbursements. Its roots are in developing economies and thus it possesses an excellent understanding of their financing needs. It understands what development truly means and has at its core a vision of a great leveler that is inclusive and not selective (NDB, 2019, 2020).

The average repayment maturity of NDB lending spread comprising maturity premium, market risk premium, and cost of funds over benchmark rate for sovereign guaranteed loans vary from 0.65 percent up to 8 years and to 1.35 percent for greater than 18–19 years. These are quite favorable lending terms for the CARICOM states. The NDB supports member countries to achieve their development aspirations, especially with respect to the UN's 2030 Agenda for Sustainable Development and the 2015 Paris Agreement on Climate Change. The CARICOM supports these very development agendas (NDB, 2019). Climate change, sustainable development, vulnerability and governance in the Caribbean are under serious analyses by Caribbean scholars and policy makers (Scobie, 2018; Rhiney, 2015).

In March 2020, there were 138 countries from Sub-Saharan Africa, Europe and Central Asia, East Asia and Pacific, Middle East and North Africa, Latin America and Caribbean, and South East Asia that were in the BRI (Green Belt and Road Initiative Center, 2020). According to the Office of the Leading Group for Promoting the Belt and Road Initiative (OLGPBRI) (2019), financial integration is an important pillar of the BRI. Thus, investment and financial models, international multilateral financial institutions, and commercial banks have played a role in expanding the channels of diversified financing, providing stable, transparent, and quality financial support for the BRI (OLGPBRI, 2019). A bigger part is being played by the sovereign wealth funds and investment funds of participating countries. The Abu Dhabi Investment Authority of the UAE, China Investment Corporation, and other sovereign wealth funds have increased their investment in major emerging participating economies. The China–EU Joint Investment Fund began operating in 2018 and injected €500 million from the Silk Road Fund and the European Investment Fund. This has helped the BRI to dovetail with the Investment Plan for Europe (OLGPBRI, 2019).

The BRI has growing support from multilateral financial cooperation such that China's Ministry of Finance and its counterparts in 27 countries including Argentina, Russia, Indonesia, the UK, and Singapore have endorsed the "Guiding Principles on Financing the Development of the Belt and Road" (OLGPBRI, 2019). The BRI countries support channeling financial resources to serve their real economy, with priority given to such areas as infrastructure connectivity, trade and investment, and industrial cooperation. Joint financing programs of BRI programs have been jointly financed by the People's Bank of China, the World Bank's International Finance Corporation, the Inter-American Development Bank, African Development Bank, European Bank for Reconstruction and Development, and other multilateral development institutions. These agencies had invested in more than 100 programs in over 70 countries and regions by the end of 2018. The China-Central Eastern European Countries (CEEC) Bank Consortium established in 2017 includes 14 financial institutions from China, Hungary, the Czech Republic, Slovakia, Croatia, and nine other Central and Eastern European countries (OLGPBRI, 2019). The China Arab States Bank Consortium founded in July 2018, was followed by China–Africa Financial Cooperation Consortium in September 2018.

The BRI promotes closer cooperation between financial institutions for example through policy-backed export credit insurance, with wide coverage that plays a special role in supporting infrastructure and basic industries. Commercial banks take deposits from wider sources, corporate financing, financial products, trade agency, and trust services. The China Export and Credit Insurance Corporation had endorsed US$600 billion on export to and investment in the participating countries (OLGPBRI, 2019). Furthermore, Chinese-financed banks, such as the Bank of China, Industrial and Commercial Bank of China, Agricultural Bank of China, and China Construction Bank, have formed extensive agent banking relations with the participating countries (OLGPBRI, 2019). The BRI banking mechanism was joined by the first German bank, Commerzbank, which signed a memorandum of understanding on cooperation with the Industrial and Commercial Bank of China (OLGPBRI, 2019).

The BRI countries have made continued efforts to consolidate and improve financial cooperation for long-term benefits and win-win outcomes by improving the financial market system. The steady supply of innovative financial products has expanded substantially the channels for financing the BRI. China has continued to open up its interbank bond market, and by the end of 2018 about RMB200 billions of Panda bonds had been issued (OLGPBRI, 2019). The Export–Import Bank of China issued a RMB2 billion green bond for global investors, and the BRICS NDB issued a RMB3 billion green bond to support the green development of the BRI. Meanwhile, stock equity, business and technical cooperation between securities and futures exchanges has advanced (OLGPBRI, 2019). The Shanghai Stock Exchange, Deutsche Börse Group, and China Financial Futures Exchange jointly founded the China Europe International Exchange in 2015, and the Shanghai Stock Exchange and Astana International Financial Center Authority of Kazakhstan have signed an agreement to co-invest in building the Astana International Exchange (OLGPBRI, 2019).

Eleven Chinese-funded banks established 76 first-grade institutions in 28 BRI countries, and 50 banks from 22 BRI countries have opened seven corporate banks, 19 branches, and 34 representative offices in China deepening financial connectivity. Two Chinese-funded securities firms have established joint ventures in Singapore and Laos. China has made bilateral currency swap arrangements with more than 20 BRI states, has Renminbi clearing arrangements with seven BRI countries, and signed cooperation agreements with the financial supervision authorities of 35 BRI countries. Meanwhile, the Renminbi's functions as a currency for international payment, investment, trade, and reserve have been strengthened. The Cross-Border Interbank Payment System (CIPS) now covers some 40 countries and regions involved in the BRI. The China–IMF Capacity Development Center and the Research Center for the Belt and Road Financial and Economic Development have been founded (OLGPBRI, 2019).

These are monumental developments in the global financial architecture spearheaded by China that the CARICOM cannot overlook as a possible alternative to the imperial monetary and financial arrangement in which the region is currently entrapped.

Conclusion

Neoliberal financialization manifests itself in the Caribbean in certain specific ways that sets it apart from developments in developed capitalist countries. While financialization already dominate the developed economies, the Caribbean states are seeking to have finance capital become the engine of economic growth. In developed capitalist economies it is easy to point to concrete outcomes of neoliberal financialization like the domination of economy and society by finance capital. Also, economic growth spearheaded by financial capital in Wall Street does not meet the working people in the main street, while the top financiers grow workers at the bottom stagnate and regress. In the Caribbean, the material conditions of financialization are actually about the key features identified above such as creating the appropriate financial architecture and capital markets.

The ruling elites have pushed aside industrialization in favor of financialization as the engine of economic growth. They have relegated financial self-determination to the dustbin of history by building financial institutions, products, and instruments in line with the financial markets of the developed capitalist countries. The aim is to deepen the neoliberal financial sector and strengthen its linkages to the global financial grid established by the managers of finance capital in the advanced capitalist states. The Caribbean financial architecture is focused on stability to insulate the region from crises that result from crashes and scams originating in the developed economies.

The recommendation is for the Caribbean to carefully review the works of Odle (1974, 1972) and Thomas (1965, 1972) to rekindle the ideas and spirit of financial self-determination. Financial independence espoused by Thomas and Odle was not designed to bring about the financialization of the region. Their focus was on the use of domestic regional funds to finance Caribbean development. The rekindling of their ideas on financial independence is really to further industrialization as a central plank in Caribbean development. This goal can be achieved if the region embraces the alternative financial arrangements provided by BRICS Bank and China's BRI in the new multipolar world order.

References

Amin, S. (2013). "Globalization, Financialization and the Emergence of the Global South," pp. 258–270 in Polanyi-Levitt, K. (ed.) *From the Great Transformation to the Great Financialization: On Karl Polanyi and Other Essays*. Halifax and London: Fernwood Publishing and Zed Books.

Bennett, K. (2008). "Issues in Financing Development in CARICOM," *Journal of Business, Finance and Economics in Emerging, Economies* 3 (2): 99–117.

Bernal, R.L. (2016). *"Chinese Foreign Direct Investment in the Caribbean: Potential and Prospects,"* Inter-American Development Bank, November.

Bhagoo-Ramrattan, V. (2015). "The Pivotal Role of the Financial Sector in the Caribbean Economy," *World Finance*, 4 September.

Canterbury, D.C. (2013). *Capital Accumulation and Migration*. Chicago, IL: Haymarket Publishers.

Canterbury, D.C. (2016). "Neoliberal Financialization: The 'New' Imperial Monetary and Financial Arrangements in the Caribbean," *The CLR James Journal* (Special Issue: Clive Y. Thomas) 22 (1/2): 113–150.

Caribbean Financial Action Task Force. (2019). "De-Risking in the Caribbean Region – A CFATF Perspective. Port of Spain, Trinidad and Tobago: CFATF Secretariat, 1 November.

CARICOM (2001). Revised Treaty of Chaguaramas Establishing the Caribbean Community including the CARICOM Single Market and Economy Signed by Heads of Government of the Caribbean Community on July 5, 2001 at their Twenty Second Meeting of the Conference of Heads of Government in Nassau, Bahamas.

CARICOM (2010). *Trade and Investment Report, 2010: Strategies for Recovery, Renewal and Reform*. Turkeyen, Guyana and Kingston, Jamaica: Ian Randle.

CARICOM (2011). *Regional Stock Exchange*. Turkeyen: Guyana: CARICOM Secretariat.

CARICOM (2013). *CARICOM Finance Ministers Tackle Growth and Development*. CARICOM Secretariat Press Release, 175/2013.

CARICOM-EIPU (2011). "Draft CARICOM Financial Services Agreement (and Quest for a Seamless Financial Landscape)," Georgetown, Guyana.

Cassell, W. Jr. (2015). "List of Major Stock Exchanges in the Caribbean," *Investopedia*, 14 July.

Collister, K.R. (2007). *A New Approach to Development Banking in Jamaica*. Santiago, Chile: CEPAL Development Studies Unit, Economic Development Division (Financiamiento del Desarrollo. Serie 193).

Cox, W. (2011). *The International Financial Architecture and Its Application to the Caribbean*. Bridgetown, Barbados: Bank of Barbados.

Cozier, J.G. (2010). "The Evolution of the Stock Market in the Caribbean: From 1969 and Beyond," Submitted in Partial Fulfillment of the Requirements for the Degree of Masters of Philosophy in Economic Development Policy and Management of the University of the West Indies, St. Augustine, Trinidad and Tobago.

ECLAC (1996). *Financial Liberalization: Its Relevance and Experiences in the Caribbean*. Port of Spain, Trinidad and Tobago: Sub-Regional Headquarters for the Caribbean, Caribbean Development and Cooperation Committee, LC/CAR/G.492.

ECLAC (2001). *The Impact of Privatization on the Banking Sector in the Caribbean*. Port of Spain, Trinidad and Tobago: Sub-Regional Headquarters for the Caribbean, Caribbean Development and Cooperation Committee, LC/CAR/G.671.

Farrell, T.W. (2010). "The Political Economy of Financial Regulation: Global and Caribbean Perspectives," *25th Adlith Brown Memorial Lecture, 42nd Annual Conference of the Caribbean Centre for Money and Finance. Financial Stability, Crisis Preparedness and Risk Management in the Caribbean*, Port of Spain, Trinidad and Tobago.

Furness, V. (2020). "Can Africa Escape a Belt and Road Debt Trap?" *Belt and Road News*, Hong Kong, 5 June.

Goldstein, J.P. (2009). "Introduction: The Political Economy of Financialization," *Review of Radical Political Economics, Special Issue: The Financialization of Global Capitalism: Analysis, Critiques, and Alternatives* 41 (4): 453–457.

Green Belt and Road Initiative Center (2020). "*Countries of the Belt and Road Initiative*," Beijing, China: Green Belt and Road Initiative Center.

Hilferding, R. (1981). *Finance Capital: A Study in the Latest Phase of Capitalist Development*. London: Routledge and Kegan Paul.

Jones, P.W. (2006). *The Caribbean Regional Stock Exchange, CSME and Economic Development*. Kingston Jamaica: Economic Development Institute.

Kautsky, K. (1911). "Finance-Capital and Crises." *Social Democrat*, London, XIV, July–December.

Lapavitsas, C. (2013). *Profiting Without Producing: How Finance Exploits Us All*. London and New York: Verso.

Lenin, V.I. (1963). *Imperialism, the Highest Stage of Capitalism*. Moscow: Progress Publishers.

Lewis, W.A. (1950). "The Industrialization of the British West Indies," *Caribbean Economic Review* 2 (1): 1–61.

Li, C. and J. Wong. (2018). *Financial Development and Inclusion in the Caribbean*. Washington DC: International Monetary Fund, Working Paper WP/18/53, March.

Luxemburg, R. (1951). *The Accumulation of Capital*. London: Routledge and Kegan Paul.

MacDonald, S.B. (2019). Is There a 'New Normal' for De-risking in the Caribbean?, Washington, DC: Center for Strategic and International Studies (CSIS), 16 October.

Marx, K. (2011). *Capital Volume I A Critique of Political Economy*. New York: Dover Publications.

New Development Bank (NDB) (2019). *National Development Bank Annual Report 2018*. Shanghai, China.

New Development Bank (NDB) (2020). *Virtual Annual Board Meeting of NDB Board of Governors*, 20 April.

Odle, M.A. (1972). *The Significance of Non-Bank Financial Intermediaries in the Caribbean: An Analysis of Patterns of Financial Structure and Development*. Kingston, Jamaica: Institute of Social and Economic Research (ISER), University of the West Indies.

Odle, M.A. (1974). *Pension Funds in Labor Surplus Economies*. Kingston, Jamaica: Institute of Social and Economic Research (ISER), University of the West Indies.

Office of the Leading Group for Promoting the Belt and Road Initiative (OLGPBRI) (2019). *The Belt and Road Initiative: Progress, Contributions and Prospects 2019*. Beijing, China: Foreign Language Press.

Petras, J. (2007). *Rulers and Ruled in the US Empire: Bankers, Zionists, Militants*. Atlanta, GA: Clarity Press.

Petras, J. and H. Veltmeyer (2001). *Globalization Unmasked: Imperialism in the 21st Century*. London: Zed Books.

Polanyi-Levitt, K. (2013). *From the Great Transformation to the Great Financialization: On Karl Polanyi and Other Essays*. Halifax and London: Fernwood Publishing and Zed Books.

Ramsaran, R. (2013). "An Overview of Global and Regional Economic and Financial Developments," pp. 21–97 in Ramsaran, R. (ed.) *The Financial Evolution of the Caribbean Community, 1996-2008*, Second Edition. St. Augustine: Caribbean Center for Money and Finance, The University of the West Indies.

Rhiney, K. (2015). "Geographies of Caribbean Vulnerability in a Changing Climate: Issues and Trends," *Geography Compass* 9(3): 97–114.

Shridath Ramphal Center (2010). *International Business and Financial Services Profile*. Cave Hill, Barbados, University of the West Indies.

Scobie, M. (2018). "Accountability in Climate Change Governance and Caribbean SIDS (Small Island Developing States)," *Environment Development and Sustainability*, (20): 769–787. https://doi.org/10.1007/s10668-017-9909-9.

Thomas, C.Y. (1972). *The Structure, Performance and Prospects of Central Banking in the Caribbean*. Kingston, Jamaica: Institute of Social and Economic Research (ISER), University of the West Indies.

Thomas, C.Y. (1965a). *Monetary and Financial Arrangements in a Dependent Monetary Economy: A Study of British Guiana, 1945-1962*. Kingston, Jamaica: Institute of Social and Economic Research (ISER), University of the West Indies.

Thomas, C.Y. (1965b). Monetary and Financial Arrangements in a Dependent Monetary Economy: A Study of British Guiana, 1945–1962, (Supplement to *Social and Economic Studies* 14(4): 1–186.

Thomas, C.Y. (1972). *The Structure, Performance and Prospects of Central Banking in the Caribbean*. Jamaica: Institute of Social and Economic Research, University of the West Indies.

Williams, M. (2004). The Development of the Caribbean Capital Market. Presented at Capital Market Seminar, Bank of Barbados. Bridgetown: Barbados.

Witter, D. (2010). "A Look at Stock Exchanges across the Caribbean," *Jamaica Observer*.

World Bank and CCMS (1998). Wider Caribbean Financial Sector Review: Increasing Competitiveness and Financial Resource Management for Economic Growth. Washington: World Bank.

Zephirin, M.G., and D. Seerattan. (1997). "Financial Innovations in the Caribbean," *Caribbean Center for Monetary Studies*. Trinidad and Tobago: St. Augustine, University of the West Indies.

9 Caribbean agriculture in the new multipolar world order

Introduction

The CARICOM does not have an agricultural policy for the new multipolar world order, the ruling elites as creatures of habit, continue with business as usual in agriculture with the US' Caribbean Basin Initiative (CBI) and the CARIFORUM–EU EPA. President Trump on October 10, 2020 signed into law H.R.991, the bipartisan extension of the Caribbean Basin Economic Recovery Act (CBERA), which extends the expiring Caribbean Basin Trade Partnership Act (CBTPA) through 2030 (The White House, 2020). The opportunities to develop a genuinely sustainable self-reliant agriculture of its own choosing are being improperly considered. This has been the case throughout the three regimes through which Caribbean agriculture has traversed – colonial, nationalist, and neoliberal (Canterbury, 2007).

This chapter opens up the debate on the prospects of CARICOM's agriculture in the NMWO focusing on the dynamics of the agrarian question that throws back to mercantile capitalism involving in recent years agricultural measures in the CBI and the CARIFORUM–EU EPA. The CARICOM must recalibrate its agricultural development to bring it in line with China's BRI agricultural measures, which allows its participants to mutually formulate their own designs for agricultural cooperation (PRC, 2017).

The analysis commences with an exposition on selected theoretical issues on agriculture in general and the Caribbean in particular from colonial times to present. The focus is on the colonial approach and Moyne Commission (1945), Lewis' (1950, 1954, 1955) approach, Thomas' (1968, 1984, 1993) considerations, neoliberalism and food security, food regime analysis and its problems, and the new political economy of agriculture and biofuels. The second part analyses agricultural measures in the CBI and CARIFORUM–EU EPA. The agricultural measures in the BRI are discussed in the third part, while the final section provides ideas toward the formulation of a Caribbean agricultural policy in the NMWO.

DOI: 10.4324/9781003092414-9

Selected theoretical issues

The colonial approach and Moyne Commission

Mercantile capitalism subjected the Caribbean to the production of a single agricultural export crop, justified by the colonial authorities on the basis of comparative advantage as the region was seen to be endowed with arable land best suited for farming. Williams and Smith (2008) noted colonial strategy promoted export-oriented agriculture on large-scale plantation. Sugar, cocoa, and coffee were produced and exported in raw form for processing in Britain (Williams and Smith, 2008). Subsequently, the rural sector became the supplier of farm food and cheap labor to domestic cities, and medium and small farmers diversified agriculture by growing non-traditional crops. The colonial approach produced a dual production structure fraught with many problems – inadequate land tenure, use, and settlement schemes, poor self-sufficient, inability to find new markets, deficient infrastructure in finance, organization, marketing, science, technology, transport, drainage, irrigation, and education, dependence on imports, and a lack of diversification. The economic and social conditions of plantation labor were dismal and eventually stimulated major anti-colonial social unrest. The colonial authorities established the Moyne Commission of Inquiry to determine the cause of the unrest and to make recommendations.

The Moyne Commission argued that it would be impossible for Caribbean agriculture to provide the essentials of life for the growing population in the region if certain negative conditions persisted including low technical knowledge, business organization and management efficiency, and the lack of systematic agriculture suited to the inherent circumstances of the area (Moyne Commission, 1945). Measures identified to overcome the problems of agriculture included land settlement schemes to ease overpopulation, restriction on rural-urban migration by opening up opportunities for employment in the countryside, and the diversification of agricultural production (Thomas, 1988). Colonial policy addressed the problems of unequal land distribution, land tenure, and housing, which were major sources of conflict in the rural sector. Government produce departments and marketing boards were established to regulate and supervise land use. The produce department stabilized farm income and retail prices, by buying up surplus produce at competitive prices and then retailing them reasonably. The structural reforms in global capitalism in the neoliberal era dismantled these latter measures on the grounds that they were state-driven.

Lewis and Thomas

The collapse of the colonial slave mode of production stimulated debate on the relationship between agriculture and industry. The Corn Laws were repealed in 1846, just eight years after the final abolition of slavery in the

British West Indies in 1838. In the period just prior to the repeal of the Corn Laws the emerging industrialist and landed aristocracy were in conflict over which type of production arrangement was more favored. The industrialist were outraged at the landed aristocracy's denunciation of the cruelty of the factory system. The industrialists argued that the Corn Laws designed to protect the landed aristocracy was a humbug to industrial progress and useless because it brought little protection to corn producers.

Marx (2011) observed that the quarrel between those two factions of the ruling class about which of them exploited labor more shamefully, was on each hand the midwife of truth. The repeal of the Corn Laws galvanized English agriculture, bringing about extensive drainage, new stall-feeding methods in live stocks, artificial cultivation of green crops, the introduction of mechanical manuring apparatus, new treatment of clay soils, increased use of mineral manures, employment of the steam-engine and of all kinds of new machinery, and more intensive cultivation generally (Marx, 2011). The agricultural population decreased simultaneously as area under cultivation increased. This intensive cultivation due to the incorporation of capital with the soil increased the wealth of capitalist farmers (Marx, 2011). Caribbean agriculture was not galvanized by the repeal of the Corn Laws, instead it was a casualty of those developments as agricultural interests in the region lost ground in Europe. Plantation agriculture remained stuck in the ways of the backward landed aristocracy in England. Thus, as European agriculture was industrialized, Caribbean agriculture remained backward with some innovation and declined.

The theoretical debate on the relationship between industry and agriculture spawned a popular view that the transition from the production of primary agricultural commodities to secondary manufactured goods was essential for economic growth and development. This view was advocated by Chenery (1955), Clark (1951), and the United Nations (1947). The thesis that economic growth and development required a transition from agriculture to industry dominated the thinking on development, from the 1950s to the 1970s. Lewis (1954, 1955) however held the view that the issue was not merely about transitioning from primary agricultural to secondary manufacturing production. Pushback also came from Fei and Ranis (1961), Johnston and Mellor (1961), Jorgenson (1961), and Mellor (1976), who "demonstrated that the one-way path leading resources out of agriculture ignored the full growth potential" of the agricultural sector (Williams and Smith, 2008).

Lewis (1954, 1955) was concerned with how agriculture, industry, and mechanical cultivation reinforce each other to benefit a country, rather than with the displacement of agriculture by industry. Lewis (1954) reasoned "if the capitalist sector produces no food, its expansion increases the demand for food, raises the price of food in terms of capitalist products, and so reduces profits." That is one sense "in which industrialization is dependent upon agricultural improvement." It is unprofitable "to produce a growing volume of manufactures unless agricultural production [was] growing simultaneously." It is for that reason "industrial and agrarian revolutions always go together and why economies in which agriculture is stagnant do not show industrial development." Lewis (1954) reasoned "if we postulate that the capitalist sector is not producing food, we must either postulate that the subsistence sector is increasing its output, or else conclude that the expansion of the capitalist sector will be brought to an end through adverse terms of trade eating into profits" (Lewis, 1954: 173). Lewis (1954) argued, his conclusion was "first cousin" to "Ricardo's problem of increasing rents ... he worried about rents increasing *inside* the capitalist sector, whereas we are dealing with rents *outside* the sector (Lewis, 1954: 173).

To understand the relationship between agriculture and industry it was necessary to determine the conditions under which mechanized agriculture is economic (Lewis, 1955). Mechanized agriculture is economic if there is a shortage of labor relative to capital, whereas, if the opposite condition is present there is a super-abundance of labor and "the main effect of introducing mechanization is to create still more unemployment, at the cost of using up scarce foreign exchange to import the mechanical equipment and its fuel" (Lewis, 1955: 129). In such a situation "the objective of economic policy is to maximize output per acre, and not output per worker" (Lewis, 1955: 129). Lewis (1955) states: "mechanization will increase output if it enables land to be brought into cultivation which could not be cultivated by hand methods." In surplus labor countries mechanical cultivation is economic "in so far as it releases for human use land which otherwise required draught animals" (Lewis, 1955). This depends "on the cost of machinery and fuel on the one hand" and on the other "the value of the crop released in this way" (Lewis, 1955).

Mechanization "is a necessary part of economic growth where labor is scarce but is only marginally relevant where labor is abundant" (Lewis, 1955: 130). The justification for mechanization is based on "the relative scarcities of labor, land and capital," whereas "the feasibility of mechanization depends next upon the land and the crop." Lewis (1955) identified some restrictions on the areas to which mechanical cultivation is applicable. With the advance of nanotechnology farm size may not be as important in the application of mechanization. Small farms can successfully employ mechanical cultivation in combination with large farms "if machinery is owned by a central agency which cultivates the land for the farmers in return for a fee, while leaving each farmer to plant, weed and reap on his own account" (Lewis, 1955: 130–131). However, "large scale agricultural operations are more efficient, and show more rapid economic growth than small scale operations," if there is economy in mechanical cultivation, large scale control of irrigation, seeds, disease precaution, processing, and marketing (Lewis, 1955: 129).

According to Lewis (1955), poorer countries can leave pure science research to the advanced industrial nations, the results of which are freely available for wholesale borrowing (Lewis, 1955: 174). Agricultural research in the tropics should concentrate on commercial crops for export to Europe, and neglected crops produced for domestic consumption (Lewis, 1955: 188). Furthermore, "economic growth results in a continuous decline of the importance of agriculture relatively to other sources of employment ... (since) other industries are continuously recruiting labor from the agricultural sector. The recruitment of labor is absolute if production is stable and relative with a rapidly growing population (Lewis, 1955: 190). Note the emphasis on commercial agriculture for export to Europe. Nowadays, however, the emphasis on commercial agricultural exports has to be beyond Europe.

Thomas (1984) reasoned the colonial slave mode of production spawned dependency relations, such that the Caribbean produced what it did not consume and consumed what it did not produce. Caribbean agricultural produce was exported, and the region imported its food. The agriculture sector does not meet the consumption needs of the growing Caribbean population. Thomas (1984) recommended fundamental structural changes in the economy, polity, and society to equilibrate Caribbean consumption and production. Thomas (1993) observed that since 1970s the Caribbean's traditional export staples – sugar, bananas, rice, cocoa, coffee, citrus – became increasingly uncompetitive, but the region has failed to develop any significant new export crops. There was a paucity in the facilities for producing and marketing food and raw materials locally.

Thomas (1993) noted that there was still need in the region for radical land reforms, basic changes in the legal and institutional structures, a science-based system of mixed farming, a technically trained agricultural workforce, marketing and distribution arrangements that cater to the needs of the broad mass of the population, credit and infrastructural provisions (such as drainage, irrigation, feeder roads) and various other facilities to minimize post-harvest losses (Thomas 1993). The region had tied up much of its "human, financial, technical, and land resources" in agriculture, but "the sector had been so badly neglected that as far back as 1970 the food balance sheet of the area had gone into deficit when over 50 percent of the food essentials consumed in the area was imported" (Thomas, 1993: 215). The neglect of small-farm agriculture was at all levels – scientific, organizational, credit and marketing. Meanwhile, the taste for imported foods was reinforced by tourism, migration, the Caribbean's proximity to the North America, social media, and the internet.

Neoliberalism and food security

The neoliberal turn in global capitalism in the 1980s devastated an already dismal Caribbean agricultural sector. The Caribbean depends on external trade which means the region's agriculture is interwoven and evolve with the shifting structures of global production, marketing, and consumption (Thomas, 1993). Caribbean agriculture became subjected to neoliberal

138 *Caribbean agriculture*

economic liberalization policies and the global institutional framework erected to facilitate those measures which concentrated on price incentives, rehabilitation of infrastructure, foreign private investment, privatization of state farms, and cost recovery. The goal was to relieve budgetary constraints and maintain infrastructure such as drainage, irrigation, and roads. Caribbean governments are obliged to comply with WTO agricultural liberalization measures and rulings. Caribbean agriculture continued to hemorrhage and decline unabated in spite of neoliberal structural adjustment in agriculture. The food crisis and food security challenges that surfaced in the neoliberal era forced Caribbean states to refocus the role of agriculture in attenuating the problems.

Apprehensions with food crisis, security, and insecurity led the Caribbean Food and Nutrition Institute (CFNI), the Caribbean Agricultural Research and Development Institute (CARDI), the UN Food and Agriculture Organization (FAO), and the CARICOM to brainstorm appropriate policies to address the situation. The main trepidation was to identify the areas of food security and insecurity and construct appropriate policies to overcome the problems identified. The CFNI with support from the US Department of Agriculture and the CARICOM Secretariat, broached the food security problem at a policy dialogue on poverty alleviation and food security strategies in the Caribbean, in 2003 (CFNI, 2005). The determination was that policies to alleviate poverty and increase food security essentially promoted economic development defined in terms of how humans satisfy their needs (Benn, 2005). The consensus was food security, nutrition, and health challenges called for a food policy agenda that synchronizes food security and health concerns in three areas – food consumption, nutrition, and health; food trade, production and safety; and food and agriculture resource allocation and public health programing (Ford, 2005). The food policy spectrum was identified as covering undernutrition, food security, the right to food, food sovereignty, food poverty, food safety, and the prevention of chronic diseases.

The FAO (2015) found CARICOM states had progressed in the reduction of undernourishment, and in meeting the global hunger targets. The number of undernourished persons declined from 8.1 million in 1990–1992, to 7.5 million in 2014–2016. The proportion of undernourished persons dropped from 27 percent to 19.8 percent. Undernourishment was extremely high 50 percent in Haiti, but it was less than 10 percent in Dominica, Bahamas, Belize, Jamaica, and Trinidad and Tobago. Barbados, Guyana and St Vincent, and the Grenadines had met the World Food Summit (WFS) global hunger targets set in 1996, and the United Nations Millennium Development Goals (MDGs) in 2000. The remaining CARICOM countries had undernourishment levels between 10 and 20 percent (FAO, 2015). Food energy in CARICOM countries exceeded the recommended population food energy guidelines (FAO, 2015).

Per capita calories consumption in Barbados and Dominica exceeded 3,000, while in the other countries the number was above 2,400. The estimated average for Haiti was about 2,000. The high caloric intake was associated with changes in food consumption in the direction of processed foods, which has contributed to the CARICOM countries ranking among the highest in the world in terms of obesity. Overweight and obesity affected higher proportions of the CARICOM population than undernourishment. The female obesity rate in the above 15 year age group was several times higher than that of the rate for males. In Haiti, obese females outnumbered obese males 16:1, and in Jamaica and St Lucia, the ratios were 6:1 and 4:1, respectively (FAO, 2015).

Food imports was by far the largest source of food for CARICOM populations, as opposed to food grown locally. CARICOM countries imported more than US$4 billion in food annually, an increase of 50 percent since 2000, and the projected increase by 2020 was US$8–10 billion, unless efforts to address the problem succeeded (FAO, 2015). But, Dorodnykh (2017) noted the CARICOM's food import bill was US$5 billion in 2017, and was projected to reach US$22 billion by 2030. More than 60 percent of the food consumed in almost all CARICOM states were imports, while half of these countries imported more than 80 percent of the food they consumed (Dorodnykh, 2017). Belize, Guyana, and Haiti produced more than 50 percent of their food consumption. The top five food imports were processes foods, grains in particular wheat and corn, and livestock products in particular meat and dairy. These account for more than US$1 billion or roughly 25 percent of CARICOM's annual food imports. Simultaneously, the national production of fruits and vegetables per capita had declined (Dorodnykh, 2017).

The population's access to food constituted another major problem which is linked to poverty. The estimates were that about 40 percent of the region's population was considered poor due to lack of access to nutritious food. More than 30 percent of the population in seven CARICOM states was below the national poverty levels, while the statistic for Haiti was 59 percent. At the same time the region was characterized by high levels of income inequality, and the consumption expenditure of the highest 10 percent of income earners averaged 16.4 times more than that of the lowest 10 percent of income earners (FAO, 2015).

Food regime analysis and its problems

Food regime analysis has forced its way into in the literature on agricultural development. Friedmann (1987) and Friedmann and McMichael (1989) first introduced the idea to provide a world-historical perspective on the role of agriculture in the development of the capitalist world economy, and on the trajectory of the state system (Friedmann and McMichael, 1989: 93). Given its world historical system perspective the take on agriculture is not the same as the critical development studies approach (Veltmeyer and Bowles, 2018). A food regime "links international relations of food production and consumption to forms of accumulation broadly distinguishing periods of capitalist transformation since 1870" (McMichael 2013: 1).

Food regimes correspond to distinct historical periods – as capitalism changes its form it gives birth to new food regimes. The first was a British-centered food regime, from 1870 to 1930, which "linked the fortunes of an emergent industrial capitalism to expanding cheap food supply zones across the world" (McMichael, 2013). The second was a US-centered food regime, from 1950 to 1970, characterized by the US "deployment of food aid to create alliances, markets and opportunities for its intensive agro-industrial model" including "national agro-industrialization, adopting green revolution technologies, and instituting land reform to dampen peasant unrest and extend market relations into the countryside" (McMichael, 2013). The third is a corporate food regime, from 1980s to 2000s characterized by market hegemony. The corporate food regime has a role in a broader "neoliberal project dedicated to securing transnational circuits of money and commodities, including food" (McMichael, 2013).

The corporate food regime governed by neoliberal free trade principles, applies unevenly across the globe. It has displaced "smallholders into a casual global labor force for capital," deepened the US-centered food regime incorporating "new regions into the animal protein chains (e.g., Brazil/China)," consolidated "differentiated supply chains into a 'supermarket revolution,'" and subdivided "quality and standardized foods to provision of bifurcated class diets" (McMichael, 2013). It has intensified the dumping of northern-subsidized food surpluses such as grains, milk powder, and animal protein parts, choke-off so-called inefficient farmers in the South, generate increasing numbers of slum-dwellers, and fuel a global counter-movement among farmers and landless workers unified around the notion of food sovereignty, which incorporates advocacy for "democratic policy regarding rights for farmer/peasants, local food security and ecological farming for soil and human health" (McMichael, 2013).

The fault lines in food regime analysis from a Caribbean perspective are first, it overlooks the dynamics of Caribbean agriculture prior to 1870 when the region was characterized by what Williams (1994) and Thomas (1984) called slavery-cum-capitalism or colonial slave mode of production, respectively. This period was essential in the formation of the modern Caribbean and the development of industrial capitalism. Second, twenty-first-century food system is regarded as truly global because food producers are in many different locations servicing consumers all over the globe. But, this is no different from the early beginnings of capitalism, when food moved across continents – European products found their way to Africa and vice versa, especially with the English and French challenges to Portuguese monopoly on the Guinea Coast (Rodney, 1970).

Third, food regimes analysis is top-down without fully grasping the working class struggle in the former colonies, making it impossible to elaborate on the class dynamics of the colonial slave mode of production characteristic of Caribbean colonies. It tells the story of agriculture from the point of view of hegemonic powers from the outside looking in, missing the true account from the inside looking out. Fifth, it sees Caribbean agriculture as evolving through three periods whereas Caribbean agriculture has a different trajectory. Caribbean agriculture was integral to the development of industrial capitalism, a fact acknowledged in food regime analysis. But, it omits to point out that Caribbean agriculture was stagnated after its contribution in that regard. Sixth, Caribbean food supplies came from abroad, although the region's agriculture was a mainstay in the development of industrial capitalism.

Seventh, the neoliberal corporate food regime is associated with de-agrarianization and the disappearance of the peasantry as a unit of analysis (Akram-Lodhi, 2018; Kay, 2018). But, the CARICOM countries never developed a peasantry in the classical sense of the term, they engaged simultaneously in wage-labor and crop cultivation. Finally, food regime analysis does not properly account for China's role in present-day world agriculture. China is merely incorporated as a part of the neoliberal corporate food regime, engaging in animal protein chains, etc. However, the agricultural system in China is based on a state-driven model, while the neoliberal corporate food regime is based on a free trade model.

The new political economy of agriculture and biofuels

The recalibration of Caribbean agricultural policy has to take cognizance of the new political economy of agriculture and biofuels (Veltmeyer and Petras, 2019). This concerns a variety of features involving a skewed imperial innovation system. First, is the concentration and centralization of agrobusinesses engaged in food and farming led by the Big Six – Monsanto, Dow, BASF, Bayer, Syngenta, and DuPont whose principal areas of investments are pesticides, seeds, and biotechnology (Veltmeyer and Petras, 2019). Second is the replacement of competition with collusion as these corporations establish elaborate licensing, cross-licensing, and subcontracting. Third is the promotion of vertical integration upward along the food chain with the establishment of food chain clusters that combine agricultural inputs with processing and marketing facilities. Fourth is their unprecedented power over agricultural research, the fruits of technological advances in agriculture, and trade agreements and agricultural policies. They position their technology as science-based solution to increase crop yields, extend the value chain of corporate capital and control over land and agricultural reduction, and avoid democratic and regulatory controls over their activities. They undercut counterhegemonic, anti-imperialist struggles for food sovereignty and agro-ecological advances by forces of resistance in agriculture, and subvert competitive markets (Veltmeyer and Petras, 2019).

Silicon Valley is a visible representation of concentration and centralization of human capital – scientific knowledge applied to production in an imperial innovation system and appropriation of production-based technologies and patents (Veltmeyer and Petras, 2019). This monopoly capital dynamic in the new political economy of agriculture is evident through mergers and acquisitions, international trade in grains, and on the expansion and advance of resource-seeking, or extractive capital such as the formation and expansion of the soy economy in Latin America (Veltmeyer and Petras, 2019).

The political economy of biofuels capitalism involves the conversion of farmland and agriculture for food production into production of biofuels. This is triggered by the use of corn not as food, but in the production of ethanol in Brazil, and the conversion of farmland to grow soy, canola, sunflower, and palm oil as a biofuel form of energy – biodiesel. According to the National Biodiesel Board (NBB), one bushel of soybeans can yield 1.5 gallons of biodiesel. Based on a yield of 44 bushels per acre, an acre of soybeans could yield 66 gallons of biodiesel, compared to 69 gallons for a 1,300-lb per acre canola yield, 84 gallons for sunflower and over 600 gallons for palm oil (Hill, Kurki, and Morris, 2006). Biofuels production and related financial speculation are factors behind the land-grab in Latin America for soy production based on transgenic seeds as a key sector of the global food regime (Veltmeyer and Petras, 2019). Biofuels production is a major driving forced in capitalist development in South America, resulting in land-grab, foreign ownership of land, concentration of capital in the agricultural sector, and attendant issues including privatization and commodification of land, rationalization of land use as a form of capital, proletarianization of peasant farmers and their produce, forced displacement of the rural poor, and the emergence of new forces of resistance (Veltmeyer and Petras, 2019).

The CBI and the CARIFORUM-EU EPA

The CBI and the CARIFORUM–EU EPA both have a bearing on Caribbean agriculture, reflecting two dimensions of the neoliberal free-trade economic agenda that are singled out for critical analysis because of their dominating and detrimental effects on the sector.

The Caribbean Basin initiative

The CBI constrains member-states within the US neoliberal economic framework, promoting the duty-free access of Caribbean agricultural produce to US markets. The commodities include fresh and frozen seafood, tropical fruit products, winter vegetables, and ethnic and specialty foods, such as sauces, spices, liqueurs, jams, and confectionery items. The CBI divides beneficiary countries into two groups and makes a separate special arrangements for Haiti (US Trade Representative, 2017). This preferential trade agreement between the US and Caribbean Basin states is subject to the activities and regulations of a complex of US institutions and laws that relate agriculture.

Caribbean agricultural exports to the US can be duty free only if they conform to stringent US laws and regulatory bodies. The regulatory environment includes the US Department of Agriculture, the Office of International Cooperation and Development (OICD), the US Trade and Investment Program (TIP), the Agribusiness Promotion Council (APC), the Agricultural Marketing Service (AMS), the Animal and Plant Health Inspection Service (APHIS), the Food Safety and Inspection Service (FSIS), the US Forest Service, the Agricultural Marketing Agreement Act of 1937, the Environmental Protection Agency (EPA), and the Food and Drug Administration (FDA) (US Department of Commerce, 2000).

US regulations mean that Caribbean agriculture has to be on the same standard as US agriculture. There are obvious problems here seeing that Caribbean farmers do not have the resources to comply with US standards. To do so they must seek foreign most likely US finance, and hand over the control of their businesses to foreign interests. It is good to bring Caribbean agriculture up to US standards but the region cannot afford to do under the neoliberal arrangements. This is a major limitation of trade agreements such as the CBI and economic partnership agreement. The developed country imposes their standards on the poor countries and offer to provide them with financial support to achieve those standards. The result is economic dependence on the foreign financiers and external political control of those states.

The CARIFORUM–EU EPA

The CARIFORUM states inserted into the CARIFORUM–EU EPA a full chapter (Chapter 5) on agriculture and fisheries (CPDC, 2016). The main objectives of the agricultural and fisheries provisions in the EPA are to increase competitiveness in agricultural and fisheries production, processing and trade, and in the traditional and non-traditional sectors. This is consistent with the sustainable management of natural resources, to be achieved by recognizing the economic and social significance of the fisheries sub-sector, as well as the importance of the utilization of the living marine resources of the CARIFORUM States. The measures appreciate agriculture and fisheries as having the potential to provide benefits including food security, employment, poverty alleviation, foreign exchange earnings, and social stability of fishing communities. The parties to the EPA have accepted that food security and enhancing livelihoods of rural and fishing communities are critical elements in poverty eradication and sustainable development. The objectives of the EPA involve the pursuance of measures to increase livelihood and food security to alleviate poverty.

The agricultural and fisheries provisions in the EPA are supposed to benefit the CARIFORUM states in four areas. The first has to do with traditional commodities – bananas, sugar, rice, and rum. These commodities originating in CARIFORUM receive preferential access to the EU for an extended period, including duty and quota free market access in the EU, the elimination of customs duty on sugar and rice, and the granting of duty and quota free entry for rum into the EU market. The EU can impose duties on certain commodities only in excess of their quotas. The CARIFORUM states exclude rum, vodka, whiskies, cordials, liqueurs, and wines, from its list of products eligible for liberalization. A Second set of benefits aims to protect rural livelihoods and food security by excluding from liberalization certain products produced by small farmers. The third set of benefits involved the development of new product lines including agro-processing for export to the EU.

A fourth set of perceived benefits has to do with the role of the EPA in fostering sustainable agricultural development through regional integration. The CARIFORUM states are spared the higher Most Favored Nation (MFN) tariffs the EU places on valued-added products relative to those imposed on basic agricultural commodities. CARIFORUM products do not qualify for duty free entry into the EU under the Everything But Arms (EBA) and Generlalized Scheme of Preferences (GSP) regimes, so MFN tariffs would have been applied to them. Fifth, the EPA is perceived to benefit the CARIFORUM states because it eliminates agricultural export subsidies on EU exports to CARIFORUM countries. In accordance with Annex I of the World Trade Organization (WTO) Agreement on Agriculture any product on which the CARIFORUM states eliminate customs duties, the EC will phase out all existing subsidies granted upon the exportation of that product to the territory of the CARIFORUM states based on modalities determined by the CARIFORUM–EC Trade and Development Committee.

Despite the presumed benefits the EPA brings CARIFORUM states, the region remains food import dependent and its agricultural sector is in the doldrums. New product lines have not been sufficiently developed, regional integration has not fostered sustainable agricultural development, and the protection of rural livelihoods and food security have not been fully achieved. The main objectives of the agricultural and fisheries provisions in the EPA have proven to be quite elusive. Caribbean agriculture needs state support until the sector becomes competitive. The EPA restricts the developmental role of the state in Caribbean agriculture. Meanwhile, the EU as a supra-national state institution plays a major protective role in European agriculture.

Belt and Road Initiative in agriculture

China's ideas on green development and agricultural production, trade and investment information sharing, and technologies in the BRI are outlined in the *"Vision and Action for Building 'One Belt One Road' in Agricultural Cooperation."* The PRC (2017) agricultural measures provide the CARICOM states a window of opportunity to concretely reverse the age old problems of Caribbean agriculture. The BRI brings something different to the table in agriculture to what the Caribbean has been accustomed in its dealings with Europe and the US historically, and manifested currently through the CBI and EPA. The principles, framework, priorities, mechanisms, actions, and future projections of the BRI indicate that the differences are substantial. The CARICOM's experiences with Europe and the US have been mercantilist, colonialist, imperialist, and capitalist now in its neoliberal form. On that basis alone the BRI on agriculture would be something brand new in the Caribbean because China has never been an imperial power in the region. The BRI allows Caribbean states and private institutions to participate in jointly shaping a global vision on agriculture. The BRI does not pretend to have the solution to the agricultural problems of the globe. It is based on the premise that with joint cooperation the agricultural problems can be identified and effectively tackled collectively by participating states.

The BRI's principles are to encourage policy coordination that fosters vision matching and policy dialogue by participating countries that are willing to converge their interests and foster the maximum common good (PRC, 2017). Governments have a special role to provide services that promote mechanisms for state-to-state cooperation to guide and work for agricultural collaboration (PRC, 2017). The principle on green and sharing allows countries to choose their own mode and path of agricultural development. While the principle on mutual benefit means that participating states will have their interests and concerns accommodated, as the advantages in agriculture of all countries are synergized, and potential for cooperation tapped.

The BRI's priorities in agriculture are to create a tripartite policy dialogue platform, promote agricultural science, technology, trade, investment, capability building, and non-governmental exchanges. This is quite different to the EPA's priority which is to promote competitiveness. The BRI promotes planned collective activity while the EPA promotes individual competitiveness. The proposed tripartite policy dialogue platform encourages the exchange of views on development by governments, institutes, and enterprises. It supports these stakeholders to work out plans and measures in further cooperation and address their problems through consultation. The tripartite policy dialogue platform is designed to provide policy support for pragmatic cooperation and implementation of BRI projects (PRC, 2017). The BRI's position on agricultural science and technology prioritizes cooperation in science and technology, while strengthening knowledge sharing, technology transfer, information communication, and personnel exchanges through multiple channels (PRC, 2017).

The building of trade routes and infrastructure jointly by participating states to integrate logistics in transportation and storage is a cornerstone idea on agricultural trade in the BRI. Also, participating countries will build on existing domestic and international mechanisms to smoothly implement their planned collaborative activities. It aims to open-up agricultural corporation and domestic cooperative experiment zones for agriculture, with respect to finance, taxation, insurance, and the inspection and quarantine of animals and plants, to bolster exchange in personnel and information, share agricultural technologies, experience, development modalities, and jointly plan and implement seven key projects (PRC, 2017). These projects are "enhancing comprehensive grain productivity," "science and technology cooperation and demonstration, joint prevention and control of animal and plant diseases and outbreaks, agricultural vertical integration, strengthening trade infrastructure, building the platform for agricultural R&D and training, and developing IT application network(s) for agriculture" (PRC, 2017).

Caribbean agricultural policy in the NMWO

The BRI, unlike the CBI and EPA, does not have any political or economic conditionalities attached to it. The BRI is based on mutual cooperation, rather than on China imposing its will on other states such as the cases with the US and the EU. The Caribbean negotiators of the EPA had to conduct their negotiations within the framework of the European version of neoliberal economics. The CBI is a US-styled free-trade imposition in the Caribbean that boxes in the region's agriculture with US interests. The CBI and EPA are therefore inherently biased toward US and EU political and economic conditionalities. The evidence is conclusive that the CBI is concerned with protecting US private and public interests than fostering agricultural development in the Caribbean Basin. Caribbean agricultural development must take place within the confines of US foreign and domestic policy. Benefits will only accrue to the Caribbean states if they satisfy US government regulations, and promote and protect the private sector and consumers in the US. The BRI however is founded on a different philosophy. It does not explicitly tie benefits to satisfying Chinese government regulations. Benefits are mutual and do not flow only in one direction. The BRI contains a more genuinely agricultural development program that also involves trade, compared with the CBI which is to promote development through the free-market.

The CBI and the BRI are similar in that they were both created by a foreign power in which the Caribbean participates. The EPA was negotiated by the Caribbean within a framework created by the EU that tied the hands of the negotiators to the EU's notion of "global Europe." The BRI allows the Caribbean to frame for itself the way it will engage with the BRI agricultural program. The CBI was created by the US and handed down to the Caribbean. The Caribbean shapes its role in the BRI while the US shapes the role of the Caribbean in the CBI. This is because the CBI has conditionalities based on the US ideology of free trade and democracy, while the BRI does not have such conditionalities.

The BRI has undoubtedly thrown a big spanner in theoretical works that analyze agriculture in the era of US and EU neoliberal economics. Chief among these is food regime analysis discussed above. Food regime analysis has a kind of Weberian anchor in that it regards great powers and corporations as the dominating forces in world historical agricultural systems. Political power in food regime analysis is really understood in a Weberian sense, in which strong states dominate weak ones. In that type of analysis, strong nations or powers do not allow their neighbors to get as strong as themselves.

An examination of the agricultural provisos in the BRI reveals that China is projecting a different view on how power is understood and used in world agriculture. China embraces the trend toward a multi-polar world (PRC, 2017), which in essence means that there has to be power-sharing in a community of states, rather than one power dominating all states. The Chinese authorities claim that their intention is to have the BRI stimulate rather than dominate world agricultural development. They do not seek to restrict the agricultural development of any country in the interest of an agro-corporations-led corporate food regime.

In formulating its agricultural strategy with the BRI the CARICOM has to focus on sustainable agriculture, with the aim to reduce imports of processed foods by producing its own substitutes. It must improve through mechanization the production of livestock, dairy products, fruits, and vegetables, conscious of the fact that mechanization and economic growth will reduce the amount of labor available for agriculture. The problem then is for the policymakers to determine how to mechanize and deciding on the types of technology to introduce in the agricultural sector. This must all be tied in with the idea of the increasing role of the state rather than a blind dependence on market forces envision in the capitalist development process.

Caribbean policymakers must first have a clear understanding of the agricultural needs of the region and the dynamics of the multipolar world order and its agricultural characteristics. This would entail comprehensive reviews of the CBI, EPA, and BRI in their agricultural dimensions to identify the ways in which they are similar or dissimilar to help policymakers determine the aspects of those programs that can coalesce in a grand program for Caribbean agricultural development in the twenty-first century. The review must bring understanding on Caribbean agricultural relations outside of the established programs created by the US and EU. Intra-regional trade in agriculture among and within the Islands and Latin America, as well as extra-regional agricultural trade with Africa and Asia must be understood with the same policy goal in mind. Caribbean agricultural exports must be refocused to embrace other regions including Europe and the US.

A second task is to identify the problems of Caribbean agriculture and to prioritize or develop some sequence in which they can be tackled as determined by the new conditions of agriculture in the new multipolar world order. These problems are well documented, but the concern here is that as hitherto identified they could have different levels of impact and understood differently in the new multipolar world order. The third task is to implement the planned program for Caribbean agricultural development that result from this review. This would entail the creation of the right institutional structures, and the reform of existing ones, to match the conditions of the current multipolar world order. There are two principal factors that constrain the Caribbean in its approach to the China and the BRI. The first is the US stance of the BRI, which regards it as a Chinese ploy to take over the world. This places pressure on Caribbean countries because of their close geographic proximity to the US. Second, some Caribbean countries recognize Taiwan as China and may not find favor with the BRI.

Conclusion

The struggle to make agriculture serve the economic development interest of the Caribbean has been quite arduous and generally unsuccessful. The problems of agriculture have remained basically the same from colonial times to present. Embracing the BRI is not the panacea for Caribbean agricultural problems, it has to be done in conjunction with domestic and regional institutions such as CFNI and NARI, CARDI, and existing agricultural trade arrangements with the EU and US. The new policy has to be a synergy of the BRI, EPA, and CBI. The focus must be on agricultural self-sufficiency to allow agriculture to shine in terms of feeding the domestic population to reduce food imports; promoting agricultural exports; improving the welfare of small farmers and the rural population; and promote economic development by freeing labor for non-agricultural production. This means policymakers have to understand off-farm migration, and how mechanization lowers price and free labor to be employed in non-agricultural production.

References

Akram-Lodhi, A.H. (2018). "The Global Food Regime," pp. 301–313 in Veltmeyer, H. and P. Bowles (eds.) *The Essential Guide to Critical Development Studies*. London and New York: Routledge.

Benn, D. (2005). "Economic Development and Poverty in the Caribbean: Theoretical Perspectives and Political Challenges," *Cajanus* 38 (2): 60–65 (in Policy Dialogue on Poverty Alleviation and Food Security Strategies in the Caribbean).

Canterbury, D. (2007). "Caribbean Agriculture Under Three Regimes: Colonialism, Nationalism, and Neoliberalism in Guyana," *Journal of Peasant Studies* 34 (1): 1–28.

Caribbean Food and Nutrition Institute (CFNI) (2005). "Policy Dialogue on Poverty Alleviation and Food Security Strategies in the Caribbean," *Cajanus* 38 (2).

Caribbean Policy Development Centre (CPDC) (2016). Understanding the CARIFORUM-EU EPA and Caribbean Agriculture, Final 30 August.

Chenery, H.B. (1955). "The Role of Industrialization in Development Programs," *American Economic Review* 45: 40–58.
Clark, C. (1951). *The Conditions of Economic Progress.* London: Macmillan.
Dorodnykh, E. (2017). *Economic and Social Impacts of Food Self-Reliance in the Caribbean.* London and New York: Palgrave/Macmillan, DOI: 10.1007/978-3-319-50188-8.
FAO (2015). *State of Food Insecurity in the CARICOM Caribbean, Meeting the 2015 Hunger Targets: Taking Stock of Uneven Progress.* Bridgeton Barbados: FAO.
Fei, J.C. and G. Ranis (1961). "A Theory of Economic Development." *American Economic Review* 51 (4): 533–565.
Ford, D. (2005). "Towards a New Food Policy Strategy for the Caribbean: Linking Food Security, Health and Surveillance," *Cajanus* 38 (2): 108–110 (in Policy Dialogue on Poverty Alleviation and Food Security Strategies in the Caribbean).
Friedmann, H. (1987). "The Family Farm and the International Food Regimes," pp. 247–258 in Shanin, T. (ed.) *Peasants and Peasant Societies.* Oxford: Basil Blackwell.
Friedmann, H. and P. McMichael (1989). "Agriculture and the State System: the Rise and Decline of National Agricultures, 1870 to the Present," *Sociologica Ruralis* 29 (2): 93–117.
Hill, A., A. Kurki, and M. Morris. (2006). Biodiesel: The Sustainability Dimensions. Butte, MT: Appropriate Technology Transfer for Rural Areas (ATTRA) Publication, National Center for Appropriate Technology.
Johnston, B.F. and J. Mellor (1961). "The Role of Agriculture in Economic Development," *American Economic Review* 51 (4): 566–593.
Jorgenson, D.G. (1961). "The Development of a Dual Economy," *"Economic Journal* 71: 309–334.
Kay, C. (2018). "Contemporary Dynamics of Agrarian Change," pp. 291–300 in Veltmeyer, H. and P. Bowles (eds.) *The Essential Guide to Critical Development Studies.* London and New York: Routledge.
Lewis, W.A. (1950). "Industrialization of the British West Indies," *Caribbean Economic Review* 2 (1): 1–61.
Lewis, W.A. (1954). "Economic Development with Unlimited Supplies of Labor," *The Manchester School* 22 (2): 139–191.
Lewis, W.A. (1955). *The Theory of Economic Growth.* London: Unwin University Books.
Marx, K. (2011). *Capital Volume I A Critique of Political Economy.* New York: Dover Publications.
McMichael, P. (2013). *Food Regimes and Agrarian Questions.* Halifax, NS: Fernwood.
Mellor, J. (1976). *The New Economics of Growth: A Strategy for India and the Developing World.* Ithaca, New York: Cornell University Press.
Moyne Commission (1945). West Indian Royal Commission Report, HMSO, Cmd 660.
People's Republic of China (PRC) (2017). "Vision and Action on Jointly Promoting Agricultural Cooperation on the Belt and Road," Beijing, May.
Rodney, W.A. (1970). *A History of the Upper Guinea Coast, 1545–1800.* New York: Monthly Review.
The White House (2020). Statements and Releases, Bill Announcement, 10 October.
Thomas, C.Y. (1968). *Dependence and Transformation: The Economics of the Transition to Socialism.* New York: Monthly Review Press.

Thomas, C.Y. (1984). *Plantations, Peasants, and State: A Study of the Mode of Sugar Production in Guyana*. California: Center for Afro-American Studies, University of California.

Thomas, C.Y. (1988). *The Poor and the Powerless: Economic Policy and Change in the Caribbean*. New York: Monthly Review Press.

Thomas, C.Y. (1993). "Agriculture in the Commonwealth Caribbean: A General Survey," pp. 215–226 in Lalta, S. and M. Freckleton (eds.) *Caribbean Economic Development: The First Generation*. Kingston, Jamaica: Ian Randal Publishers.

United Nations (1947). *Report of the Sub-Commission on Economic Development of the United Nations Economic and Employment Commission (ECM 147)*. New York.

US Department of Commerce. (2000). *International Trade Administration, Guide to the Caribbean Basin Initiative*. Washington DC, November.

US Trade Representative (2017). *Twelfth Report to Congress on the Operation of the Caribbean Basin Recovery Act*, 29 December.

Veltmeyer, H. and P. Bowles (2018). *The Essential Guide to Critical Development Studies*. New York and London: Routledge.

Veltmeyer, H. and J. Petras (2019). *Latin America in the Vortex of Social Change: Development and Resistance Dynamics*. Oxford and New York: Routledge.

Williams, E. (1994). *Capitalism and Slavery*. Chapel Hill NC: The University of North Carolina Press.

Williams, T.O. and R. Smith. (2008). "Rethinking Agricultural Development: The Caribbean Challenge," paper presented at the *40th Annual Monetary Studies Conference*, Basseterre, St Kitts, 11–14 November.

10 PetroCaribe and the CARICOM–China development alternative

Introduction

The growing Caribbean literature on China–CARICOM relations focuses on their economic implications, and consequences for the CARICOM's interactions with the EU and the OACP (Bernal, 2016, 2012, 2010; Montoute, 2013, 2011). The literature covers the increasing volume and types of Chinese investments in the CARICOM and the competition between China and Taiwan to gain the support of the CARICOM states in international forums. This chapter purposely analyses CARICOM–China relations in a different light by locating them within the framework of the new multipolar world order while drawing attention to US-led efforts to demolish PetroCaribe and to the possibility of the US doing the same thing to China–Caribbean alternative development projects (Canterbury, 2015). The proposition is that an energy self-sufficient US must find markets for its energy products, and the Caribbean is an ideal client which must be weaned-off of PetroCaribe. The US attacks on the BRI is to deter the CARICOM states and other developing countries from engaging with state-led development alternatives with China. The argument is that unless the appropriate safeguards are put in place CARICOM–China development projects could suffer the same fate as PetroCaribe.

The PetroCaribe energy development alternative is outlined followed by attempts by the US to dismantle it by sponsoring alternative US–Caribbean energy arrangements, and destabilizing Venezuela. The following section analyzes China's current economic role in the Caribbean with a focus on projects it finances, and the CARICOM states in the BRI.

The PetroCaribe energy development alternative

PetroCaribe is an Energy Cooperation Agreement signed between the Bolivarian Republic of Venezuela and Governments of the Caribbean (BRVGC) in 2005. It is a state-led development alternative in which Venezuela supplies oil to member-countries at discount prices. It engages member-countries in infrastructure projects such as construction of power generation plants,

DOI: 10.4324/9781003092414-10

fuel distribution, and Liquefied Petroleum Gas (LPG) filling, natural liquefied gas regasification, and petrochemical plants. It fosters social projects in the areas of the environment, tourism, education, health, roads, housing, agriculture, culture, and sports (BRVGC, 2005). The current PetroCaribe countries are Antigua and Barbuda, Belize, Cuba, Dominica, Grenada, Guatemala, Guyana, Haiti, Honduras, Jamaica, Nicaragua, Dominican Republic, Saint Kits and Nevis, Saint Vincent and the Grenadines, Suriname, the Bahamas, Saint Lucia, and Venezuela. In 2010, PetroCaribe supplied approximately 45 percent of the energy needs of member-countries.

PetroCaribe was created out of concern about global economic trends and in particular the policies and practices prevailing in industrialized countries that could lead to more exclusion of the Third World smaller countries with economies that are more dependent on international developments (BRVGC, 2005). The initiative is premised on fair trade, complementariness, solidarity, social justice, and common will to develop. It was hailed as the only true alternative that developing countries have to get secure and reliable access to energy sources (BRVGC, 2005). PetroCaribe is regarded as a shield against misery and is premised on the principles of unity, solidarity, cooperation, complementarity, energy security, socio-economic development, sovereignty use of energy resources, environmental awareness, and looks toward the South (BRVGC, 2005).

The institutional structure of PetroCaribe comprises the Ministerial Council made up of Ministers of Energy or their equivalent of member-countries. The primary functions of the Ministerial Council include the coordinating of corresponding policies, strategies, and plans, set priorities of the organization, accountability, and overseas membership. PetroCaribe aims to reduce the great gaps of exclusion, social and economic inequality of peoples, with traditional patterns of cooperation to understand and address poverty as a structural and multidimensional phenomenon (BRVGC, 2005).

The Bolivarian Alternative for Latin America and the Caribbean (ALBA) – Caribbean Fund was established to help finance PetroCaribe projects. The financing mechanisms and compensations of PetroCaribe are based on bilateral payments and long-term financing. The grace period established for this financing is two years, and short-term payment 90 days. Deferred payment is 17 years, including the two-year grace period, as long oil price remains under 40 dollars per barrel. If price exceeds 40 dollars per barrel the payment period is extended to 25 years including the two-year grace period, reducing the interest to 1 percent. If the price of oil is greater than or equal to $100 per barrel 50 percent of the oil supplied by PetroCaribe would be financed over 25 years at 1 percent interest, and the buyer must pay the other 50 percent within 90 days. Venezuela could accept part of deferred payment in goods and services, for which it would offer preferential prices. The products included sugar, banana, or other goods or services which are affected by the trade policies of rich countries (BRVGC, 2005).

The US and PetroCaribe

The US attempt to dismantle PetroCaribe is analyzed under two separate headings – the US–Caribbean Energy Summit, and US destabilization of Venezuela.

The US–Caribbean energy summit

According to Goldwyn and Gill (2014), the US should use the Energy and Climate Partnership of the Americas (ECPA) Summit (the Caribbean Energy Security Summit) "to kick start a Caribbean energy transition" from dependence on PetroCaribe, and to "coordinate with the IFIs to promote policy reform." Goldwyn and Gill (2014) recommended six actions the US must take in its fight against PetroCaribe. First the US must "treat the Caribbean's energy uncertainties as both a priority and an opportunity" and take appropriate actions in this connection. Second, the US should "declare exports of LNG and crude oil to be in the US national interest." Third, the US should "take a serious look at a natural gas strategy for the Caribbean," and fourth "target the 2015 ECPA Summit to kick start a Caribbean energy transition." Fifth, the US should "plan for a potential cutoff of PetroCaribe financing," and sixth "coordinate with the IFIs to promote policy reform" in the region (Goldwyn and Gill, 2014).

The then US Vice President Joe Biden hosted the Caribbean Energy Security Summit in Washington, DC. It was attended by the governments of "Antigua and Barbuda, Aruba, Bahamas, Barbados, Belize, Canada, Colombia, Curacao, Dominica, Dominican Republic, France, Germany, Grenada, Guyana, Haiti, Jamaica, Mexico, New Zealand, Spain, St. Kitts and Nevis, St. Lucia, St. Vincent and the Grenadines, Suriname, Trinidad and Tobago, United Kingdom, United States, together with the Caribbean Community (CARICOM) Secretariat, Caribbean Development Bank, European Union, Inter-American Development Bank (IDB) Group, International Renewable Energy Agency, Organization of American States, and the World Bank Group" (The White House, 2015). The Joint Statement issued at the end of the summit was clear that the US heeded the advice of Goldwyn and Gill (2014).

The measures to transform the Caribbean's energy systems were situated within the framework of existing national and regional energy plans, in particular, the CARICOM Energy Policy (CARICOM, 2013) adopted by the CARICOM in March of 2013, and the Caribbean Sustainable Energy Roadmap and Strategy (C-SERMS) (Auth et al., 2013). The CARICOM Energy Policy focuses on security of energy supplies, energy pricing policy, the impact on relative competitiveness in the CARICOM Single Market and Economy (CSME), and purchasing and transportation arrangements. Its other concerns are natural gas, renewable energy, investment requirements and coordinated investments in the Regional Energy Sector, energy efficiency, environmental impact, and rationalization of the Regional Energy Sector (CARICOM, 2013). The C-SERMS was created "to facilitate the process of translating intentions" of the CARICOM Energy Policy into action. The C-SERMS is "designed to build on existing regional efforts and to provide CARICOM member states with a coherent strategy for transitioning to sustainable energy" (Auth et al., 2013).

The Caribbean Energy Security Summit expressed its commitment to support the transformation of the energy systems of Caribbean states, to share lessons learned through new and expanded regional information networks, and to report progress in relevant forums. In accordance with national laws, the plan identified six steps toward transforming the energy systems of Caribbean states. First is the pursuit of "comprehensive, planning-based and research-driven approaches to energy transition." Second, the Caribbean must undertake the "necessary and specific reforms, including the recommendations from the 2013 CARICOM Energy Policy." This is essential "to support policy and regulatory environments that facilitate the introduction of new technologies favoring sustainable and clean energy that provide legal certainty for investors and improved predictability in price and supply for users" (The White House, 2015).

A third element necessary for Caribbean energy transformation is the "alignment of national legal and regulatory approaches to facilitate greater clean energy investment throughout the region, provided that countries can access finance and other resources on affordable terms, to set the stage for future electrical interconnection in keeping with the goals of Connect 2022" (The White House, 2015). Connect 2022 is a hemispheric initiative proposed at the Summit of the American in 2012 and launched by Columbia and the US to Connect the Americas by 2022 to ensure "citizens, businesses, schools, and hospitals have the electricity they need at a price they can afford." It "establishes a decade-long goal to achieve universal access to electricity through enhanced electrical interconnections, power sector investment, renewable energy development, and cooperation" (US State Department, 2015).

The fourth factor identified for Caribbean energy transformation is the promotion and affordable development of "no- or lower carbon electricity generation through wind, solar, geothermal power, hydropower, bioenergy, ocean energy, energy recovery from waste, and other clean energies," and "energy efficiency measures," while recognizing "that alternative fuels, such as natural gas, can play a useful bridging role." The fifth factor identified in the Joint Statement is "open, transparent, competitive and criteria-based processes, including liberalization where cost effective, to procure energy investment and facilitate access to finance for cleaner and climate resilient energy projects and infrastructure." Finally, "data and energy information exchange and coordination with, between, and among countries and stakeholders" is advocated "to minimize duplication and enable the monitoring and evaluation of energy projects to maximize the impacts of efforts toward

PetroCaribe and the CARICOM–China development 155

fully integrated, low carbon and climate-resilient energy transition plans" (The White House, 2015).

The outcome of the US–Caribbean Energy Summit has engendered reactions both in favor and in opposition to it. First, according to Sanders (2015), the prediction of the death of PetroCaribe and "the ascendency of the US as the dominant player" in the Caribbean's geopolitics" may be premature. In Sanders' (2015), view the Energy Summit "did not result in a great deal of enthusiasm," and "the atmosphere generated by the meeting was one of disappointment on the Caribbean side." Sanders (2015) observed "the greatest disappointment was that the US government offered no official financial resources to help Caribbean countries to develop renewable energy sources or to transform their energy-generating systems to use natural gas." Instead, "Vice President Biden, in obvious references to Venezuela and PetroCaribe remarked about 'governments dependent on a single, increasingly unreliable, external supplier' and 'no country should be able to use natural resources as a tool of coercion against any other country'" (Sanders, 2015: 1). Undoubtedly, the US' position is that the Caribbean must exit PetroCaribe, realign with the US, and purchase energy in the free market to guarantee the region's energy self-sufficiency and security.

Second, notions of "legal certainty for investors" and "improved predictability in price" are conditionalities deemed essential for Caribbean energy transformation. But, such conditionalities are alien to the PetroCaribe and China models, whose effectiveness are derived from a shared commitment to the economic development of the CARICOM countries and not necessarily price movements. PetroCaribe has a built-in mechanism to deal with price fluctuations in oil rather than depending on price predictability as a condition for investment. The China model does not depend on political conditionalities that provide the legal guarantees before Chinese capital is invested in the Caribbean. China claims that now it can afford to, it wants to support the economic development of its fellow Third World states purely on the basis that those countries, supported China when China was at a time of need.

Third, the call for "liberalization where cost effective" is an indication that Caribbean energy transformation is hinged on marketization measures. Whereas, it was the failure of these very liberalization measures that stimulated alternative development approaches such as PetroCaribe. However, rather than providing concrete proposals to address the liberalization vulnerabilities of the CARICOM states, the US–Caribbean Energy Summit merely reinforces the failed neoliberal policies by advocating that liberalization is essential to transition in the Caribbean energy sector. Further evidence of liberalization in the Caribbean's energy sector is gleaned from the proposals to attract investment.

According to Familiar (2015), "many donors and investors are supporting" energy reforms in the Caribbean and "this is why a Caribbean Energy Investment Network" was proposed at the Energy Summit, "to develop a new architecture of cooperation for energy security in the region." Familiar (2015) stated the "new network would not only support greater cooperation across islands and between governments, donors, international financing institutions, and investors but would also help identify concrete steps that Caribbean nations and development partners can take to attract investments for sustainable energy initiatives."

US destabilization of Venezuela

The US has many weapons in its arsenal to bring about regime change in the Caribbean including direct military intervention as in Haiti and Grenada. It relies on financing the electoral campaigns through non-governmental organizations such as the National Endowment for Democracy (NED) and the Atlas Network to put in power regimes it favors (Veltmeyer and Petras, 2019). The Guyana elections in 2015 is a case in point where the NED and the International Republican Institution (IRI) funded the political opposition as a means to effect regime change replacing the PPP with the APNU+AFC government. The PPP had won power under the umbrella of neoliberal democratization, pursued Washington Consensus policies, and remained in office for 23 years (Canterbury, 2018). The US tactics to bring about regime change in Venezuela involve an attempt at a military coup which was discovered and scuttled, and an economic war that sank Venezuela into a crisis of unprecedented proportions.

The US with the assistance of Saudi Arabia engineered a collapse in oil prices to undermine the oil-dependent economies of Russia, Iran, and Venezuela. Caught in the squeeze Venezuela became vulnerable to regime change as the economic crisis worsened (Veltmeyer and Petras, 2019). Venezuela was caught in the crosshairs of the US imperialist offensive (Veltmeyer and Petras, 2019). The economic sanctions imposed by the US through legislation and executive action on Iran, Russia, and Venezuela aim to either eliminate (Iran) or restrict (Venezuela) crude oil trade by as much as 3.3 million to 4.0 million barrels per day (Brown, 2020). The sanctions prohibit US transactions with *Petroleos de Venezuela S.A.* (PdVSA), forcing Venezuela to find alternative buyers (Brown, 2020).

The US strategy versus Maduro includes violent street mobs and mobilizing large retailers to provoke artificial shortages. With the aid of international mass media and corporate funded NGOs Maduro is accused of being an "authoritarian" (Veltmeyer and Petras, 2019). President Trump has recognized the head of Venezuela's National Assembly, Juan Guaidó, as the country's interim president, ceased to recognize the Maduro regime (Margesson and Seelke, 2019), and is forcing the Caribbean states to do the same. The social unrest and economic crisis in Venezuela has led to a call for the Caribbean countries to look beyond PetroCaribe and to move back into the US fold. According to Goldwyn and Gill (2014), "the United States has already become the dominant supplier of petroleum products to the Caribbean region, a consequence of the shale oil boom." In 2012, "US product exports to PetroCaribe states totaled 160,000 bpd." This was "well above Venezuela's 121,000 bpd in combined crude and product exports" (Goldwyn and Gill, 2014).

Although at the time US law prohibited exports of crude oil, US energy exports were said to "provide Caribbean states with a stable source of petroleum products." The US needed to disrupt PetroCaribe in the interest of its "security, climate, and economic interests in the stability and prosperity of the Caribbean" (Goldwyn and Gill, 2014). According to Goldwyn and Gill (2014), there were indications that Venezuela was seeking to mitigate the costs of PetroCaribe by tightening credit terms. Goldwyn and Gill (2014) noted that maturities were reportedly shortened to 15 and 17 years from the previous 25 years, while interest rates had reportedly risen from 1–2 percent to 3–4 percent. Goldwyn and Gill (2014) argued that these emerging trends and the potential that they may persist provided yet another incentive to the US to lead international efforts to begin transitioning PetroCaribe member states away from dependence on the program.

Venezuela's socioeconomic woes have worsened as US sanctions on the country expanded under the Trump Administration. As of June 1, 2020 the Treasury Department imposed sanctions on at least 144 Venezuelan or Venezuelan-connected individuals, Venezuela's state-owned oil company, government and central bank, and the State Department has revoked the visas of hundreds of individuals and their families (Seelke, 2020). The situation in Venezuela has created a regional migration crisis as people flee the country (Margesson and Seelke, 2019).

The dismantling of PetroCaribe by promoting US–Caribbean energy agreements and destabilizing Venezuela is not being accompanied with any financial assistance from the US to replace it. The Trump Administration claims that financial difficulties in the US thwarted the implementation of its Caribbean policies (Sullivan et al., 2020). Yet, the US claims that the Americas – the US, Mexico, and Canada – are the new epicenter of energy and not the Arabian Peninsula (Sanders, 2015). If this is so then why the US does not propose an energy alternative for the Caribbean that is similar or better than PetroCaribe? The answer must be that the US neoliberal capitalist model does not support development alternatives, which are not driven by free-market capitalist principles. The US wants the Caribbean to secure its energy supplies from US companies at market price and not based on any concessionary arrangement. Jessop (2015) indicated that US energy policy "does not seek to throw US money at the region but to suggest that by ensuring the right investment climate and an enabling environment the Caribbean can attract private sector investment to change its energy profile" (Jessop, 2015).

The US efforts to dismantle PetroCaribe is a clear indication that externally fermented social unrest in donor states such as Venezuela and China can disrupt alternative development projects in recipient countries.

The lesson here is that all of the money that Venezuela pumped into the Caribbean through PetroCaribe will not bring real benefits to Venezuela. A possible point of consolation for Venezuela however is that its contribution to economic development in the Caribbean is based on a development alternative that really seeks to help others rather than bring profit for a few. The proximity of the Caribbean to the US and the common history of the region could push countries to close ranks behind the regional hegemon. Undoubtedly, this is a problem that China could face in the future, for which it must plan in anticipation in the event of an economic downturn in that country.

It is believed that the current political instability and economic crisis in Venezuela will prevent the country from continuing to provide its CARICOM neighbors with the generous economic development assistance it does through PetroCaribe. Furthermore, a change in government in Venezuela could lead to new economic policies that would downgrade or altogether abandon PetroCaribe. The fall in oil prices is blamed for the economic crisis in Venezuela as the country earns less oil revenue to finance its state-led economic policies (Sullivan, 2015) of twenty-first-century socialism. Whereas, for many years Washington has been pursuing a strategy of "regime change" in Venezuela fermenting social unrest and economic crisis (Petras, 2013, 2015). The George Bush Administration classified Venezuela as being a part of "an axis of evil" and the democratically elected Venezuelan president the late Hugh Chavez was overthrown but reinstated by the people through mass street demonstrations. The Obama Administration classified Venezuela as a national security threat to the US, and the Trump Administration is taking actions to put an end to the danger.

China in the Caribbean

China has been financing development projects in the Caribbean long before the BRI came on stream in 2013. The Chinese-funded projects were not all part of the BRI although some of them commenced in 2013 and 2014. We present two distinct periods in which China had been active economically in the Caribbean – pre-BRI and under the BRI. The US is hostile to the BRI as well forcing even the heavily indebted Argentina that needs the support to think twice about joining (Dalto, 2020).

China-financed projects

Guyana signed an agreement with the People's Republic China (PRC) in 1971 on the Mutual Establishment of Commercial Offices and established diplomatic relations in 1972. China and Guyana exchanged trade missions in 1971, and Jamaica followed suit in 1972, Trinidad and Tobago in 1974, and Barbados in 1977 (Jhinkoo, 2013). In 1984, the governments of Guyana and China signed five documents on economic cooperation, cultural exchange, the establishment of a joint commission on economic, trade, scientific and technical cooperation, transformation of the textile mill built with Chinese assistance, and the provision of cotton under loans by China. Then in 1997 China established diplomatic relations with the Commonwealth of the Bahamas, and in 1998, China joined the Caribbean Development Bank as a non-regional member. In the 2000s however China–CARICOM relations underwent rapid change for the better.

In 2005, the Bahamas was the recipient of US$1Bn investment from the Hong Kong-based Hutchison–Whampoa to develop the Freeport container port (Ward, 2019). Hutchison-Whampoa, which took-over operational control of the Panama Canal in 1999, owned and operated the container port regarded as the largest in the world. In 2003, a Chinese navy ship visited Jamaica with several Chinese nurses and doctors to perform humanitarian work in the island. The following year the governments of Dominica and China established diplomatic relations. China promised to grant Dominica US$100M to develop infrastructure including the construction of a sports stadium and a new grammar school, and the rehabilitation of the principal road that connects Roseau, the capital city of Dominica, and the Princess Margaret Hospital, the primary medical facility in the island. China deployed military personnel in the Western Hemisphere for the first time in its history by sending a peacekeeping police contingent to Haiti, after an earthquake devastated the island in 2004. Haiti is one of the Caribbean islands that recognize Taiwan as an independent country. The first China–Caribbean Economic and Trade Cooperation Forum was held in February 2005 (Jhinkoo, 2013).

In the second half of decade between 2006 and 2010, China escalated its activities in the CARICOM. China made a concessionary loan of US$100M to Trinidad and Tobago at an interest rate of 2 percent for 20 years with a five-year moratorium, in January 2006. In December of that year, Bosai Minerals Group the Chinese mining company, bought Canadian IAMGOLD's stake in Guyana's Omai Bauxite Mining (OBMI). Bosai owns 70 percent of OBMI and the Guyana government's National Industrial and Commercial Investments Limited (NICIL) the remaining 30 percent. The following year Costa Rica and Grenada severed ties with Taiwan in favor of China, and the second China–Caribbean Economic and Trade Cooperation Forum was held (Jhinkoo, 2013).

Sinopec the Chinese state oil company established in Trinidad a subsidiary called SOOGL Antilles (Trinidad) Limited in 2008. Then SOOGL acquired 45.4 percent interest in the offshore East Brighton Block, a 107 km^2 area off the south west coast of Trinidad in the Gulf of Paria. The Trinidad and Tobago state-owned Petrotrin owns 30 percent, and Primera East Brighton a CL Financial Subsidiary owns the remaining 24.5 percent of the block. But, it is SOOGL that is the designated operator in an area, believed to be rich in hydrocarbons. In the same year China joined the IDB agreeing to contribute $350M to the IDB Group to bolster key programs at a time when the world economy was under duress. Then, in November 2008, China launched its first-ever policy paper on Latin American and the Caribbean region that outlines China's desire to develop a comprehensive and cooperative relationship fostering equality, mutual benefit, and common development with the countries in the region. The areas of cooperation highlighted in the policy paper include trade, investment, finances, agriculture, infrastructure, resources and energy, tourism, customs, quality inspection, culture, and education (Jhinkoo, 2013).

China signed with Jamaica in 2010 a US$500M investment pact for road, housing, and other developmental projects in the island. In the same year, two Chinese companies signed a memorandum of understanding with Suriname for US$6Bn worth of projects which include a deep sea harbor and a railroad to Brazil. The 2011 report by the Economic Commission for Latin America and the Caribbean on foreign direct investment in the region stated that Chinese companies invested about US$15Bn in the area in 2010, making China the third-largest investor with a share of 9 percent. The year 2011 was characterized by activities that deepened China–Caribbean relations.

The Arthur Lok Jack Graduate School of Business in Trinidad and Tobago signed a memorandum of association with China's International Cooperation Centre to deepen educational ties (Jhinkoo 2013). Baha Mar Ltd., a private company contracted the China State Construction Engineering Corporation as the general contractor to construct a US$3.5Bn mega resort in the Bahamas. Michael Hong Architects primarily planned and designed the 2,250 rooms project, which includes a golf course, retail space, a convention center and what the developer says will be the largest casino in the Caribbean (Jhinkoo 2013). The Export-Import Bank of China provided US$2.45Bn toward the project.

The eleventh Guyana–China Joint Commission on Economic Trade and Technical Cooperation was held in 2011, to celebrate its 27th anniversary. The Export–Import Bank of China provided $210M to the National Academy for the Performing Arts (NAPA) in Trinidad and Tobago to undertake remedial infrastructural works, through a financial agreement between the governments of China and Trinidad and Tobago (Jhinkoo, 2013). Also, in the same year, the Chinese company Chaoyang (25 percent) in partnership with Total (30 percent), and BHP (45 percent), announced the start-up of Phase 2 gas development of the Greater Angostura gas field in Trinidad and Tobago with a design capacity of 280 million cubic feet of gas per day (7.9 million cubic meters per day). Also, China granted to Barbados approximately BDS$6.15M for various small-scale development projects. And the contracting and engineering firm China National Complete Plant Import Export Corporation (Complant) acquired assets in Jamaica's sugar industry, as China announced plans to invest approximately US$156M for the renovation of three sugar factories and land in Jamaica (Jhinkoo 2013).

Three other activities rounded off Chinese investment in the Caribbean in 2011. These were a US$7.9M grant to Jamaica, the China Investment Corporation's (CIC) acquisition of a 10 percent stake in the Atlantic LNG plant at Point Fortin, Trinidad and Tobago for EURO 600 million (TT$5.5Bn), and the third China–Caribbean Economic and Trade Cooperation Forum (CCETCF). China announced at the third CCETCF that it would provide a US$1Bn loan to Caribbean countries to support local economic development, and a US$1M donation to the CARICOM Development Fund. Also, China announced that it would support measures to increase Caribbean exports to China, provide help to build seismic and tsunami warning systems in the region, and offer training opportunities for 2,500 persons. Furthermore, China promised training for doctors and nurses, improved measures to increase tourism flow between the regions, the provision of resources to boost agriculture and fisheries, and support for the development of alternative, small-scale energy projects such as solar power (Jhinkoo, 2013).

A new National Stadium, funded and built by China was opened in the Bahamas in 2012. The year 2013 was very active in terms of the projects that China undertook in the region. Funding through China's Co-financing Fund for Latin America and the Caribbean, to support public and private sector projects that promote sustainable economic growth in the region, were approved by the IDB and the People's Bank of China. The proposed $2Bn contribution by China was intended to co-finance a total of up to $500M of IDB public sector loans and up to $1.5Bn for loans made by the Bank to private sector entities (Jhinkoo, 2013).

These were followed by a state visit to Trinidad and Tobago by Chinese President, Xi Jinping (Associated Press, 2013). A memorandum of understanding was signed by Beijing Oriental Yuhong Waterproofing Technology Co Ltd and Lake Asphalt of Trinidad and Tobago to establish a manufacturing plant in La Brea was another major project in 2013 (Associated Press, 2013). Also, China awarded a US$250M loan to build a children's hospital and signed a memorandum of understanding to advance co-operation in energy, mineral, and infrastructure development, among other areas, with the government of Trinidad and Tobago (Associated Press, 2013). President Xi Jinping announced on that occasion that the CARICOM countries, which support the People's Republic of China's One China Policy would benefit from US$3Bn in concessional loans from China (Bernal, 2016).

Two other key events in the same month were the third Annual Avalon Invest Caribbean Now 2013 Forum in New York at which there was a panel on China–Caribbean relations. Chinese officials urged the Caribbean region to take advantage of the fact that China is now the new number one tourism source market in the world. That June as well, the first China–Latin America and Caribbean Agricultural Ministers Forum was held in Beijing (Ministry of Foreign Affairs China, 2016). China pledged US$50M to support cooperation in agricultural projects between Latin America and the

Caribbean (Jhinkoo, 2013). China hosted the Jamaican Prime Minster the Honorable Portia Simpson Miller on an official five-day visit in August 2013. Then in September, the China–Caribbean 2013 trade mission was planned to help Caribbean premiers, ministers of governments, investment agencies, and C-level private sector business leaders, meet with top Chinese officials from varied ministries (Jhinkoo, 2013).

The following year, a China–Latin American Forum was held in Jamaica, organized by the China Foundation for International Studies and the Chinese People's Institute of Foreign Affairs. Thereafter, Dominica and China finalized a pair of agreements covering EC$18M in financial assistance. In addition, 23 trade union leaders from the Caribbean traveled to Beijing to participate in a seminar of China–Caribbean Trade Union Leaders, which was hosted by the All-China Federation of Trade Unions. In 2014, it was reported that Chinese investors were investing more than US$1Bn to develop Antigua and Barbuda's first mega-resort, on the 1,600-acre multi-hotel and residential and commercial project creating 1,000 jobs on the island. The project includes several luxury hotels, hundreds of private homes, a school, hospital, marinas, golf courses, an entertainment district, a horse racing track, and a casino (Business Insider, 2014).

The China–Community of Latin American and Caribbean States (CELAC) Forum was established in 2014. The inaugural ministerial meeting of the China–CELAC Forum was held in Beijing in January 2015. The China–CELAC Forum cooperation plan for 2015–2019 adopted by the ministerial meeting identified trade, investment, and financial cooperation as the key engines driving their relations as well as six major areas of cooperation, namely energy, agriculture, infrastructure, manufacturing, innovation, and information technology (Baiyi, 2015). China promised to quicken the provision of a US$20Bn infrastructural loan, US$10Bn concessional loan, and US$50M agricultural loan. According to Baiyi (2015), in addition to economic cooperation, China also promised to do more to boost political and cultural ties. China promised in five years to offer 6,000 scholarships and 6,000 training opportunities to Latin American and Caribbean countries, invite 1,000 leaders of political parties to visit China, and implement a training program called Bridge for the Future, which is expected to link up 1,000 Chinese and Latin American young leaders (Baiyi, 2015).

The CARICOM states in the BRI

In recent years Antigua and Barbuda, Jamaica, Guyana, Barbados, Trinidad and Tobago, and Suriname have agreed to officially join the BRI. In May 2018, Trinidad and Tobago became the first Caribbean country to sign on to the Belt and Road Initiative. Premier Li Keqiang and Trinidad Prime Minister Keith Rowley sign a Memorandum of Understanding at the Great Hall of the People in Beijing. Trinidad and Tobago is China's largest trade partner in the English Caribbean area along with Jamaica. Suriname and China signed a Memorandum of Understand on enhanced cooperation in the fields of infrastructure construction, agriculture, forestry, fishing, law enforcement, human resources, and public health in July 2018. Suriname has also adopted the Chinese Spring Festival as a national holiday.

The Cooperation Agreement with Guyana was signed by Foreign Minister Carl Greenidge and China's Ambassador to Guyana Cui Jianchun in July 2018. Greenidge described Guyana's infrastructure as grossly inadequate which served as a constraint to investment and the attraction of economic opportunities. The China Harbor Engineering Company (CHEC) is working on a US$150M expansion of the Cheddi Jagan International Airport. Guyana, in 1972, became the first Caribbean country to establish diplomatic relations with China. China is becoming entangled in Guyana's natural resource wealth, with as many as 4 billion barrels of oil found off its coast, making the nation poised to become a serious oil producer (Ward, 2019). The China National Offshore Oil Corporation owns 25 percent of potential oil findings in the country, while the Bosai Mineral Group is expanding magnesium and bauxite operations.

In February 2019, He Lifeng, chairman of the National Development and Reform Commission (NDRC), and Jerome Walcott, Minister of Foreign Affairs and Foreign Trade of Barbados, held talks in Beijing. The two sides exchanged views on jointly building Belt and Road cooperation between China and Barbados. In April 2019, Tian Qi, China's ambassador to Jamaica, and Kamina Johnson-Smith, Minister of Foreign Affairs and Foreign Trade in Jamaica signed a Memorandum of Understanding. Qi hoped that the two countries can focus on development, improve their cooperation level, fulfill the sustainable development goals in the 2030 Agenda, and better promote connections between China and Caribbean countries in policy, infrastructure, trade, finance, and people-to-people exchanges. The CHEC has built roads zigzagging through Jamaica, including a US$730M highway linking Kingston to Ocho Rios, and has earmarked another US$348M for a highway along the underdeveloped southern coast (Ward, 2019). Jiuquan Iron and Steel announced plans in 2019 to invest in Jamaica over US$3Bn in an aluminum refinery and smelter, adding to a US$300M refinery purchased in 2016 (Ward, 2019).

June 2018 Prime Minister of Antigua and Barbuda Gaston Browne signed a Memorandum of Understanding with China, becoming the first country in the Organization of Eastern Caribbean States (OECS) to do so. The agreement signed by ambassador Wang Xianmin and ambassador Brian Stuart-Young, mentions projects such as roads, bridges, civil aviation, ports, energy, and telecommunications to be undertaken in Antigua and Barbuda. In September 2018, Grenada signed on to the BRI. Grenada's Minister for Foreign Affairs, Peter David said the initiative is a strategy of the Chinese Government that focuses on connectivity and cooperation with different regions of the world. The Minister said objectives would be met with a $40Bn fund investment in infrastructure. The Belt and Road

Initiative the Minister said facilitates the movement of goods and capital between developing areas of the world (Caribbean Investment Journal Network, 2019).

The Foreign Ministers and government representatives from the People's Republic of China, Grenada, Antigua, and Barbuda, the Commonwealth of The Bahamas, Barbados, the Commonwealth of Dominica, the Cooperative Republic of Guyana, Jamaica, the Republic of Suriname, and the Republic of Trinidad and Tobago gathered on October 28–29, 2019 in St. George's, Grenada, for the China–Caribbean Conference for Cooperation on the Belt and Road Initiative and issued a joint statement (Joint Statement of the China–Caribbean Conference on BRI Implementation, 2019). Among other things the signatories to the agreement agreed that the BRI embodies the spirit and principles of peace and cooperation, openness and inclusiveness, equality, mutual learning, and benefit, as well as principles of extensive consultation, joint efforts, shared and mutual benefits, the concept of open, green, and clean cooperation, and the pursuit of high standard, people-centered and sustainable development which strengthen the connectivity and the expansion of the world economy (Joint Statement of the China–Caribbean Conference on BRI Implementation, 2019). They agreed to remain committed to the aforementioned spirit, principles, and concepts to expand and strengthen cooperation inter alia in development policy coordination, infrastructure connectivity, trade, investment finance, and closer people-to-people bond, so as to strengthen global partnership, and for Caribbean countries to strengthen their development policy coordination (Joint Statement of the China–Caribbean Conference on BRI Implementation, 2019).

China has pledged billions to revamp infrastructure in the capital of Haiti, one of Taiwan's oldest allies. Haitian President Jovenel Moise's regime has signaled that its friendship with Taipei should not be taken for granted: 'Taiwan is a long-time friend … [but] Haiti is looking for where its interests lie'" (Ward, 2019). Meanwhile, Huawei has agreed to partner with the Caribbean mobile phone company Digicel, to expand 4G and 5G coverage to Jamaica, Trinidad and Tobago, Barbados, and Guyana. Huawei Marine has laid over 3,500 km of underwater cables from the Bahamas to Haiti (Ward, 2019).

Conclusion

The Caribbean states must have a vested interest in the development projects China is financing in the region. These projects are bringing much needed development to the region that Europe and the US have engaged for centuries but failed to transform on an equitable basis. The Caribbean now has to turn to Venezuela and China to bring more advanced infrastructure to the region and expand trade, and diversify its economy to reduce dependence on tourism, agriculture, and on the US and European markets. Seemingly, the US feels compelled to thwart the role of Venezuela and China in the economic development of the Caribbean, and to confine the region to exploitation by American capitalism.

The Caribbean states are being warned they will be saddled with Chinese debt if they sign on to the BRI. But, the situation in Jamaica provides a good counter argument to the view that China is creating a debt trap for the Caribbean. Jamaica's debt was 147 percent of its GDP, mostly owed to the IFIs such as the IMF, World Bank, and the IDB. Money owed to Beijing's EXIM Bank accounted only for 3.9 percent of Jamaica's overall debt, even though the country is China's largest partner in the Caribbean (Ward, 2019). The Caribbean would be the biggest losers if the US succeeds with its sinister plans. The loss for China would be the benefits America derives from Chinese investments in the Caribbean.

References

Associated Press (2013). "China President Xi Jinping Makes First Ever Visit to Trinidad," 1 June.

Auth, K., M. Konold, E. Musolino, and A. Ochs. (2013). *Caribbean Sustainable Energy Roadmap (C-SERMS), Phase 1: Summary Recommendations for Policymakers*. Georgetown and Washington: CARICOM and Worldwatch Institute and Inter-American Development Bank.

Baiyi, W. (2015). "Latin America Is the Latest Focus of China's Major-Power Diplomacy," China.org.cn, 23 January.

Bernal, R.L. (2010). "The Dragon in the Caribbean: China–CARICOM Economic Relations," *The Round Table* 99 (408): 281–302.

Bernal, R.L. (2012). "China and Small Island Developing States," *African-East Asian Affairs The China Monitor* (1): 3–30.

Bernal, R.L. (2016). *Chinese Foreign Direct Investment in the Caribbean*. Potential and Prospects, Inter-American Development Bank, November.

Bolivarian Republic of Venezuela and Governments of the Caribbean (BRVGC) (2005). *PetroCaribe Energy Cooperation Agreement*. City of Puerto la Cruz: Bolivarian Republic of Venezuela.

Brown, P. (2020). *Oil Market Effects from US Economic Sanctions*. Iran, Russia, Venezuela, Washington DC: Congressional Research Service, 5 February.

Business Insider (2014). "China is Building a $1 Billion Mega-resort in the Caribbean," 19 August.

Canterbury, D.C. (2020). "China and the Caribbean Community in the 21st Century: Lessons from PetroCaribe," pp. 115–142 in Chinese American Professors' Association in Connecticut, *Proceedings of the First Interdisciplinary Conference: China in the 21st Century*. (7 March 2015, Henry Lee Institute of Forensic Science, University of New Haven, Connecticut). Middletown, DE.

Canterbury, D.C. (2018). *Neoextractivism and Capitalist Development*. London and New York: Routledge.

Caribbean Investment Journal Network (2019). "The Caribbean Engages the Belt and Road Initiative," 1 December.

CARICOM (2013). "CARICOM Energy Policy," Georgetown, Guyana, 1 March.

Dalto, V. (2020). "Argentina Ponders BRI Endorsement Amid Tricky Debt Restructuring," *Diálogo Chino*, London: UK, 12 August.
Familiar, J. (2015). "Unlocking the Caribbean's Energy Potential," *Caribbean360*, 1 February.
Goldwyn, D.L. and C.R. Gill (2014). "Uncertain Energy: The Caribbean's Gamble with Venezuela," *Atlantic Council*, July.
Jessop, D. (2015). "US Energy Policy and the Caribbean," *News Americas*, 5 February.
Jhinkoo, J. (2013). "Highlighting the China–Caribbean Relationship," *Port of Spain: Caribbean Center for Money and Finance Newsletter*, 6 (2).
Joint Statement of the China–Caribbean Conference on BRI Implementation (2019). St. George's, Grenada, 28–29 October.
Margesson, R., and C.R. Seelke. (2019). The Venezuelan Regional Migration Crisis, Washington DC: Congressional Research Service, 15 February.
Ministry of Foreign Affairs China (2016). "Basic Information about China–CELAC Forum, Department of Latin American and Caribbean Affairs Ministry of Foreign Affairs of China," April.
Montoute, A. (2011). "Emerging Players in the Caribbean What Implications for the Caribbean, Their Relations with the EU and the ACP?" European Center for Development Policy Management, June.
Montoute, A. (2013). "Caribbean–China Economic Relations: What Are the Implications?" *Caribbean Journal of International Relations & Diplomacy* 1 (1): 110–126.
Petras, J. (2013). "US–Venezuela Relations: A Case Study of Imperialism and Anti-Imperialism," Venezuelananalysis.com, 23 October.
Petras, J. (2015). "US and Venezuela: Decades of Defeats and Destabilization," *The People's Voice.Org.*, 5 March.
Sanders, R. (2015). "The Unhelpful Geopolitics of Energy in the Caribbean," *Caribbean360*, 1 February.
Seelke, C.R. (2020). *Venezuela: Overview of US Sanctions*. Washington DC: Congressional Research Service, 2 June.
Sullivan, M.P. (2015). *Latin America and the Caribbean: Key Issues for the 114th Congress*. Washington DC: Congressional Research Service, 28 January.
Sullivan, M.P., Beittel, J.S., Meyer, P.J., Seelke, C.R., Taft-Morales, M., and Villarreal, M.A. (2020). *Latin America and the Caribbean: U.S. Policy and Issues in the 116th Congress*. Washington DC: Congressional Research Service, 21 May.
The White House (2015). *Caribbean Energy Security Summit Joint Statement*. Washington DC: Office of the Press Secretary, 26 January.
US State Department (2015). *Connecting the Americas 2011 Initiative*. Washington DC.
Veltmeyer, H. and J. Petras (2019). *Latin America in the Vortex of Social Change: Development and Resistance Dynamics*. Oxford and New York: Routledge.
Ward, J. (2019). "Caribbean Countries Turn to China's Belt and Road," *East Asian Forum*, 23, July.

11 China–US policies and the CARICOM

Introduction

The policies formulated by China and the US for the Caribbean and possible effects of US–China relations on the CARICOM are the primary focus of this chapter. The argument is US security concerns to obtain natural resources are the motivating factors driving America's policy in the Caribbean, whereas China's are more of a developmental nature. The current aggressive policies the US adopts toward China will have a disruptive effect on CARICOM–China relations and negative consequences for development alternatives in the region. After 9/11, the US pivoted toward the Middle East in the "war on terrorism" and US resources to economically support the Caribbean became even scarcer. The Obama Administration welcomed China in the Caribbean as the US underwent the shocks of the 2007/2008 global financial and economic crises. The US maintained nonetheless several complaints about the economic shortcomings in China's state-led embrace of the neoliberal free trade model. The Trump Administration has taken an aggressive stance against China despite the positive economic effects the country has in the US and the Caribbean. The US and China are currently engaged in a trade war that promises to be very disruptive in the new multipolar world order.

The argument is developed by first undertaking a descriptive analysis of China's policy toward the Caribbean. Second, the US' policy toward the region is analyzed with attention paid to both the Obama and Trump Administrations. Third, the analysis shifts to US–China relations and the CARICOM where the focus is on some of China's alleged economic transgressions and President Trump's tariff war. Fourth, the final part focuses on some germane issues for CARICOM–China relations that derive from Chinese and American policies and interactions in the region.

China's policy toward the Caribbean

China's current policy toward the Caribbean is laid out in a policy paper for Latin America and the Caribbean that was announced in November 2016

DOI: 10.4324/9781003092414-11

(PRC, 2016). The policies follow on China's first policy paper on the region issued in 2008 whose goal was to establish a comprehensive and cooperative partnership featuring equality, mutual benefit, and common development of the two sides (PRC, 2016). The relations between China and the region became much stronger with frequent high-level exchanges and political dialogues, developments in trade, investment, finance, and other areas, and closer cultural and people-to-people exchanges with the establishment of a comprehensive and cooperative partnership of equality, mutual benefit, and common development in 2014 (PRC, 2016).

The five salient features of China's policy toward the Caribbean are political sincerity and mutual trust, win–win cooperation in the economic arena, mutual learning in culture, close coordination on international issues, and mutual reinforcement between China's cooperation with Caribbean states and its bilateral relations with individual countries (PRC, 2016). Seemingly, China's relation with the Caribbean has a single political conditionality – the "one China principle" which is an "important political foundation for China to develop its relations with other countries" (PRC, 2016). The cooperation priorities are driven by trade, investment and finance, energy and resources, infrastructure construction, agriculture, manufacturing, scientific and technological innovation, and information technology. The policy intends to stimulate new models for capacity cooperation in terms of logistics, electricity, and information, facilitate interactions among enterprise, society, and government, expands financing channels, and improve and upgrade cooperation between China and the region (PRC, 2016).

China's policies toward the Caribbean are in the political, economic, and social realms. The policies could have a direct political impact by strengthening high-level exchanges of experiences on governance, legislatures, political parties, local governments, and inter-governmental dialogue and consultation mechanisms. The Chinese political model could very well turn out to be a useful replacement of the Westminster model that has failed Caribbean countries such as Guyana. The electorate in Guyana vote in two racial blocs and the race group with the largest number of voters can win national elections indefinitely in the Westminster model. The political impasse in Guyana after the March 2, 2020 national elections cries out for major alteration to the Westminster model in that country.

China's economic policy covers cooperation on scientific and technological innovation, space, maritime, customs and quality inspection, trade and investment promotion institutions and business associations, and economic and technical assistance. The focus on trade involves industrial investment and capacity cooperation, financial institutions, energy and resources, infrastructure, manufacturing, and agriculture. The economic policies promote reciprocity and mutual benefits in the trade of specialty products, goods with competitive advantages or high added-value, and technology-intensive products, and strengthen trade in services and e-commerce (PRC, 2016). In the area of industrial investment and capacity cooperation China proposes to encourage its enterprises to expand and optimize investment in the region on the basis of equality and mutual benefit, and uphold "the principle of business-led and market-oriented cooperation for mutual economic and social benefits" (PRC, 2016). It will "support the efforts of Chinese enterprises to invest and start business," and encourage them to "align high-quality capacity and advantageous equipment of China with the needs" of the region, "in order to help the countries in need to enhance their capacity for independent development" (PRC, 2016).

China proposes to support its financial institutions to strengthen their business exchanges and cooperation with national, regional, and international financial institutions in the region, and to establish branch networks. According to the PRC (2016), China will enhance dialogue cooperation between central banks and financial regulatory authorities, expand cross-border local currency settlement, and promote monetary cooperation, including Renminbi (RMB) clearing arrangements. On the basis of bilateral financial cooperation China proposes to establish relevant financing arrangements with Caribbean states and to support key areas and major projects (PRC, 2016).

The expansion and deepening of cooperation and sustainable development in energy and resources is a major area of policy focus. Upstream businesses will be promoted to explore for and develop energy and natural resources. This is regarded as necessary to consolidate the foundation for cooperation and expand resources potentials, and simultaneously extend support for downstream industries such as smelting, processing, logistics trade, and equipment manufacturing to improve added value of products. China proposes to explore with the Caribbean states "the establishment of mechanisms for long-term supply of energy and resources products and local currency pricing and settlement, to reduce the impact of external economic and financial risks" (PRC, 2016).

There is a strong focus in China's policy toward the Caribbean on developing the region's infrastructure. The achievement of this goal requires the strengthening of "cooperation on technical consultation, construction and engineering, equipment manufacturing and operation management in the fields of transportation, trade logistics, storage facilities, information and communication technology, energy and power, water conservancy, housing and urban construction" (PRC, 2016). China proposes to support and encourage "enterprises and financial institutions to actively participate in the planning and construction of logistics, power and information passages" and "explore new ways of cooperation, such as the public–private partnership (PPP) model, so as to promote the connectivity of infrastructure" in the Caribbean (PRC, 2016).

According to the PRC (2016), China will play a major role in the development of the Caribbean's manufacturing sector by encouraging its enterprises to participate in major resources, energy development, and infrastructure construction projects. These projects will be undertaken as the foundation on which "to build production lines and maintenance service bases in [Latin America and the Caribbean] for construction materials, non-ferrous metals, engineering machinery, locomotives and rolling stock, electric power and communication equipment, with the purpose of reducing costs for resources and energy development and infrastructure construction" (PRC, 2016). Enterprises that cover the whole industrial chain in the manufacture of automobiles, new energy equipment, motorcycles and chemical industry will be encouraged. This will be done "so that the two sides can complement each other, increase local employment, upgrade the level of industrialization and promote local economic and social development" (PRC, 2016). The business-led and market-oriented principles will lead the way in "the joint construction of industrial parks, logistics parks, high-tech industrial parks, special economic zones and other industrial agglomeration areas," to help with regional industrial upgrading (PRC, 2016). The platforms and environment will be built to encourage exchanges and cooperation between small and medium-sized enterprises in China and the Caribbean.

The promotion of agricultural trade is essential to businesses in China and the Caribbean. These enterprises will be encouraged to push for "exchanges and cooperation in agricultural science and technology, personnel training and other fields," deepen team work in "livestock and poultry breeding, forestry, fishery and aquaculture, and jointly promote food security" (PRC, 2016). China proposes to establish and enhance "agricultural technology demonstration programs, promote the development and demonstration of modern agricultural technologies, and enhance agricultural technology innovation, agricultural production and processing capacity and international competitiveness" in China and the Caribbean (PRC, 2016). Agricultural policy seeks to improve bilateral mechanisms for agricultural information exchanges and cooperation," while "giving full play to the role of the special fund for agricultural cooperation between the two sides, and encourage more agricultural cooperation projects (PRC, 2016).

The focus in the social realm covers issues such as social governance and social development, cooperation on environmental protection, climate change and disaster reduction, poverty reduction, and health. In the cultural and people-to-people field, the focus is on cooperation in cultural and sports exchanges, education and human resources training, exchanges and cooperation in press, publication, radio, film and television, tourism, academic think-tank exchanges, non-governmental exchanges, and consular cooperation (PRC, 2016). The international collaboration aspect of the policy focuses on international political affairs, global economic governance, implementation of the 2030 Agenda for Sustainable Development, response to climate change, and cyber security (PRC, 2016). Other policy foci cover peace, security, and judicial affairs with a focus on military exchanges, and judicial and police affairs; collective cooperation; and trilateral cooperation (PRC, 2016).

China has put in place a comprehensive set of policies to help the Caribbean in its all-round economic, political and social development. These measures have surpassed those of the Moyne Commission that has been used as the standard in debates about landmark policy recommendations for the Caribbean. The difference is that the reform measures proposed by the Moyne Commission were what the colonial authorities recommended for their colonies. China's proposals are seen as coming from an outside source, seeking to spread its influence in the area. China's policies cannot be implemented without the sensible cooperation and participation of Caribbean states.

The Caribbean's embrace of the Belt and Road Initiative (BRI) has to consider the level of development of the region's economic, political and social institutions, structure of production, consumption, and trade (commerce, exchange). The goal must be transformation of the institutional structures where there is an established need and the cultivation of new infrastructure to support new lines of products, production, trade, and changes in tastes. The Caribbean has to cultivate relationships with China from the standpoint of what the region has, what is possible to enhance what it has, and to acquire new vestiges in social and economic development.

US policies toward the Caribbean

The four essential pillars of President Obama's policies toward the Caribbean were the promotion of "economic and social opportunity; ensuring citizen security; strengthening effective institutions of democratic governance; and securing a clean energy future" (Sullivan, 2015). President Obama's policies showed "substantial continuity" with "some of the same basic policy approaches as the Bush Administration" (Meyer, 2014). However, there were some significant changes under Obama to reflect "an overall emphasis on partnership and shared responsibility" (Meyer, 2014). A major change was that President Obama substantially broke with the long-standing US sanctions-based policy toward Cuba, and moved toward diplomatic engagement with the island (Meyer, 2014). The increasing independence of Caribbean states, their diversified "economic and diplomatic ties with countries outside the region," and their establishment of regional organizations such as the Community of Latin American and Caribbean States (CELAC) that excludes the US, provide the context for US policy toward the region (Meyer, 2014).

The Obama Administration had a charm offensive in the Caribbean that included moves to normalize US relations with Cuba, the 2013 visit by US Vice President Joseph Biden to the Caribbean, the 2015 Caribbean Energy Security Summit in Washington, and President Obama's visit to Jamaica and Panama in April 2015. US Vice President Biden signed the United States–CARICOM Trade and Investment Framework Agreement (TIFA) in 2013. The TIFA "provides a strategic framework and principles for dialogue on trade and investment issues of mutual interest" to the US and the CARICOM. The US–CARICOM Trade and Investment Council established by the TIFA "will guide implementation of the Agreement" (The White House, 2013).

While in Jamaica President Obama unveiled his clean energy partnership with the CARICOM and announced a US$70M program to invest in "education, training, and employment initiatives for young people throughout Latin America and the Caribbean" (Somanader, 2015). The President revealed "The 100,000 Strong in the Americas initiative, with the goal of having 100,000 US students studying across the Americas and 100,000 students in this region studying in the US by 2020" (Somanader, 2015). President Obama launched "The Young Leaders of the Americas Initiative," which proposed to "provide 250 fellowships each year to help participants develop joint business and civil society initiatives" (Somanader, 2015).

The Trump administration defines the Caribbean as "Antigua and Barbuda, Aruba, Bahamas, Barbados, Belize, Curacao, Dominica, Dominican Republic, Grenada, Guyana, Haiti, Jamaica, Saint Lucia, Sint Maarten, St. Kitts and Nevis, St. Vincent and the Grenadines, Suriname, and Trinidad and Tobago" (US State Department, 2020). The Caribbean is regarded as the US' "third border" characterized by common interests and societal ties. The US is the Caribbean's primary trading partner and in 2018 the US realized a US$12.3Bn trade surplus on US$35.3Bn of trade with the Caribbean, 10 percent more than 2017 (US State Department, 2020).

Caribbean–US relations under the President Trump are equally characterized by continuity and change. The US continues to project its hegemonic power contained in its new strategy for engaging the Caribbean. The strategy is outlined in a state department report to the congress entitled: *Caribbean 2020: A Multi-Year Strategy to Increase the Security, Prosperity, and Well-Being of the People of the United States and the Caribbean*. The six priority areas are security, diplomacy, prosperity, energy, education, and health (US State Department, 2020; Sullivan et al., 2020).

The security priorities are to deny Islamic State in Iraq and Syria (ISIS) "a foothold in the region, dismantle illicit trafficking networks, enhance maritime security, confront violent and organized crime, and increase the sharing of threat information among countries" (US State Department, 2020). Countering transnational criminal and terrorist organizations involves partnering with Caribbean governments to strengthen "mutual national security and advance the safety" of "citizens by pursuing programs to dismantle transnational criminal and terrorist organizations, curb the trafficking and smuggling of illicit goods and people, strengthen the rule of law, improve citizen security, and counter vulnerability to terrorist threats" (US State Department, 2020). This involves support for "law enforcement and border-control agencies, defense forces, and regional security institutions with training, equipment, institution-building programs, technical assistance, and operational collaboration to strengthen partnership," and "improve cooperation, accountability, and trust between the security forces and public" (US State Department, 2020).

Security matters include bolstering "partnerships with governments and civil society to prevent, investigate, and prosecute terrorism; counter terrorist financing and facilitation networks; reduce the vulnerability to radicalization; and improve border security," by increasing "governments' capacity to investigate and prosecute domestic and transnational crime, assist victims, dismantle criminal organizations, and expand rehabilitation options for juvenile offenders (US State Department, 2020). With respect to regional cooperation on security the US proposes to "define a common operational framework to tackle shared threats, including combating maritime drug trafficking and promoting law enforcement information sharing" (US State Department, 2020).

Advancing citizen security involves crime and violence prevention by partnering with "governments to build the resilience of at-risk youth and communities by providing educational, economic, and social opportunities" (US State Department, 2020). It calls for governance to "support efforts to prevent and prosecute corruption, increase government effectiveness, and build national and regional crime monitoring institutions to ensure crime prevention programs are well-targeted" (US State Department, 2020).

Through diplomacy the US intends to raise and focus its political level dialogue with the Caribbean on its six priorities. "The United States–Caribbean Strategic Engagement Act of 2016 reflects broad interest in more robust and regular engagement between Caribbean leaders and the US government. Increased, institutionalized engagement will lead to more effective coordination of the disparate components of the US–Caribbean relationship and forge greater multilateral cooperation at the Organization of American States and United Nations" (US State Department, 2020). The US proposes to enhance its engagement with the region through US–Caribbean dialogue by convening "an annual consultative meeting with Caribbean leaders" with the "support and participation of relevant interagency and Congressional leaders" to provide a venue for advancing the agenda outlined" in the US strategy for engagement in the Caribbean (US State Department, 2020).

Through its diplomatic engagement in the Eastern Caribbean, the US proposes, if funding becomes available in the future, to "explore expanding its diplomatic and consular presence in Eastern Caribbean countries that do not currently host a permanent US diplomatic mission" (US State Department, 2020). Through Caribbean-American diaspora diplomacy the US proposes to "tap into the robust Caribbean diaspora community in the United States to promote the goals" of the US strategy for engagement in the Caribbean (US State Department, 2020).

The aim is to increase prosperity in both the US and the Caribbean through sustainable growth, open markets for US exports, and private sector-led investment and development. The US proposes to support US exports and job creation, and engage with the Caribbean in a mutually beneficially manner "to promote sustainable economic policies and job-creating, private sector-led growth, utilizing trade preference programs and key forums such as the US-CARICOM Trade and Investment Council" (US State Department, 2020). To improve the trade and investment climate the US proposes to "hold a trade and investment conference with Caribbean countries focused on increasing bilateral trade and improving the region's investment climate and regulatory environment" (US State Department, 2020). US exports will be promoted through a "Direct Line program to highlight US export and investment opportunities" (US State Department, 2020).

Small business and infrastructure development will be pursued to "increase private sector job growth and create new markets for US businesses," and "advance the growth and formalization of small- and medium-sized enterprises and seek opportunities to empower women and youth entrepreneurs" (US State Department, 2020). Connectivity will be achieved through expanding "internet access in the Caribbean by increasing engagement with policy and regulatory authorities, as well as US information-technology leaders, to promote broadband development and deployment" (US State Department, 2020). The US proposes to engage Caribbean agriculture by supporting "compliance with regulations and standards to increase agricultural trade and improve food safety for US consumers" (US State Department, 2020). The US proposes to "work to conclude more Open Skies agreements with Caribbean nations by the end of 2020 to facilitate travel and commerce" and with respect to sustainable tourism "foster healthy, well-managed, and productive marine and coastal ecosystems- the backbone of the Caribbean tourism industry" (US State Department, 2020).

The US vows to lessen the Caribbean's reliance on Venezuelan heavy fuel oil by providing the region with cleaner, cheaper alternative energy, through its exports of natural gas and renewable energy technologies. The US provided an economic argument in its bid to replace Venezuela as the Caribbean's energy supplier. According to the US State Department (2020), Caribbean consumers pay on average three times as much for electricity as US consumers, the effect of which is a drag on the region's economies. This situation provides an opportunity for Caribbean states to benefit from cooperating with the US on energy (US State Department, 2020). The US will supply the region with "low cost, reliable sources of energy, including renewable and natural gas, to spur economic development that will create new opportunities for globally competitive US energy firms and exports" (US State Department, 2020).

The US proposes to strengthen energy governance and improve energy planning through a number of reforms. Energy sector reforms "will provide targeted technical support to countries with the capacity and interest in pursuing energy sector and utility reforms to spur private investment and US energy technology exports" (US State Department, 2020). Regulatory reforms are touted as a means to "continue integrated resource planning efforts and regulatory reforms to encourage governments and utilities to make transparent and economically viable decisions regarding capacity improvements that mitigate risk for US investors and lower costs for consumers (US State Department, 2020). Regional energy planning is encouraged to "support efforts by CARICOM and others to strengthen the regional platform coordinating energy planning to achieve economies of scale" (US State Department, 2020).

The energy measures include leveraging public finance to mitigate energy investment risk. In this case, the US proposes to leverage its, and "international public finance resources to help energy project developers mitigate technical and political risks, thereby reducing the region's reliance on imported fuels and creating openings for US private sector investment and PPPs" (US State Department, 2020).

The education priority concentrates on "exchanges and programs for students, scholars, teachers, and other professionals that provide mutual benefits to US and Caribbean communities and promote economic development and entrepreneurship" (US State Department, 2020). The idea is to have "educational and cultural programs between the Caribbean and the United States build stronger economic partnerships, counter vulnerability to crime and extremism, promote the export of US higher education services, and advance cooperation on science, technology, and development" (US State Department, 2020). The priority on education involves advancing economic partnerships to promote growth through PPP. The US proposes to "support public-private sector collaborations that facilitate higher education and workforce development strategies in the United States and the Caribbean, as well as the efforts of US colleges and universities to recruit qualified students from the region" (US State Department, 2020).

To build security capacities and messaging the US speaker program "will leverage US experts, digital communication, and other messaging resources to reduce crime and counter violent extremism" (US State Department, 2020). Competitiveness in the hemisphere will be enhanced by sending "US academic experts to the region to develop early literacy curricula." Exchanges "will foster educational collaboration between US and Caribbean professionals, students, and scholars," while educational policy training "will provide technical assistance programs and virtual tools to teachers, policymakers, and civil society" (US State Department, 2020).

The US proposes to continue partnering with Caribbean states on health issues including the fight against infectious diseases like HIV/AIDS and Zika. The health priority focuses on "improving health security, advancing public health, and strengthening resilience to emergencies and disasters in the Caribbean" to serve "US national security and economic interests." The view is "secure and stable health systems build the productivity of Caribbean populations and contribute to economic prosperity" (US State Department, 2020). Under the new Caribbean-US Resilience Partnership the US "is taking a whole of government approach to help create a healthier and more resilient Caribbean." The US proposes to improve its own security by strengthening global health security. To this effect the US Global Health Security Agenda (GHSA) is intended to "improve the safety of US citizens and promote the health of Caribbean citizens," by assisting CARICOM countries "to prevent, detect, and respond to infectious disease threats and comply with the International Health Regulations" (US State Department, 2020).

In terms of resilience, the idea is to "work with Caribbean countries to combat non-communicable diseases and to develop their emergency response capacity and infrastructure resilience to natural and man-made disasters" (US State Department, 2020). Advancing the President's Emergency Plan for AIDS Relief (PEPFAR) the US proposes to "assist Caribbean countries to achieve the "90-90-90" goals of the Joint United Nations Program on HIV/AIDS by 2020, including focused HIV/AIDS programming, effective partner management, and implementation of new policies" (US State Department, 2020).

A comparison of the policies of China and the US toward the Caribbean reveals that President Trump's strategy to engage the region is brazenly nationalistic intended for US recolonization of the region. In every area, education, security, agriculture, energy, and health the US is only concerned with its own prosperity. The ideology of American bran capitalism, is at the heart of US policy toward the Caribbean, while China's is seemingly ideologically neutral. The US believes China is definitely projecting its power and influence in the Caribbean but China has a clear interest in the economic and social development of the region. The US six priority areas of security, diplomacy, prosperity, energy, education, and health are vintage "America first" Trumpism. President Trump's intention to engage with the Caribbean to promote US interest is not different to what previous US administrations have done. The difference is the brazenness with which the Trump Administration is asserting US power in the Caribbean. China on the other hand is keen to point out that its policies are designed to further political, economic, social, and cultural development of the region. China's policies propose to further international cooperation, peace, security and judicial affairs, collective, and trilateral cooperation.

The current US strategy arguably is a throwback to the Monroe Doctrine through which the US opposed forces other than itself from dominating the Caribbean. But, Trumpism has come a little too late in that the world has changed in decisive ways since the emergence of neoliberal globalization. The Monroe Doctrine coincided with the rise of European colonialism and the US growing influence in the Americas, but Trumpism comes at a time when the US' influence is waning as the center of gravity of economic power has shifted from America and the EU, toward China and other BRICS countries. The European Union, China, and Russia are not the only threats to US hegemony in the Caribbean. It is evident that the US feels threatened by the specter of states such as China, Cuba, Brazil, and Venezuela in the Caribbean.

US–China relations and CARICOM

The US and China established diplomatic relations in January 1979 and by July of the same year signed a bilateral trade agreement. The two nations provided mutual most-favored-nation treatment, beginning 1980 (Morrison, 2019). In 1979, US–China trade had an estimated total of US$4Bn, while China was the US' 24th largest trading partner, 16th export market, and 36th largest source of imports. About three and a half decades later China was the US' largest trading partner with total US merchandise trade estimated at US$636Bn, in 2017. China was the US' third-largest export market, and its biggest source of imports (Morrison, 2019). The rapid growth in economic relations between the US and China is attributed to China's economic reforms including the liberalization of its trade regime in the late 1970s. Thus, total US–China merchandise trade rose from US$2Bn in 1979 to US$636Bn in 2017 (Morrison 2019).

Nowadays, participation in China's market is regarded as critical for US companies to remain globally competitive. It is cheaper for US companies to use China as the final point of assembly for their products, or to use Chinese-made inputs for production in the US. Consumers in the US derive all-round benefits from the low production costs of US companies operating in China or utilizing Chinese-made inputs, as well as from US import of low-cost Chinese goods. The US$1.2 trillion (as of April 2018) of US Treasury securities held by China makes that country America's largest foreign holder, which helps to keep interest rates in the US low (Morrison, 2019).

Undoubtedly, the economic role of China in the Caribbean was seen to be equally important by the Obama Administration, which it seems, went out of its way to welcome China's presence in the region as a good thing without regard to a possible threat (Brandt et al., 2012). Campbell (2014) claims there were "many opportunities for the US to benefit from China's economic engagement" in the Caribbean. This was particularly the case with China's "investments in and financing of port infrastructure and shipping and its involvement in humanitarian aid and disaster relief efforts" (Campbell, 2014).

Campbell (2014) and Brandt et al. (2012) see China's activities in the Caribbean as presenting opportunities to the US, but, they admonish US policymakers to closely monitor China's, growing involvement in the region (Brandt et al., 2012; Campbell, 2014). Campbell (2014) expresses the view that "Beijing likely judges it has an opportunity to fill a vacuum caused by a decrease in US and European trade, investment, and other business ties following the global economic crisis" (Campbell, 2014). It is claimed there exists a pervasive narrative in "the Caribbean countries that the US has neglected the region while China has embraced it" (Campbell, 2014).

The opinion is expressed however that such a storyline is "misleading" because "current US trade and diplomatic ties with the region are more robust than those of China" (Campbell, 2014). In addition, the persistence of the view that the US is neglecting the region could "limit the effectiveness of US policy in the Caribbean" (Campbell, 2014). Brandt et al. (2012) argue, "China's emphasis on building South–South cooperation has given governments and businesses in the Latin American and Caribbean (LAC) region an alternative to the United States." In their view "the United States is still viewed as a preferred economic partner by many LAC nations," but "there is evidence that US market share of LAC trade is declining while Chinese lines of credit and foreign direct investment in LAC are growing substantially" (Brandt et al., 2012).

The US maintained major grouses with China despite the positive economic role of China in America and the Caribbean. These ideological complaints and attempts by the US to address them have relevance for China–Caribbean relations. The US argues that China is the cause of the trade tensions between the two countries because of China's intransigence behavior. The US accuses China of failing to completely transition to a free market economy. China has not gone far enough with its economic and trade liberalization program and continues to maintain or imposed state-directed policies which distort trade and investment flows (Morrison, 2019).

The US policymakers claim that China engages in "widespread cyber economic espionage against US firms" (Morrison, 2019). The US alleges that China does not effectively enforce intellectual property rights (IPR), and engages in discriminatory innovation policies (Morrison, 2019). China is said to have a "mixed record on implementing its WTO obligations," and utilizes excessive "industrial policies (such as subsidies and trade and investment barriers) to promote and protect industries favored by the government" (Morrison, 2019). The Chinese government is accused for its "interventionist policies to influence the value of the currency." The claim by the US authorities is that the foregoing measures implemented by the Chinese government "adversely impact US economic interests [and] have contributed to US job losses in some sectors (Morrison, 2019). President Trump accuses China of spreading COVID-19 which he calls the "China Virus" to the US.

Morrison (2014) identified four broad categories of proffered solutions advocated to address these perceived problems with China in the era of President Obama. First is the US should adopt "a more aggressive stance on China, such as increasing the number of dispute settlement cases brought against China in the WTO, or threatening to impose trade sanctions against China unless it addresses policies (such as IPR infringement and cyber theft of trade secrets) that hurt US economic interests" (Morrison, 2014).

Second, the US should intensify its negotiations with China "through existing high-level bilateral dialogues, such as the US–China Strategic and

Economic Dialogue (SED), which was established to discuss long-term challenges in the relationship" (Morrison, 2014). Furthermore, the US should "seek to complete ongoing US negotiations with China to reach a high-standard bilateral investment treaty (BIT), as well as to finalize negotiations in the WTO toward achieving China's accession to the Government Procurement Agreement (GPA)" (Morrison, 2014).

Third, the US should "encourage China to join the Trans-Pacific Partnership (TPP) negotiations and/or seek to negotiate a bilateral free trade agreement (FTA) with China, which would require it to significantly reduce trade reforms and investment barriers" (Morrison, 2014). Finally, the US should "continue to press China to implement comprehensive economic reforms, such as diminishing the role of the state in the economy and implementing policies to boost domestic consumption" (Morrison, 2014).

The Trump Administration has opted for the more aggressive option in its policies toward China. The US describes its relations with China in terms of "great power competition," which includes "a prolonged standoff over trade, severely straining ties on the 40th anniversary of the two countries' establishment of diplomatic relations (Lawrence, Martin, and Schwarzenberg, 2019). China and the US lead the world via the size of their economies, their defense budget, and their global greenhouse gas emissions, and are permanent members of the UN Security Council, and were each other's largest trading partners in 2018 (Lawrence, Martin, and Schwarzenberg, 2019).

The Trump Administration's National Security Strategy (NSS) formulated in 2017 set the tone for US–China relations. It posits that the US is in competition with China, Russia, North Korea, Iran, and "transnational threat groups." This new situation requires the US to "rethink the policies of the past two decades." These policies are said to be "based on the assumption that engagement with rivals and their inclusion in international institutions and global commerce would turn them into benign actors and trustworthy partners" (Lawrence, Martin, and Schwarzenberg, 2019). The NSS regards China and Russia as "revisionist powers" that "challenge American power, influence, and interests, attempting to erode American security and prosperity" (Lawrence, Martin, and Schwarzenberg, 2019). The Trump Administration "has sought to identify and respond to perceived threats from China," even as China has stepped up its "cooperation on such issues as stemming the flow into the US of fentanyl, a class of deadly synthetic opioids, and maintaining pressure on North Korea to curb its nuclear weapons and missile programs" (Lawrence, Martin, and Schwarzenberg, 2019).

The Trump Administration focuses on reducing US bilateral trade deficit, enforcing the US trade laws and agreements and promoting free and fair trade (Morrison, 2019). President Trump has resorted to increasing tariffs to achieve those outcomes. The President decreed on March 18, 2018, a 25 percent and 10 percent tariff on steel and aluminum, respectively, based on Section 232 national security justifications. President Trump then announced on March 22 that he would take action against China under Section 301 over its IPR policies which are harmful to the US. The President stated that he would "seek commitments from China to reduce the bilateral trade imbalance and to achieve "reciprocity" on tariff levels" (Morrison, 2019).

China, the largest producer of steel and aluminum, announced on April 1, "that it had retaliated against the US action by raising tariffs (from 15 percent to 25 percent) on various US products, which together totaled US$3 billion in 2017" (Morrison, 2019). The US Trade Representative (USTR) announced on June 12 the US' "two-stage plan to impose 25 percent ad valorem tariffs on US$50 billion worth of Chinese imports" (Morrison, 2019). In stage one, "US tariffs would increase on US$34 billion worth of Chinese products and effective July 6," while in stage two, there would be tariff increases "on US16 billion worth of Chinese imports, mainly targeting China's industrial policies" (Morrison, 2019).

China retaliated with "its own two-stage list of counter-retaliation of equal magnitude," forcing President Trump to threaten "10 percent ad valorem tariffs on another US$400 billion worth of Chinese products" (Morrison, 2019). As the Trump Administration implemented the first round of tariff increases on July 6, China retaliated in kind. The tariff war between the US and China threatens to "reduce US–China commercial ties, disrupt global supply chains, raise import prices for US consumers and importers of Chinese inputs, and diminish economic growth in the US and abroad" (Morrison, 2019).

The US and EU issued on July 25 a joint statement aimed at China saying the two sides are working "together with like-minded partners to reform the WTO and to address unfair trading practices, including intellectual property theft, forced technology transfer, industrial subsidies, distortions created by state owned enterprises, and overcapacity" (Morrison, 2019).

Issues for CARICOM–China relations

The central issue for CARICOM–China relations is the ways in which the US' aggressive retaliation against China's perceived economic intransigence would impact China's immense contribution toward the economic development of the Caribbean. An analysis of China–US policies toward the Caribbean and US–China relations bring to the fore several pertinent observations into considerations.

First, China became active in the Caribbean at a time when the US experienced its worst economic crisis since the Great Depression. While the US was in the throes of the 2007/2008 global financial and economic crises it had no choice but to tolerate development alternatives in the Caribbean provided by PetroCaribe which filled an important void in the region's energy financing, and China. But, as soon as the US achieved energy self-sufficiency it began to push to dismantle PetroCaribe and sell US energy in the Caribbean. Now that US policy toward China is aggressive both Chinese and Venezuelan alternative development approaches in the Caribbean are under severe threat. China and the Caribbean must be aware of this threat as they pursue development alternatives projects.

CARICOM–China development projects could suffer in like-manner to the "smash and grab" and "open robbery" technique the Trump Administration pursued in its bid to have American companies assume 100 percent ownership of the TikTok operations in the US (Tribbitt and Tobin, 2020). President Trump declared TikTok a threat to America's national security claiming that the Chinese-owned app whose parent company is ByteDance Ltd., collects vast amounts of data on Americans which it can be forced by the government of China to share with the Chinese state. The Pentagon and some US private corporations have ordered their personnel to delete the app from their phones, but no proof has been supplied that TikTok shares information on US citizens with the Chinese government (Tribbitt and Tobin, 2020). Already the US Southern Command has used US national security as the ground on which to objected to Chinese infrastructure projects in the Caribbean.

President Trump subsequently announced that US companies Oracle and Walmart will have "total control" over TikTok Global, if a deal between Oracle, Walmart, and TikTok's parent company, ByteDance is approved (Kovach, 2020). Americans will hold four of the five seats on the board of TikTok Global, with ByteDance's CEO occupying the fifth seat (Kovach, 2020). The deal will position Americans as 53 percent owners of TikTok global on the following basis. Oracle and Walmart will own 12.5 percent and 7.5 percent, respectively of TikTok Global (Kovach, 2020). American investors own 41 percent of ByteDance, which will own 80 percent of TikTok Global (Kovach, 2020). The US can employ similar tactics as in the case of TikTok to smash and grab CARICOM–China development projects.

The second observation is that US policies toward the Caribbean centers on American security. The US war on terrorism is a driving force in US policy toward the region. The economic development of the Caribbean takes second place to securing the US' borders. The US focus on energy is also a matter of securing the American way of life. The Caribbean region, in which Venezuela can be located along with Trinidad and Tobago, and Guyana two CARICOM oil-producing countries has the world's largest oil reserves that the US is determined to control. The US' education and health policies are also about securing the US from crime, violent extremism, and diseases.

Third, Chinese policies are more of a developmental nature concentrating on the political, economic, and social realms. They focus is on issues like political exchanges, governance, legislatures, political parties, local governments, and inter-governmental dialogue and consultation. Trade, industrial investment and capacity, financial institutions cooperation, energy and natural resources, infrastructure, manufacturing, and agriculture are primary concerns. China's policy in the region promotes social and cultural development and international collaboration.

Fourth, the Trump Administration has taken up a hostile position against China to address the accusations that China engages in economic practices that are harmful to the US economy. But, the US takes actions that are equally harmful to other countries including economic sanctions that ruin the economies of states it considers enemies. Venezuela is a current example where US sanctions have condemned millions to starvation and to flee their country into uncertain futures. US hostility toward China will have a negative impact on China–Caribbean relations because China could become skeptical in its dealings with the region considered America's "third border."

Fifth, the Trump Administration's policies to regard China as a competitor changes the equation concerning China's role in the Caribbean. It means that China is no longer welcomed as it was under the Obama Administration when it filled an important void created by the US' pivot toward the Middle East in the "war on terrorism." As a competitor, the US will do everything in its power to keep China out of the economic and political affairs of the Caribbean.

Sixth, if China were to fully transition to a market economy, and alter the economic role of its state that would definitely hurt China–CARICOM relations. This is because China's government-sponsored investments, concessional loans, grants, debt cancellation, and in-kind aid programs will have to operate on neoliberal market principles, driven by the profit motive. The CARICOM must take cognizance of other possible difficulties that could also arise. Some of these challenges that are analyzed in the context of China–Africa economic relations relate to labor, environment, and technology transfer issues. Would Chinese construction and mining projects in the CARICOM countries help to increase the skill level of the CARICOM labor force, transfer technology to the region, and degrade the environment?

Seventh, the US demand for the Chinese state to separate itself from Chinese businesses is hypocritical. US imperialism in terms of US private businesses investing abroad is exclusively dependent on the US state. Indeed, the Trump Administration is guilty of the same crime it is accusing China of committing. President Trump's "America first" doctrine is a state directed dogma in which the state and private businesses work hand-in-hand. The tax cuts to promote US businesses, the government bailout of US private companies, the policies favorable to private businesses all reflect the marriage between the state and private capital in America.

Finally, the tariff war between the US and China could harm China's ability to assist the Caribbean due to rising cost of operations of Chinese businesses.

Conclusion

Undoubtedly, President Trump like his predecessors Presidents Barak Obama and George Bush Jr. placed security at the center of US policy toward the Caribbean. The focus on security has to do with the fact that these were the US Presidents in the era of the US' "war on terrorism." US investments in Caribbean social and economic development projects are out of security concerns, which link the profit motive with security. Social and economic development in the Caribbean are treated as a deterrence to terrorism taking root in the region. The US promotes health in the Caribbean because it does not want Americans to be infected with diseases coming from the region. Education is promoted because it wants to teach Caribbean people about how not to become terrorists and to have the US private education sector invest in the region. Clean energy is promoted in the Caribbean because the US wants to sell energy products to the region. Prosperity in the US and Caribbean means open markets to support US exports and job creation. Diplomacy is pursued to bring the CARICOM states in line with US policies toward the region.

Understandably, China does not have a security threat from the Caribbean and so has different interests in the region. Its policies are more concerned with securing resources and promoting economic development. China's tit-for-tat tariff war with the US is further evidence of the new multipolarity, the fact that America no longer stands by itself as the sole superpower but is sharing power with others. The negativity emerging from current US–China relations as America tries to punish the Chinese for their perceived economic intransigence, might reduce China's ability to deliver on its economic assistance to the Caribbean. These are some of the issues that the CARICOM has to be concerned within its development pursuits.

References

Brandt, J., N. Adams, C. Dinh, A. Tuck, D. Kleinfield-Hayes, D. Hottle, N. Aujla, K. Kaufman, and W. Ren (2012). *Chinese Engagement in Latin America and the Caribbean: Implications for US Foreign Policy.* American University School of International Service, US State Department.

Campbell, C. (2014). "China's Expanding and Evolving Engagement with the Caribbean," *US–China Economic and Security Review Commission Staff Report*, 16 May.

Kovach, S. (2020). "TikTok Deal Puts US Owners in Charge, But Chinese Parent Company Still Has Some Say," *NCBC*, 21 September.

Lawrence, S.V., M.F. Martin, and A.B. Schwarzenberg. (2019). *U.S.-China Relations.* Washington DC: Congressional Research Service, 8 August.

Meyer, P. (2014). *US Foreign Assistance to Latin America and the Caribbean: Recent Trends and FY2015 Appropriations.* Washington DC: Congressional Research Services Report, 10 September.

Morrison, W.M. (2014). *China's Economic Rise: History, Trends, Challenges, and Implications for the United States.* Washington DC: Congressional Research Service, Report 9.

Morrison, W.M. (2019). *US-China Trade Issues.* Washington DC: Congressional Research Service, 30 July.

People's Republic of China (PRC) (2016). *China's Policy Paper on Latin America and the Caribbean.* Beijing: Ministry of Foreign Affairs.

Somanader, T. (2015). "Barack in Jamrock: The Young Leaders of the Americas Meet with the President in Jamaica," The White House.Gov, 10 April.

Sullivan, M.P. (2015). *Latin America and the Caribbean: Key Issues for the 114th Congress*. Washington DC: Congressional Research Service, 28 January.

Sullivan, M. Beittel, J.S., Meyer, P.J., Seelke, C.R., Taft-Morales, M., and Villarreal, M.A. (2020). *Latin America and the Caribbean: U.S. Policy and Issues in the 116th Congress*. Washington DC: Congressional Research Service, 21 May.

The White House. (2013). Fax Sheet: United States Support for Economic Growth and Development in the Caribbean. Washington DC, 28 May.

Tribbitt, M. and M. Tobin. (2020). *Why Is Donald Trump Threatening Popular Video-Sharing App TikTok?* New York: Bloomberg, 11 August.

US State Department (2020). *Caribbean 2020: A Multi-Year Strategy to Increase the Security, Prosperity, and Well-Being of the People of the United States and the Caribbean*. Washington DC.

12 Conclusion: Economic policy for the new multipolar world order

Introduction

The principal proposition of this book is that a transition has taken place from a US-led unipolar neoliberal global order to a new multipolar world order characterized by the US, EU, China, and Russia with a decided shift in economic power from the West to the East, but the CARICOM states continue to cast their economic policy within the neoliberal framework. The thesis is argued by locating the historical origins of capitalist development in the Caribbean in European imperial expansion. The Caribbean had to cope with the subsequent rise of US imperialism prior to and during the Cold War and the "new American century" doctrine, which was replaced by the "make America great again" creed. The thesis argument is advanced with analyses of the academic debates on, and the characteristic features of the new multipolar world order, the theoretical frameworks that accompanied capitalist development in the Caribbean, the Caribbean Forum-Europe Union Economic Partnership Agreement (CARIFORUM–EU EPA) and Brexit, neoliberal financialization, agriculture, the PetroCaribe, and the CARICOM–China development alternative and the implications of China–US relations for the CARICOM. It is appropriate to conclude this book by suggesting some concrete ideas on Caribbean economic policy for the new multipolar world order.

The purpose of this concluding chapter is to provide some ideas that could go into the formulation of a Caribbean alternative approach to development commensurate with the global economic realignment that is taking place with the BRICS led by China's Belt and Road Initiative – a state and measured private sector development model. It argues that for the CARICOM countries to successfully embrace such a model they will have to take measures to transform the class and power dynamics in their societies to make them more favorable to working people. This would require a radical transformation in the state and society that allows working people to play a direct role in their future development involving BRI projects, unlike the situation that obtained under colonialism and neocolonialism that marginalized workers. The Caribbean private sector known for its tardiness will not be given the responsibility to lead the economic development

DOI: 10.4324/9781003092414-12

of the region. The state has to take the lead and then involve the private sector in a measured way ensuring that people's basic needs are met, which must be the goal of production instead profit.

There is no uniform view on the constitution of the new multipolar world order, but there is general agreement that the world order has changed – the US is no longer the sole superpower, the preeminent force that can push its economic, political, and even military agendas on the rest of the world. It is a well-established fact that the center of gravity of economic power has shifted from the West to the East. The liberal order established after World War II is under serious challenge or otherwise at an end. Its demise is hastened by Trumpian nationalism which is overseeing the collapse of the Bretton Woods institutions that have furnished the rules that govern the international system. With the demise of these institutions new poles of economic power China, Russia, the EU have emerged along with the US requiring new organizations to govern the new multipolar world order.

The fall of the Trump Administration at the US 2020 national elections has not changed the foregoing observations on the collapse of the US-led neoliberal order. The defeat of President Trump merely represents a shift in the type of capital that controls state power in the US. The administration of President Joseph Biden and Vice President Kamala Harris most probably symbolizes a restoration of neoliberal capital over the state in the US, and the defeat of the type of fascistic national capitalism that the Trump Administration represented. But, this change does not mean that the US has returned to the apex of a unipolar global order. The US will have to continue to share the world stage with China, Russia, and the EU. President Biden has actually acknowledged this fact in his first address to a joint-session of the US House and Senate commemorating his first 100 days in office. In a remarkable return to Keynesianism the Biden Administration proposes to restore the US' economic competitiveness by injecting trillion of dollars into the US economy to be paid for by taxing America's super rich. The neoliberal advocates also employed Keynesian policy to bail out the financial sector in the great recession of 2007/2008, paid for by working people.

The argument for Caribbean economic realignment is strengthened by the recent events to overturn the results of the November 2020 US Presidential elections, the signing of the China–EU investment agreement, and the economic impact of COVID-19 in the Caribbean. The analysis proceeds with a brief discussion on these events, ahead of considerations on economic realignment, CARICOM's strategic framework and sustainable development goals, and an approach to development alternatives for the NMWO.

The attempted coup d'état, China–EU agreement, and economic impact of COVID-19

On January 6, 2021 a riotous mob stormed the US Capitol Building, the seat of power in America in an attempted coup d'état. The objective of the attempted coup was to overturn the results of the November 2020 US Presidential election won by President Joseph Biden and Vice President Kamala Harris, and retain the looser, the incumbent President Trump, in power. President Donald Trump falsely claimed that the election was rigged and stolen from him and urged his supporters to overrun the Capitol building in Washington while both Houses of the Congress were in sessions to carry out their function to rubberstamp the Electoral College win for President-elect Biden and Vice President-elect Harris. In what appeared to be a well-coordinated attack by President Trump's supporters involving retired and active duty police and military personnel, elected officials in the Congress and State legislatures, and ordinary civilians five persons were killed in the process including a policeman. A sixth person died by suicide a few days after the melee – he was a policeman on duty at the Capitol building during the attack.

The obvious take away from the attempted coup is that the US political system is inherently unstable. This instability was in full view of the public as the US buckled under the divisiveness, bigotry, and vitriol of the Trump Administration, which culminated in the attempted coup. The evidence of social and economic instability is clearly visible from the Trump Administration's handling of the COVID-19 pandemic. At the time of writing, in the US more than 32,031,068 million persons were infected by the disease, another 571,297 killed by it. The current daily rate of COVID-19 deaths once exceeded 3,000, but currently more than 237,360,493 Americans have been vaccinated against the disease.

The pandemic has caused widespread social and economic dislocation in the US through business closures and high unemployment, while the deeply divided Congress fails to provide adequate economic relief to the people. The US has lost its credibility in the new multipolar world order and can no longer be depended on as a stable democracy. The Caribbean has to look elsewhere in the NMWO in fulfillment of its social and economic objectives.

The Comprehensive Agreement on Investment (CAI) signed between China and the EU December 30, 2020, further begs the question for a comprehensive CARICOM–China economic agreement. The EU is seeking unpresented access to Chinese markets for its investors. The Caribbean states have to do the same while encouraging the transfer of Chinese technology to the region. The debate on whether the economic relations between China and the Caribbean states have to be driven by market principles and US-styled democracy has to be tempered given the strong role the state plays in the NMWO. The stout role for the state in social and economic development has become even more evident in the attempts to combat the COVID-19 pandemic. The Chinese state has successfully constrained the COVID-19 virus and the country's economy is back to normal, while the US and EU continue to falter from the disease.

The economic impact of the COVID pandemic on the Caribbean region has increased calls for governments to take pungent action to stimulate economic activity, bring much needed relief to small businesses, and provide urgent welfare assistance to the poor and vulnerable. The COVID-19 pandemic has "impacted every aspect of life beyond the health sector" in the Caribbean (ECLAC, 2020). According to ECLAC (2020), there were 203,645 positive cases of COVID-19 and 3,731 deaths in the Caribbean Development and Cooperation Committee (CDCC) member and associate member countries as at 24 September 2020. The Dominican Republic and Puerto Rico accounted for 83.4 percent of all positive cases and 78.9 percent of related deaths. All Caribbean countries have reported cases of COVID-19, but there were no reported deaths in Anguilla, Dominica, Grenada, Saint Kitts and Nevis, Saint Lucia, or Saint Vincent and the Grenadines (ECLAC, 2020).

The wide-ranging impacts on leading sectors in the Caribbean subregion's economy have been devastatingly evident in the tourism industry. Border closures, stay-at-home requirements, the sharp fall in visitor and domestic spending, the near shut down of the domestic economy due to COVID-19 have had a debilitating effect on the Caribbean tourism industry. The losses in the tourism industry, which is the mainstay of many economies in the subregion is estimated to reduce the gross domestic product (GDP) by approximately 7.9 percentage points. According to ECLAC (2020), this is due to the near shutdown of the tourist industry in most Caribbean countries. ECLAC (2020) has estimated a 57 percent contraction in Trinidad and Tobago's energy sector, while the loss in revenue in the transportation sector has badly affected regional airlines forcing them to seek government support. Productivity losses in the education sector amounted to US$85.7M due to school closures, while there has been an increase in security and social protection challenges, and rise in cybercrimes (ECLAC, 2020).

The dependence of Caribbean economies on direct and overall contributions of tourism to their gross domestic product ranges from as low as 1.1 percent and 2.6 percent respectively, in Suriname, to as high as 30.4 percent and 73.6 percent, respectively, in Aruba. The average direct and overall contributions of tourism to the GDP in the Caribbean were 11.8 percent and 28.5 percent, respectively in 2019 (ECLAC, 2020). Also, one in six jobs, a majority of which are held by women are accounted for by the tourism sector (ECLAC, 2020).

ECLAC (2020) used the contribution of inbound stayover and domestic tourists in the region to estimate the impact of COVID-19 on the economy. Three recovery scenarios – optimistic, base, and pessimistic, were forecasted concerning the decline in tourist arrivals for 2020. The scenarios for inbound stayovers were 58 percent, 71 percent, and 76 percent for foreign arrivals, while those for domestic tourism were 30 percent, 50 percent, and 70 percent. The average losses in tourism activity were estimated to lower GDP growth by 6.1 percentage points, 7.4 percentage points, and 7.9 percent in the optimistic, base, and pessimistic scenarios, respectively. The economies that depend on tourism the most – Aruba, the British Virgin Islands, and the US Virgin Islands, will all experience declines in their growth rate by over 15 percentage points in the base scenario. Meanwhile, the larger countries such as Trinidad and Tobago, Guyana, and Suriname, with more diversified economies which are less dependent on tourism, and more on commodity exports will be least affected.

Caribbean governments acted with haste to implement short-term measures to mitigate the social and economic impact of COVID-19. The measures to support the tourism industry include "supplementary income support to tourism industry workers and SMEs [small and medium-sized enterprises], easing of financial obligations through loan and national insurance deferrals, cash flow support through banks and credit unions, and suspension of tariffs and value-added taxes" (ECLAC, 2020: 15). Meanwhile, Caribbean leaders are pursuing the establishment of a "common border re-opening protocol and to develop a collective approach to assessing international financing" (ECLAC, 2020: 15). The COVID-19 alleviations efforts in the tourism industry cannot continue into the long-run due to the severity of the crisis and economic constraints faced by regional governments that continue to operate in the neoliberal policy framework that restrains direct government intervention in the economy. More sustainable efforts are necessary to protect businesses and employment in the tourism sector. This requires a stronger role for the government in the economy and greater collaboration with China's BRI.

The Caribbean's trajectory in the international capitalist system

The point of departure for an analysis concerning alternative development policies for the Caribbean in the new multipolar world order is an understanding of the trajectory of the Caribbean in the international capitalist system. The Caribbean was integral to the development of the capitalist colonial slave mode of production. The region produced commodities to satisfy external markets, and not for their domestic consumption. The result was the importation of consumption goods, simultaneously with the export of their produce. The region continues to utilize its natural resources as exports and not for domestic consumption. This production and consumption dynamic has resulted in the region producing what it does not consume and consuming what it does not produce. It also represents a disjuncture between resource use and resource endowment. This dynamic which persists to the present time was integral to the nature and objective of peripheral capitalism in the Caribbean. Thus, as the Caribbean territories evolved from their occupation by medieval European powers in the sixteenth century to colonies and independent states they were always fully a part of the capitalist system.

The region transitioned form the colonial slave mode of production at the end of indentureship, but entered into dependency relations with European powers and subsequently the US. The CARICOM states gained political independence fully caught-up in the Cold War between the former USSR and the US espousing socialist/community and capitalist ideologies,

190 *Conclusion*

respectively. The Caribbean states played both sides of the ideological divide, but there was a backlash when Eastern European communism collapsed. The US came out of that conflict as the winner and brought the entire region in line with its neoliberal economic measures. The neoliberal global order the US created has collapsed and a new multipolar world order has arrived.

The emergent capitalist class structure and political development

The emergent class structure of capitalist development in the region was such that the capitalist resided in Europe, but recruited their paid servants who were dispatched to the Caribbean to oversee the plantations. These individuals worked in close collaboration with the colonial officials who directed the state in the region. At some stage locals were allowed to participate in the government due to limited franchise based on property ownership. The local state officials were therefore drawn from the propertied or middle layers of Caribbean society. That form of direct European colonial rule changed with the advent of self-government based on universal adult suffrage. The colonial state continued to oversee the affairs of the state in the region under self-rule. But, undoubtedly, the introduction of universal adult suffrage changed the class dynamics in Caribbean politics. It extended political participation beyond the limitations of property ownership.

This meant that individuals from the various emergent economic and social classes could now compete for control of the state power. It became a reality that the elites who won state power at national elections included individuals from both middle and working class backgrounds. But, self-government under universal adult suffrage had its own characteristics. The state came under the control of a governor appointed by the British monarch to represent the colonial authorities, and an elected premier and parliament representing different class interests in the domestic population. Real political power resided in the hands of the European colonial state – military, judiciary, and parliament. The colonial governor had veto powers over the domestic parliament, and the Privy Council in England was the final judicial authority.

The next phase in political development was the granting of neocolonial political independence to Caribbean countries. The ruling elites now comprised the domestic middle and working class, with absentee colonial state officials. In the absence of a colonial officials in the form of a governor representing the European monarch, the local rulers who took power governed on behalf of the imperial forces in England in a classic neocolonial arrangement. There were two other simultaneous developments nonetheless, which impacted the evolution of class dynamics in the region. The first was that the ruling elites began to make moves to rule in their self-interest. They sought to use state power to build an economic base for themselves and close allies. The second development was that economic policies became more nationalistic, as the ruling elites searched for ways to break out from the neocolonial trap. The nationalist protectionist policies they pursued have stimulated a pushback by the European powers and the US. The EU and US used their leverage over the Caribbean to force market fundamentalist structural adjustment policies on the region.

Now that structural adjustment has failed, the Caribbean is being dragged into the struggle between two rival approaches to capitalist development. One based on a fascistic type of capitalism that has emerged in Europe and the US that promotes bilateralism, nationalism, protectionism, and the dismantling of neoliberal globalization. The other holds on to neoliberal principles, promotes a neoliberal rules-based global free trade arena, and multilateralism in support of the current economic initiatives of the UN's sustainable development goals (SDGs). The Caribbean faces three choices, to embrace either of those two approaches, or to institute a state-directed development approach that downplays the unfettered private sector as the engine of economic growth.

A case for economic realignment

The economic structure in the Caribbean and the social and political edifice erected on it are all geared toward promoting capitalist development in general and in the region in particular. The mercantile capitalist economic system that the Caribbean helped to create and sustain by participating as a supplier of specific agricultural products particularly sugar locked the region in a particular pattern of economic structure and economic relations with European powers. Domestically, the main means of production was the plantation system, in which slave labor produced the economic surplus supervised by a handful of managerial-type workers. This was a type of primitive accumulation in which capital was accumulated off of slave labor in a system characterized as slavery-cum-capitalism or a colonial slave mode of production. Economic policy in that system was mercantilist, pure and simple, the level of technology employed in production was rudimentary, the social institutions were almost non-existent and where they emerged they catered to the interests of the plantation owners and managers. The economic institutions that controlled trade and commerce, money and banking, agriculture, industry, labor, production, property relations, and the corresponding legal infrastructure served the interests of plantation owners and managers.

The economic structure was gradually reformed from mercantilism to cater to the free trade interest of the powerful industrialists in England. This reform generated major changes in the social, political, and economic institutional structures in the region. This was the first time in a real sense that economic activity has begun to cater to both external and domestic interests. But, still the economy was geared toward foreign interests and capitalist development, and remains so today even though political independence arrived in the region more than 50 years ago. The current multipolar world order represents the first time that Caribbean countries are participating as independent states in an international economic environment in which they could shape economic policy in their self-interest.

The CARICOM states, unless they deliberately choose to do so, no longer have to follow the discredited economic adjustment programs dictated by international capitalism in the past 50 years. A new multipolar world order has emerged, yet economic policy in the Caribbean continues to be formulated within the mold of the US-led unipolar global free-market economic framework. The Caribbean is in this dilemma because of the dynamic nature of the theory and practice of neoliberal economics.

The dynamism stems from two sources one being the inevitability of change within the theory itself, and the other comes from the outside due to the stern critics of the theory that caused its policy advocates to undertake reform. The reform does not change the overall objectives of the theory to promote economic restructuring on the bases of the free market and private sector through the appropriate measures on taxes, exchange rate stabilization, capital market liberalization, public sector reform to reduce cost, free trade, private sector promotion, etc. In essence the reform has been the implementation of measures to reduce poverty and inequality, in response to critics and the blatant hardships structural adjustment heaped on working people.

The reforms implemented by the advocates of structural adjustment in response to their critics, are not intended to abandon neoliberal economic theory but to stay the course, while trying to cause the least possible disruptions. These reforms are now accompanied by policies in line with the UN's sustainable development goals also regarded as global goals to end poverty, protect the planet and ensure all people enjoy peace and prosperity by 2030.

Caribbean economic policy tends to focus on two broad areas. First are those initiatives associated with structural adjustment even though that term has fallen into disrepute and is no longer in use by the IFIs, and second, measures to tackle poverty and inequality and procedures to achieve the UN sustainable development goals.

The glaring omission that should constitute a third set of policy initiatives has to do with a coordinated CARICOM approach to the BRICS and especially China in the new multipolar world order. The region already has an economic partnership with the EU and individual states entered into structural adjustment programs (SAPs) with the IMF and World Bank. But, there is yet to be a detailed coordinated CARICOM agreement with the BRICS or leading BRICS countries. The attitude of the CARICOM states in the new multipolarity must be shaped by economic historical facts. After playing a fundamental role in the development of capitalism on a world-scale the economic development of the CARICOM states were left behind Europe. Given that history with the West the question is: can the CARICOM see any good for their peoples by realigning their economic relations with the East, and especially because of the shifting balance of economic power from the West to the East?

Economic realignment of the CARICOM countries must be understood as the pursuit of policies with the BRICS, the EU and US-dominated IFIs to achieve a set of specific goals. These goals are to align the region's consumption patterns with the basic needs of the population. The realignment must not only reconcile the disjuncture between consumption and basic needs, it must strive to resolve the divergence in the model of resource use and endowment, and the configuration of property ownership and the social relations. The achievement of these realignment goals would require a reorganization of the economic structure such that the accumulation of capital does not merely accrue to a tiny minority but to the sundry population as coordinated and distributed through the state and state-monitored private sector. The CARICOM needs to join in the push for the establishment for new rules-based institutional mechanisms to govern the new multipolar world order. Caribbean states must have a seat at the decision-making table in the new rules-based international system.

The CARICOM's strategic framework to deepen integration and build resilience

The current development framework for the CARICOM states is contained in the community's strategic framework to deepen integration and build resilience, and policies to fulfill the UN's SDGs. The current economic initiatives in the CARICOM are intended to reposition and beneficially integrate the community within the global arena (CARICOM, 2014). The intellectual authors of this grand development strategy endorsed by the CARICOM's ruling elites, chose "global arena" instead of "global order" in which to integrate the Caribbean. But, the "global arena" has been under the dictates of the US-led unipolar neoliberal order since the collapse of the former Soviet Union in 1989–1994. It is now characterized by a new multipolar world order with the emergence of the EU, China, and the other BRICS countries in strong competition with the US. It was by some strange logic that advocates of neoliberal capitalism argued that the developing countries were outside of the global capitalist system and needed to be integrated into it, whereas in fact the developing countries are already a part of the capitalist system.

The neoliberal logic to integrate countries into something in which they are already a part, really has to do with implementing economic reforms in the developing states to deepen their exploitation by the ruling classes in the rich capitalist countries and their collaborators in the developing states. There is therefore nothing original about the initiative to integrate the CARICOM into the global arena. The intellectual source of the policy framework, prescriptions, and goals for this integration is provided by neoliberal economic theory. The idea originated in the neoliberal absurdity, despite the overwhelming evidence to the contrary, that the CARICOM economies were outside the neoliberal globalization process into which they had to be incorporated to achieve economic development. This idea was bought and spread by Caribbean scholars like Bernal (2013) who argue that to develop the Caribbean must strategically reposition itself (integrate) in the global economy.

Integrating the community into the global arena or world order has to be considered against two well-known alternative viewpoints. The first concerns studies of imperialism and economic development spearheaded by Eric Williams (1994) that outline the evidence in support of the argument that the African slave trade was central to capitalist development. The states that formed the CARICOM today have therefore been integral to the development and progression of the global capitalist order. The second alternative perspective is the idea that the underdeveloped states such as those in the CARICOM needed to delink from or break with the international capitalist system to achieve economic development (Rodney, 2011). The idea of delinking from capitalism in favor of constructing a socialist alternative is also associated with dependency theory advocated by Samir Amin (1990).

The strategic framework for the CARICOM to work together to deepen integration (regional integration and into neoliberal globalization) and build resilience has the following stated mission. The objective is to affirm the collective identity and facilitate social cohesion of the people of the community, and realize the community's human potential with the ideal Caribbean person being fully employed and fully enjoying human rights (CARICOM, 2014). It seeks to ensure that social and economic justice and the principles of good governance are enshrined in law and embedded in practice, while striving to systematically reduce poverty, unemployment, and social exclusion and their impacts (CARICOM, 2014).

The strategic framework promotes the mainstreaming of all aspects of sustainable development to unleash the collective strength of the region (CARICOM, 2014). The environmental, economic, and social dimensions, as well as the creation of an atmosphere for innovation, the development and application of technology, productivity and global competitiveness are regarded as essential to the mainstreaming of sustainable development (CARICOM, 2014). The strategic framework advocates the optimum sustainable use of the region's natural resources on land and in the marine environment, and the protection and preservation of the health and integrity of the environment (CARICOM, 2014).

The mission is to encourage citizens to willingly accept responsibility to contribute to the welfare of their fellow citizens and to the common good, by practicing healthy living and lifestyles, respect for the rule of law, protect the assets of the community, and abhor corruption, crime, and criminality in all its forms (CARICOM, 2014). The strategic framework seeks for the CARICOM to project "one voice" on international issues, and to increase savings and the flow of investment within the community (CARICOM, 2014).

Conclusion 195

The core values of the strategy to integrate the CARICOM into the global arena are unity/togetherness, equity, integrity, people-centeredness, performance-driven/results, good governance, and good environmental management (CARICOM, 2014). The strategic priorities are strong economic growth and reduction in poverty and unemployment; improved quality of life; reduced environmental vulnerability; and an integrated community with equity for all (CARICOM, 2014). Targeted interventions will be applied to mitigate and overcome the high debt, low growth, vulnerabilities to environmental shocks, and the general need for re-balancing intra-regional trade in the CARICOM to meet the desired development outcomes (CARICOM, 2014).

The integrated strategic priorities to address the development objectives are based on a resilience model. The idea is to build economic, social, environmental, and technological resilience, and to strengthen the identity and spirit of the CARICOM, and community governance (CARICOM, 2014). The six elements in the resilience model are mutually reinforcing. They include the overall objective to achieve strong economic growth, improved quality of life, reduced environmental vulnerability, and an integrated community with equity for all (CARICOM, 2014).

The problem is that the global arena under the dictates of the US-led hegemon, in which the strategic framework is intended to integrate the Caribbean, has decidedly changed. Although the objectives and mission of the strategic framework remain relevant they have to be reoriented toward the current dynamics of the new multipolar world order. The shift in economic power from the West to the East is acknowledged in sections of the literature, but there is no explicit mention or analysis of the CARICOM in the light of this realignment. The same is true for the community's economic relation with the BRICS, and in particular China's belt and road initiative launched in 2013. There is insufficient analysis of CARICOM-BRICS economic relations, the BRICS being formed in 2006. Also, there is no discussion of the role of Russia in the global arena as a power pole and the CARICOM's engagement with it.

By seeking to be integrated into a declining neoliberal global arena the community's current economic initiatives are therefore out of sync with the present-day reality of international economic relations. The primary reason for this disjuncture of aspirations and reality is the fundamental contradiction in the positions taken by regional policymakers. The incongruity is that simultaneously they are striving to integrate the community into the global arena, they acknowledge the existence of a rebalancing of global economic power in which China is poised to soon become the leading world economy.

In the midst of this contradiction, the ruling elites want to integrate the community into the "value chains" that characterize global production, and the mega-markets associated with global production networks. These networks are the proposed Trans-Pacific Partnership (TPP), the Regional Comprehensive Economic Partnership (RCEP) in Asia, the

Trans-Atlantic Trade and Investment Partnership (TTIP), and the Trade in Services Agreement (TISA). These initiatives are intended to harmonize the rules governing the operations of the various production networks. The CARICOM ruling elites believe that these initiatives are in response to the growing dominance of the emerging economies in world production and trade, and that the rules governing those initiatives could erode the policy space for the community which are outside of the mega-markets.

This could be interpreted as a further contradiction in the economic policy perspectives of the CARICOM – on the one hand, they want to integrate the region in the neoliberal global arena, while on the other that global order has rules that work against the community. Meanwhile, the Trump Administration has backed away from the TTIP and TPP. But, it is expected that the victory of President Joseph Biden and Vice-President Kamala Harris in the US presidential election in November 2020 that the US will resume its pursuit of a neoliberal agenda, albeit in a multipolar world dynamic.

It must be noted that the strategic plan for the community between 2015 and 2019 was written in the mold of neoliberal structural adjustment while the balance of power has shifted from the neoliberal global to a multipolar world order. While structural adjustment and stabilization have not produced sustained economic growth in states with severe macro-economic imbalances, the current regional approach has been to promote the removal of significant micro-economic constraints on competitive production – a neoliberal agenda.

The CARICOM and the UN sustainable development goals

The ruling elites in the CARICOM have formulated development strategy within the framework of neoliberal economic theory, paid insufficient attention to the emergence of the new multipolar world order, and seeks to fulfill the UN's SDGs which are a blueprint to achieve a better and more sustainable future for all. The SDGs represent a new way of building resilience and integrating economic, social, and environmental dimensions world-wide including justice and peace (UNDP, 2016). The seventeen goals and 169 targets that comprise Agenda 2030 and the SDGs, seen through the lens of multidimensional progress, are regarded as having "considerable relevance to the Caribbean." The SDGs are to "be tailored and prioritized to address region specific issues, serve a catalytic role in stimulating resource flows to and within the region, and be a multidimensional, medium-term anchoring development framework for the region as a whole" (UNDP, 2016).

This requires the elimination of the gap between policies and outcomes to ensure that the SDGs are achieved. The gap between policies and outcomes represents "an even more consequential deficit than that historically associated with the region's current and fiscal accounts" (UNDP, 2016). Implementing "the SDGs can contribute to the reduction or elimination of the gap between measures taken and outcomes achieved" (UNDP, 2016). This will be achieved through "greater reliance on evidence-based policy making; on transparency of results; and the development of and adherence to accountability frameworks" (UNDP, 2016).

The CARICOM has a vision for a "single, comprehensive and integrated agenda that is responsive to the diverse development realities with which individual countries and regions are confronted" (UNDP, 2016). In that context they indicated their priority concerns as climate change, energy security, water security, sustainable agriculture, food security and nutrition, employment, economic growth and diversification, debt sustainability, health (addressing both communicable and non-communicable diseases), gender equality, and the empowerment of women, challenges facing youth and children, crime and security, and governance (UNDP, 2016). These priorities are to be featured in the development agenda to address critical challenges that constrain the development prospects and performance of the CARICOM (UNDP, 2016). The 2030 Agenda for Sustainable Development addresses all of the expansive agenda of the CARICOM's ruling elites. Arguably, however, debt sustainability, crime and security, and governance as envisioned by the CARICOM ruling elites, were not addressed extensively and substantively as may have been warranted (UNDP, 2016).

The 17 interconnected SDGs to be achieved by 2030 address global challenges including poverty, inequality, climate change, environmental degradation, peace, and justice in order to leave no one behind. The first goal is the eradication of poverty through inclusive economic growth to provide sustainable jobs and promote equality. The goal to achieve zero hunger focuses on the food and agriculture sector considered central for hunger and poverty eradication. The goal to achieve good health and well-being involves ensuring healthy lives and promoting the well-being for all at all ages is essential to sustainable development. Furthermore, obtaining a quality education is considered as the foundation to improving people's lives and sustainable development.

Meanwhile, gender equality is regarded as a fundamental human right, and a necessary foundation for a peaceful, prosperous and sustainable world. The provision of clean, accessible water and sanitation for all are also fundamental in this connection. Energy is regarded as central to every major challenge and opportunity, which requires that the commodity is affordable and clean. With respect to decent work and sustainable economic growth the challenge is to create the conditions that allow people to have quality jobs. In this same vein achievement in sustainable development necessitates investments in infrastructure which are crucial for industry and innovation. The reduction of inequalities requires universal policies that pay attention to the needs of disadvantaged and marginalized populations. The goal to promote sustainable cities and communities, recognizes the need for a future in which cities provide opportunities for all, with access to basic services, energy, housing, transportation, and more.

Meanwhile, their goals to have responsible production and consumption, and climate action remains a major challenge affecting the globe. This also involves careful management of life below water, an essential global resource and key feature of a sustainable future. Also, life on land requires measures to sustainably manage forests, combat desertification, halt and reverse land degradation, and halt biodiversity loss. The goal to achieve peace, justice, and strong institutions requires access to justice for all, and building effective, accountable institutions at all levels. Finally, the challenge is to revitalize the global partnership for sustainable development.

The SDGs represent a paradigm shift on how scholars and policy makers have thus far agreed on how to increase human well-being. Previously growth in income was regarded as the corner stone in increasing human well-being. The new paradigm focuses on the enrichment of human lives by enhancing their choices rather than material wealth or income. This new "beyond income" paradigm focuses on human resilience that expands thinking about progress and multidimensions of well-being in a new holistic, sustainable development agenda. This is what is adapted to the needs and aspirations of the CARICOM. Thus, for example, the SDG goal to eradicate poverty is linked to several factors and targets such as full employment, the reduction in youth unemployment, and the augmentation of education or training. The targets for social protection are universal health care coverage, a healthy life for all, appropriate social protection, and recognition of unpaid domestic work.

The targets for demographics are appropriate social protection, recognition of unpaid domestic work, development of inclusive infrastructure, and sustainable urbanization. The education target is to ensure education for all, while those for social exclusion are inclusion of all, education on cultural diversity, and equal rights to economic resources. The targets for adverse events are the reduction in the effects of disaster, strengthen resilience to natural disasters, and the reduction of exposure to adverse effects (UNDP, 2016).

The development vision for the CARICOM in the twenty-first century focuses on the community's response to the challenges of the sustainable development goals. This is particularly significant in the light of the multidimensional and holistic scope of the SDGs. This requires measures which "through their synergies and interconnectedness, reduce human vulnerability and proneness to multidimensional poverty, halt and reverse the erosion of human development gains, promote growth in competitiveness and output, and address environmental degradation" (UNDP, 2016).

Approach to development alternatives for the NMWO

The CARICOM's strategic framework to deepen integration and build resilience, as well as the agency's adoption of the UN's sustainable development goals are well intended, but problematic because they do not properly address issues concerning the class and power structures in the region. The development challenge for the CARICOM involves building resilience and the SDGs, but it cannot be about the Caribbean's integration into the neoliberal global arena. The development challenge is about breaking with the old ways of pursuing economic progress and creating alternative approaches that are appropriate for the new multipolar world order. This is what is referred to as realigning the economic activities of the CARICOM with the new sources of international economic power. And because the CARICOM states will have a role in determining their modus operandi within the NMWO, alternative structures of power to the domination of the strong by the weak, will emerge. This does not mean that the region has to insulate or isolate itself from the West. Realignment is to assess the economic benefits of the community's participation in the process of capitalist development, and to deliberately break with the measures that work against the CARICOM's economic progress. The next step is to assess the economic dynamics of the new multipolar world order and to engage with them on the basis of what best suits the region.

The goals of realignment – the perspective of breaking with capitalist measures that work against the CARICOM, and embracing new economic policies that are made possible by the new multipolarity – are simply to reverse the long-standing problems that hinder Caribbean development. The realignment needs to bring a convergence of the CARICOM's consumption patterns with those of the basic needs of the people, resolve the divergence in its resource use and factor endowment, and reverse the pattern of property ownership and associated social relations in the new multipolar world order. The achievement of these goals would require a reorganization of the economic structure such that the accumulation of capital does not merely accrue to a tiny minority but to the region as a whole in some form of a more inclusive approach to development in which wealth is distributed more evenly. The global arena into which the ruling elites in the CARICOM want to integrate the region is one in which inequality in wealth and income is increasing and having debilitating effects on working people (Piketty, 2014).

The objective of Caribbean economic policy in the NMWO must be to put food on the tables of working people, provide them with decent well-paying jobs and sufficiently adequate access to health, clothing, housing, utilities, security, education, and recreation. Its aim must be to protect the environment, stimulate sustainable production, guarantee and defend the human, economic and social rights of everyone, insulate workers from poverty and inequality, and shield them from any form of authoritarian political rule. It must privilege a worker-controlled state over the market, people over profit, and the practical concerns about economic and social development, over capitalist free-market ideology.

The ideological approach that favors the free market over working people has failed the Caribbean, perpetuating inequality, dependence, and poverty. The Caribbean has to try an alternative worker-controlled state directed approach simultaneously with measured private investments. The state has to take the lead in development not merely to lay the foundations on which private capital builds, or because the capitalist class lacks the appropriate experience, or is more focused on commerce rather than manufacturing. The rapid economic advancement of China is evidence that a state directed approach with a measured private sector is indeed an effective development alternative to free market capitalism.

The developmental role of the state in the rich capitalist countries is undeniable (Chang, 2009; Reinert, 2019). But, the Caribbean does not have to follow the examples of the state-directed capitalist approach discussed by those authors. In those examples, the state facilitates the flourishing of capitalist enterprises, and the capitalist classes that own and or control those businesses have command over the state and rule in their self-interest. In the model proposed here the state has to be in the control of working people, and systematically guide economic expansion to bring about economic and social development, eradicate poverty, eliminate inequality, and wipe out dependence. The worker-controlled state directed private sector model driven by a true concern for economic development rather than profit has to form the foundation of the CARICOM's economic policy for the new multipolar world order. Thomas (1988) believes the state, due to existing polarity with the private sector, has to play a significant role in development in the context of a participatory political process that enhances the ordinary worker's status as a citizen, producer, and consumer of wealth.

The Caribbean's approach to development in the new multipolarity must dovetail with Thomas' (1988) view to converge domestic resource use and consumption. New strengths must be added to agriculture, manufacture, tourism, services provisions, education, etc., by matching factor endowment with Caribbean needs. Thus, when development programs or projects are formulated with the BRI and NDB, they must be based on utilizing Caribbean resources to produce for domestic consumption and exports. Agricultural development projects for example must be geared toward satisfying domestic demand as well as exports, and not be purely for exports as is fueled by the current land-grab phenomenon. The same situation must obtain for manufacturing and services provisions, as production is guided not by profit, but by the needs of the masses who along with producers must be cultivated to meet the new approach to development.

The alternative conception of Caribbean development outlined by Thomas (1988) promotes worker ownership and control of production. This conception is adopted as a framework for the construction of Caribbean economic policy in the NMWO. According to Thomas (1988), the development involves the planned and effective execution of the right to work, as well as the reversal of colonial and post-colonial authoritarian traditions. Reproducing the material conditions of life within a self-reliant and endogenous pattern of growth is necessary to reverse the region's authoritarian tradition. Democratic power must form the basis of work, politics, social organization, the exercise of fundamental rights such as freedom of expression and organization, respect for the individual's privacy, and the abolition of repression and torture.

Caribbean economic policy in the NMWO must address the class and power structures that continue to marginalize working people. Workers through their civil organizations that have a seat at the decision-making table have to exert influence on the state to bring about these outcomes. The oppressive class and power structures have to be dismantled to favor working people who combine with nature to produce the wealth that is appropriated by the rich and powerful. Development requires a system of ownership, control, and production oriented towards satisfying the basic needs of the working majority. Economic policy must seek to preserve the stability of the environment and sustainability in accordance with the UN Sustainable development goals. Also, the external context in development must be recognized given the reality the Caribbean's colonial past and geographic proximity to the US.

References

Amin, S. (1990). *Delinking: Towards a Polycentric World*. London: Zed Books.

Bernal, R.L. (2013). *Globalization, Trade, and Economic Development: The CARIFORUM-EU Economic Partnership Agreement*. New York: Palgrave Macmillan.

CARICOM (2014). *The Caribbean Community Five-Year Strategic Plan 2015-2019: Repositioning CARICOM*, Volume 1. Turkeyen, Guyana: CARICOM Secretariat, 3 July.

Chang, A.-J. (2009). *Bad Samaritans: The Myth of Free Trade and the Secret History of Capitalism*. New York: Bloomsbury Press.

Economic Commission for Latin America and the Caribbean (ECLAC) (2020). "The Caribbean Outlook: Forging a People-Centered Approach to Sustainable Development Post-COVID-19," (LC/SES.38/12), Santiago.

Piketty, T. (2014). *Capital in the Twenty-First Century*. Cambridge Mass. and London: The Belknap Press of Harvard University Press.

Reinert, E.S. (2019). *How Rich Countries Got Rich ... And Why Poor Countries Stay Poor*. New York: Public Affairs and Hachette Book Group.

Rodney, W.A. (2011). *How Europe Underdeveloped Africa*. Baltimore, MD: Black Classic Press.

Thomas, C.Y. (1988). *The Poor and the Powerless: Economic Policy and Change in the Caribbean*. New York: Monthly Review Press, 1988.

United Nations Development Program (UNDP). (2016). *Multidimensional Progress: Human Resilence Beyond Income Caribbean Human Development Report*. New York.

Williams, E. (1994). *Capitalism and Slavery*. Chapel Hill and London: The University of North Carolina Press.

Index

AAMS *see* Association of African and Malagasy States
ACS *see* Association of Caribbean States
Afghanistan, NATO's Resolute Support Mission in 47
Africa-Asia Bandung Conference (1955) 99
African Development Bank 128
Africa Union (AU) 95
Agenda for Sustainable Development (2030) 127, 170, 196, 197
Agribusiness Promotion Council (APC) 143
Agricultural Bank of China 68, 128
Agricultural Marketing Agreement Act of 1937, 143
Agricultural Marketing Service (AMS) 143
Ali Administration 56
All-China Federation of Trade Unions 162
Americanness 40
Amin, S. 113
AMS *see* Agricultural Marketing Service
Animal and Plant Health Inspection Service (APHIS) 143
Annual Avalon Invest Caribbean Now 2013 Forum 161
Antigua and Barbuda 32; Belt and Road Initiative and 22; China-financed projects 162; Memorandum of Understanding with China 163
APC *see* Agribusiness Promotion Council
APHIS *see* Animal and Plant Health Inspection Service

APNU+AFC coalition government 52–55, 57, 58
Arab Spring 64
Aristide, J.-B. 32
Article 38, 121
Aruba 188
ASEAN *see* Association of South East Asian Nations
Asian Development Bank 68
Asian Infrastructure Investment Bank 68
Association of African and Malagasy States (AAMS) 99
Association of Caribbean States (ACS) 9
Association of South East Asian Nations (ASEAN) 67
Astana International Exchange 128
Astana International Financial Center Authority of Kazakhstan 128
AU *see* Africa Union
Australia 47

Baha Mar Ltd. 160
Bahamas 32, 50; China-financed projects in 159, 160; Commonwealth of the Bahamas 159, 164; undernourishment in 138
Baiyi, W. 162
Balding, C. 70–71
Bank of China 128
Barbados 32, 138; Belt and Road Initiative and 22; BRI and 163; CARICOM stock markets in 120; China-financed projects in 158; Double Tax Treaties 22; import substitution industrialization 86; per capita calories consumption in 138; plantation dependence economy model 87

Barclays 116
BASF 141
Bayer 141
Beijing Oriental Yuhong Waterproofing Technology Co Ltd 161
Belize 32; food imports in 139; industrialization and development 84; undernourishment in 138
Belt and Road Initiative (BRI) 2, 8, 12, 22–23, 67–69, 112, 126, 133, 147, 148, 151, 158, 171, 185, 189, 200; in agriculture 144–146; CARICOM states in 162–164; critics of 70–71; threats to 51–52
Benn, D. 92
Bennett, K. 120
Bernal, R.L. 39, 194
Better Utilization of Investment Leading to Development (BUILD) Act 71
BGLU *see* British Guiana Labor Union
Biden, J. 153, 155, 171, 186, 187, 196
bilateral investment treaty (BIT) 179
biofuels, new political economy of 141–142
BIT *see* bilateral investment treaty
Böhm-Bawerk, E. 82
Bolivarian Alternative for Latin America and the Caribbean (ALBA)–Caribbean Fund 152
Bolivarian Republic of Venezuela and Governments of the Caribbean (BRVGC) 151–152
Bolivia 17
Brandt, J. 177, 178
Brazil 63; ethanol production in 142
Bretton Woods 2, 10, 41, 91
Brexit 3, 7, 9–11, 64, 95; and Caribbean reactions 103–109; class analysis of 104–105
BRI *see* Belt and Road Initiative
BRICS 2, 7, 10, 22, 61, 62, 64, 95, 109, 112, 176, 185, 193, 195; New Development Bank (NDB) 12, 68, 112, 126–129, 200
BRICS Bank 112, 126, 130
Britain 53, 64; accession to EEC 99; mercantilism 78–79
British Guiana Labor Union (BGLU) 81
British Royal Commission of Inquiry (1897) 82
British Virgin Islands 188
British West Indies, abolition of slavery in 134–135
British West Indies Federation 5
Brown, D. 63
Browne, G. 163
BRVGC *see* Bolivarian Republic of Venezuela and Governments of the Caribbean
BUILD *see* Better Utilization of Investment Leading to Development Act
Burma 48
Bush, G.W., Jr. 18, 26, 28, 32, 73; Administration 48, 158, 171
Business Identifier Codes (Bank Identifier Codes) 29
Butler, S. 63
ByteDance Ltd. 181

CAI *see* Comprehensive Agreement on Investment
CAIB *see* Caribbean Association of Indigenous Banks
CAIPA *see* Caribbean Association of Investment Promotion Agencies
CAIR *see* Caribbean Association of Insurance Regulators
Campbell, C. 177
Canada 53, 157
capital accumulation 1, 15, 19–21, 80, 113
capitalist development 77–92; challenges to colonial policy 83–88; import substitution industrialization 85–86; Lewis on industrialization and development 84–85; plantation dependence economy model 86–87; search for "another development" 87–88; classical political economy critique 79–80; emergent class structure of 190–191; Keynesian revolution 83; Marx's critique of political economy 80–81; mercantilism 78–79; neoclassical critique 81–82; new thinking on development 91–92; theoretical premises 89–91; neoliberal era 88–92
capital–labor relations 19–21
CAP *see* Common Agricultural Policy
CAPS *see* CARICOM Association of Pension Supervisors
CARDI *see* Caribbean Agricultural Research and Development Institute

204 *Index*

Caribbean: capitalist development 77–92; counterterrorism in 34–35; make America great again 39–58; neoliberal financialization in 112–130; in New American Century 25–36; political economy in 2; reactions to Brexit 105–108; terrorism in 30–31; *see also individual entries*
Caribbean Agricultural Research and Development Institute (CARDI) 138
Caribbean agriculture, in new multipolar world order 133–148; agriculture and biofuels, new political economy of 141–142; Belt and Road Initiative 144–146; Caribbean Basin Initiative 142–143; CARIFORUM–EU EPA 143–144; colonial approach and Moyne Commission 134; food regime analysis 139–141; neoliberalism and food security 137–139; policy 146–148
Caribbean 2020: A Multi-Year Strategy to Increase the Security, Prosperity, and Well-Being of the People of the United States and the Caribbean 172
Caribbean Association of Indigenous Banks (CAIB) 125
Caribbean Association of Insurance Regulators (CAIR) 125
Caribbean Association of Investment Promotion Agencies (CAIPA) 125
Caribbean Basin Economic Recovery Act (CBERA) 133
Caribbean Basin Initiative (CBI) 8, 133, 142–143, 146
Caribbean Basin Trade Partnership Act (CBTPA) 133
Caribbean Catastrophe Risk Insurance Facility (CCRIF) 125
Caribbean Center for Monetary Studies (CCMS) 117, 119
Caribbean Center for Money and Finance (CCMF) 117, 122, 125
Caribbean–China Consultations process 23
Caribbean–China Economic and Trade Forum 23
Caribbean Community (CARICOM) 1–10, 14, 22, 23, 25, 60, 92, 101, 107, 110, 117, 153; economic indicators in 5–7; and make America great again 50–57; in new multipolar world order 2, 8–10; strategic framework to deepen integration and build resilience 193–196; US arm-twisted 31–34; *see also individual entries*
Caribbean Confederation of Credit Unions (CCCU) 125
Caribbean development 4, 87, 91, 92, 101, 112, 118, 130, 188, 199, 200; financial sector in 120–122; imperialist frameworks of 14–23
Caribbean Development and Cooperation Committee (CDCC) 188
Caribbean Development Bank (CDB) 122, 125, 126, 153, 159
Caribbean Exchange Network (CXN) 123
Caribbean Financial Action Task Force (CFATF) 25, 31, 125; Annual Report for 2001–2002, 31
Caribbean Food and Nutrition Institute (CFNI) 138
Caribbean Forum (CARIFORUM) 98–102; emergence of 97–99
Caribbean Forum-European Union Economic Partnership Agreement (CARIFORUM–EU EPA) 8, 11, 50, 95–96, 98–103, 106, 108–110, 133, 143–144, 185
Caribbean Free Trade Area (CARIFTA) 5
Caribbean Group of Bank Supervisors (CGBS) 125
Caribbean Group of Securities Regulators (CGSR) 125
Caribbean Regional Negotiating Machinery (CRNM) 95
Caribbean Single Market Economy (CSME) 107, 120, 122, 153
Caribbean Sustainable Energy Roadmap and Strategy (C-SERMS) 153, 154
Caribbean-US Resilience Partnership 175
CARICOM Association of Pension Supervisors (CAPS) 125
CARICOM-BRICS economic relations 195
CARICOM College(s) of Regulators 125
CARICOM Development Fund (CDF) 125, 161
CARICOM Energy Policy (2013) 153, 154
CARICOM Financial Services Agreement 119, 121

CARICOM–French Outermost Region (FCOR) trade 102
CARICOM Investment Code 121
CARICOM Regional Stock Exchange (CRSE) 123
CARICOM Tax Administrations 121
CARIFORUM *see* Caribbean Forum (CARIFORUM)
CARIFORUM–EC Consultative Committee 101
CARIFORUM–EC Trade and Development Committee 144
CARIFORUM–EU EPA *see* Caribbean Forum-European Union Economic Partnership Agreement
CARIFORUM–EU Trade and Development Committee (TDC) 101
CARIFTA *see* Caribbean Free Trade Area
Carter Center 52
CBERA *see* Caribbean Basin Economic Recovery Act
CBI *see* Caribbean Basin Initiative
CBTPA *see* Caribbean Basin Trade Partnership Act
CCBG *see* Committee of Central Bank Governors
CCCU *see* Caribbean Confederation of Credit Unions
CCF *see* Congress for Cultural Freedom
CCMF *see* Caribbean Center for Money and Finance
CCMS *see* Caribbean Center for Monetary Studies
CCRIF *see* Caribbean Catastrophe Risk Insurance Facility
CDB *see* Caribbean Development Bank
CDCC *see* Caribbean Development and Cooperation Committee
CDF *see* CARICOM Development Fund
CELAC *see* China–Community of Latin American and Caribbean States Forum
Central America: US invasion of 16
Central Banks of the Caribbean Community 117
CFATF *see* Caribbean Financial Action Task Force
CFNI *see* Caribbean Food and Nutrition Institute

CGBS *see* Caribbean Group of Bank Supervisors
CGSR *see* Caribbean Group of Securities Regulators
Chaoyang 160
Chaudhury, D.R. 71
Chavez, H. 158
Chebankova, E. 62
CHEC *see* China Harbor Engineering Company
Chenery, H.B. 135
Chile 17
China 41, 48, 49, 60, 63, 64, 97, 155, 157, 158, 176, 192; Belt and Road Initiative 2, 8, 12, 22–23, 51–52, 67–71, 112, 126, 133, 144–148, 151, 158, 162–164, 171, 185, 189, 200; in the Caribbean: China-financed projects 158–162; China–EU agreement 186–189; China–US relations on the CARICOM 177–180; debt diplomacy 70, 126; Double Tax Treaties 22; food regime analysis 141; indentured laborers 20; International Cooperation Centre 160; Made in China (MIC) 2025, 67–70; Ministry of Finance 127; multipolar globalization 4; Mutual Establishment of Commercial Offices 158; policy toward the Caribbean 167–171, 180–182; State Council 68
China–Africa Financial Cooperation Consortium (2018) 128
China Arab States Bank Consortium (2018) 128
China–Caribbean Conference for Cooperation on the Belt and Road Initiative 164
China–Caribbean Economic and Trade Cooperation Forum (2005) 159
China-Central Eastern European Countries (CEEC) Bank Consortium (2017) 128
China–Community of Latin American and Caribbean States (CELAC) Forum 23, 162, 171
China Construction Bank 128
China Development Bank 68
China Europe International Exchange 128
China Financial Futures Exchange 128
China Foundation for International Studies 162

206 *Index*

China Harbor Engineering Company (CHEC) 163
China–IMF Capacity Development Center 129
China Investment Corporation 68
China Investment Corporation (CIC) 161
China–Latin America and Caribbean Agricultural Ministers Forum 161
China–Latin American Forum 162
China National Complete Plant Import Export Corporation (Complant) 160
China National Offshore Oil Corporation 163
Chinese People's Institute of Foreign Affairs 162
Chollet, D. 48
CIC *see* China Investment Corporation
CIPS *see* Cross-Border Interbank Payment System
Clark, C. 135
clash of civilizations 26–27
classical political economy critique 79–80
Claver-Carone, M. 56
Clean Power Plan (CPP) 43
CL Financial Limited 119
COFAP *see* Council for Finance and Planning
Cold War 50, 62, 185, 189
Coles, T.J. 104
Collister, K.R. 124
Colombia 17
colonial finance 114–119
colonial policy, challenges to 83–88
colonial slave mode of production 4, 9, 14, 19–21, 79, 114, 134, 137, 140, 189, 191
Commerzbank 128
Committee of Central Bank Governors 122
Committee of Central Bank Governors (CCBG) 125
Common Agricultural Policy (CAP) 99
Common Market 5, 14, 25, 101
competitive insertion 9
Comprehensive Agreement on Investment (CAI) 187
Conant, C.A. 15–16, 21
Congress for Cultural Freedom (CCF) 27
Connect 2022, 154
Conservative Party 107

Controlled Substances Act 45
Corn Laws 134–135
Costa Rica 159
COTED *see* Council for Trade and Economic Development
Cotonou Agreement 100
Council for Finance and Planning (COFAP) 121, 122
Council for Trade and Economic Development (COTED) 109
counterterrorism 28, 30, 34–35, 48
COVID-19, economic impact of 186–189
Cozier, J.G. 123
CPA *see* EU–OACP Cotonou Partnership Agreement
CPP *see* Clean Power Plan
CRNM *see* Caribbean Regional Negotiating Machinery
Cross-Border Interbank Payment System (CIPS) 129
CRSE *see* CARICOM Regional Stock Exchange
C-SERMS *see* Caribbean Sustainable Energy Roadmap and Strategy
CSME *see* Caribbean Single Market Economy
Cuba: Double Tax Treaties 22; plantation dependence economy model 87; US military interventions 16; US relations with 171

DACA *see* Deferred Action for Childhood Arrivals
David, P. 163
Declaration of Port of Spain on Strengthening Cooperation on Strategies to Sustain and Advance the Hemispheric Fight against Terrorism 35
Deferred Action for Childhood Arrivals (DACA) 44
Deutsche Börse Group 128
Devonshire-Ellis, C. 23
Digicel 164
Diplomatic Academy of the Caribbean 107
Dominica 32; Belt and Road Initiative and 22; per capita calories consumption in 138; undernourishment in 138
Dominican Republic: COVID-19 pandemic 188

Dominican Republic (DR) 50; Belt and Road Initiative and 22; as CARIFORUM exporter 100; US military interventions 16
Dorodnykh, E. 139
Dow 141
Dow Jones Industrial Average Index 42
DR *see* Dominican Republic
Draft CARICOM Investment Code 119
DuPont 141
Duvalier, F. 34

East Coast Program 44
Eastern and Southern African (ESA) 98
Eastern Caribbean Central Bank (ECCB) 125
Eastern Caribbean Securities Exchange (ECSE) 123
EBA *see* Everything But Arms
EC *see* European Communities
ECCB *see* Eastern Caribbean Central Bank
ECLAC *see* Economic Commission for Latin America and the Caribbean
Economic Commission for Latin America and the Caribbean (ECLAC) 85–86, 117, 160,188
Economic Partnership Agreements (EPA) 67, 100–103
economic power, global realignment of 7
economic realignment 191–193
ECPA *see* Energy and Climate Partnership of the Americas
ECSC *see* European Coal and Steel Community
ECSE *see* Eastern Caribbean Securities Exchange
EEC *see* European Economic Community
Egypt 19
Energy and Climate Partnership of the Americas (ECPA) 153
England *see* United Kingdom (UK)
Environmental Protection Agency (EPA) 43, 44, 143–146
EPA *see* Economic Partnership Agreements; Environmental Protection Agency
ESA *see* Eastern and Southern African
EU *see* European Union
EU–OACP Cotonou Partnership Agreement (CPA) 98

EURATOM *see* European Atomic Energy Community
Europe, indentured laborers 20
European Atomic Energy Community (EURATOM) 96
European Bank for Reconstruction and Development 128
European Coal and Steel Community (ECSC) 96
European Communities (EC) 96
European Council 96
European Economic Commission 104
European Economic Community (EEC) 96, 105, 107
European Parliament 96, 97
European Union (EU) 2, 3, 41, 53, 60, 72, 73, 176; birth trajectory of 96–97; bloc imperialism 66–67; economic power 7; UK withdrawal from 104–105
Everything But Arms (EBA) 144
Export–Import Bank of China (EXIM Bank) 68, 128, 160, 165
Exxon Mobil Corp 56

Fabbrini, S. 64
Familiar, J. 155–156
FAO *see* Food and Agriculture Organization
fascistic capitalism 39
FATF *see* Financial Action Task Force
FDA *see* Food and Drug Administration
Fei, J.C. 135
Financial Action Task Force (FATF) 30, 31, 125
Financial Crimes Enforcement Network (FinCEN) 29
financial sector growth, and region's economy 122–123
financial self-determination 114–119; struggle for 116–119
financial war on terrorism 29–30
FinCEN *see* Financial Crimes Enforcement Network (FinCEN)
Fisk, D. 32
Food and Agriculture Organization (FAO) 138
Food and Drug Administration (FDA) 143
food regime analysis 139–141
Food Safety and Inspection Service (FSIS) 143

food security, neoliberalism and 137–139
France 16, 64
Freedomlab 63
free trade agreement (FTA) 179
Friedmann, H. 139
FSIS *see* Food Safety and Inspection Service
FTA *see* free trade agreement
Fukuyama, F. 18

G7, 65
G-20, 48, 63, 65
GCC *see* Gulf Cooperation Council
GDP *see* gross domestic product
Generlalized Scheme of Preferences (GSP) 143
GEOCOM *see* Guyana Election Commission
Georgetown Agreement (1975) 99
Germany 64
GHSA *see* Global Health Security Agenda
Gill, C.R. 153, 156–157
Gleaner, The 23
Global Center for Combating Extremist Ideology 47
Global Health Security Agenda (GHSA) 176
global hegemon 25–27
Goldstein, J.P. 113
Goldwyn, D.L. 153, 156–157
Gorsuch, N. 45
Government Procurement Agreement (GPA) 179
GPA *see* Government Procurement Agreement
Granger Administration 55, 56
Great Depression 83, 180
Greenidge, C. 163
Grenada 32, 34, 159; BRI and 163–164
gross domestic product (GDP) 5–7, 121, 188
GSP *see* Generlalized Scheme of Preferences
Guaidó, J. 50, 51, 55, 156
Gulf Cooperation Council (GCC) 49
Gulf of Mexico 43
Guyana 34, 138, 168, 189; Belt and Road Initiative and 22–23; China-financed projects in 158–159; China's Cooperation Agreement with Guyana 163; food imports in 139; Guyana–China Joint Commission on Economic Trade and Technical Cooperation 160; Guyana Defense Force 55, 56; import substitution industrialization 86; industrialization and development 84; Ministry of Foreign Affairs 55; Omai Bauxite Mining (OBMI) 159; political impasse in 52–57
Guyana Election Commission (GEOCOM) 53, 54

Haass, R.N. 64
Haiti 19, 25, 32, 34, 50, 142; China-financed projects in 164; food imports in 139; per capita calories consumption in 139; undernourishment in 138; US military interventions 16
Hall, K.O. 92
harmonized systems (HS) 103
Harris, K. 186, 187, 196
Harry W. Colmery Veterans Educational Assistance Act 46
Heath, E. 104
Heritage Foundation 104
Hess Corp 56
Hijazi, A. 47
Hilferding, R. 112
Hobbesian Leviathan 36
Hobson, J.A. 15
Holness, A. 23, 50
Hong Kong 79
HS *see* harmonized systems

IAC *see* Insurance Association of the Caribbean
ICC *see* International Criminal Court
ICE *see* Immigration and Customs Enforcement
IDB 109, 161, 165
IDCs *see* Industrial Development Corporations
IFIs *see* international financial institutions
ILANUD *see* United Nations Latin American Institute for the Prevention of Crime and the Treatment of Offenders (ILANUD)
IMF 10, 51, 61, 89, 109, 122, 165
Immigration and Customs Enforcement (ICE) 44

imperialist frameworks of Caribbean development 14–23
imperialist war of 1914–1918, 17
import substitution industrialization (ISI) 85–86
indentured labor 4, 20
India 47, 63, 97; indentured laborers 20
Indonesia 63
Industrial and Commercial Bank of China 68, 128
Industrial Development Corporations (IDCs) 86
Institute of Social and Economic Research (ISER) 117
Insurance Association of the Caribbean (IAC) 125
intellectual property rights (IPR) 178, 180
Inter-American Development Bank 128
Inter-American Drug Abuse Commission 31
international capitalist system, Caribbean's trajectory in 189–193; economic realignment 191–193; emergent capitalist class structure and political development 190–191
International Criminal Court (ICC) 32
International Finance Corporation 128
international financial institutions (IFIs) 61, 122, 165, 193
international organizations (IOs) 61
International Republican Institution (IRI) 52, 156
International Ship and Port Facility Security (ISPS) 32
Intra-CARICOM Double Taxation Agreement 121
Investment Plan for Europe 127
IOs *see* international organizations
IPR *see* intellectual property rights
Iran 156
Iraq 19, 40, 46
IRI *see* International Republican Institution
ISER *see* Institute of Social and Economic Research
ISI *see* import substitution industrialization
ISIS *see* Islamic State in Iraq and Syria
Islamic State in Iraq and Syria (ISIS) 46, 172
ISPS *see* International Ship and Port Facility Security

Jagan, C. 34
Jamaica 32, 34, 50, 162; Belt and Road Initiative and 22, 23; CARICOM stock markets in 120; as CARIFORUM exporter 100; China-financed projects in 158, 160, 161; Double Tax Treaties 22; import substitution industrialization 86; per capita calories consumption in 139; plantation dependence economy model 87; undernourishment in 138
Japan 47, 48, 64
Jessop, D. 157
Jevons, W.S. 82
Jianchun, G.C. 163
Johnson-Smith, K. 163
Johnston, B.F. 135
Jorgenson, D.G. 135
Justo, L. 17–18

Kadir, A. 53–55
Kautsky, K. 112
Kelshall, C.M. 30
Keqiang, L. 68, 162
Keynesian revolution 83
Keynes, J.M. 83
Keystone XL and Dakota Access Pipelines project 43
Khan, A. 92
Kissinger, H. 18
Kozyrev, A. 62
Kratochvíl, P. 62

labor theory of value 80, 82
LAC *see* Latin American and Caribbean
Lal, D. 90
Laos 48
Lapavitsas, C. 113, 119
Latin America 3, 7, 10, 14, 15, 95, 167; biofuels production in 142; political economy 16; soy economy in 142; US military missions 18
Latin American and Caribbean (LAC) 178
law of self-preservation 15
LEAD program 52, 57
Lenin, V.I. 112
Levitte, J.-D. 64, 66
Levitt, K. 92
Lewis, W.A. 86, 87, 90, 116, 117, 133–137; on industrialization and development 84–85

Index

Lifeng, H. 163
Liliendaal Declaration on the Financial Sector 125
Lima Group 50
Lindahl, F. 92
Liquefied Natural Gas (LNG) 43
LNG *see* Liquefied Natural Gas
Lomé Conventions 97–99
Luce, H.R. 18, 27
Luxemburg, R. 112

Macron, E. 71
Maduro, N. 50, 56; Administration 47, 156
MAGA *see* make America great again
make America great again (MAGA) 39–58; beginning of 41–48; CARICOM and: division over Venezuela 50–51; political impasse in Guyana 52–57; threats to the BRI 51–52; mindset 39–41; in new multipolarity 41; US disengagement myth 48–50
Manley, M. 34
Maritime Transport Security Act (MTSA) 32
Marshall, A. 82
Marx, K. 112, 135; critique of political economy 80–81
Mattis, J. 7
Mazda 43
McFarland, K.T. 39, 40
McMichael, P. 139
MDB *see* multilateral development banks
MDC *see* more developed countries
MDGs *see* Millennium Development Goals
mechanized agriculture 136
Meeks, B. 92
Mellor, J. 135
Menger, C. 82
mercantilism 77–79, 191
Merger Treaty of 1967, 96
Mexico 157; US invasion of 16
Meyer, S.P. 27
MFN *see* Most Favored Nation
Michael Hong Architects 160
Millennium Development Goals (MDGs) 100, 138
Miller, S. 162
Moise, J. 164
Monroe Doctrine 10, 15, 16, 21, 176
Monsanto 141
more developed countries (MDC) 86
Morgenthau, H.J. 62
Morrison, W.M. 178
Most Favored Nation (MFN) clause 100, 144
Mottley, M. 51
Moyne Commission 133, 171; colonial approach and 134; Moyne Commission of Inquiry 134; Moyne Commission Report 83
MTSA *see* Maritime Transport Security Act
Mukherjee, S.R. 40
multilateral development banks (MDB) 126
multipolar globalization 4
Murray, D. 63
Mussolini, B. 27

NAFTA *see* North American Free Trade Agreement
National Biodiesel Board (NBB) 142
National Drug Take Back Day 45
National Endowment for Democracy (NED) 52, 156
National Industrial and Commercial Investments Limited (NICIL) 159
National Public Safety Partnership 44–45
Nationwide Public Health Emergency 45
NATO *see* North Atlantic Treaty Organization
Navigation Acts 78
NBB *see* National Biodiesel Board
NDB *see* New Development Bank
NED *see* National Endowment for Democracy
neoclassical critique 81–82
neoliberal era, capitalist development in 88–92; new thinking on development 91–92; theoretical premises 89–91
neoliberal financialization 112–130; alternative sources of 126–129; in Caribbean development 120–122; colonial finance and financial self-determination 114–119; dynamics of 119–125; financial sector growth and region's economy 122–123; non-banks and financial instruments 123–124; regional financial

architecture 124–125; theoretical considerations 112–114
neoliberal globalization 1–4, 7–10, 14, 15, 18, 39–41, 48, 65, 66, 70, 81, 91, 92, 109, 176, 191, 194
neoliberalism, and food security 137–139
New Development Bank (NDB) 12, 68, 112, 126–129, 200
new multipolar world order (NMWO) 1–5, 8–12, 14, 15, 19, 60–74, 114, 133, 187; approach to development alternatives for 198–201; Caribbean agricultural policy in 146–148; Caribbean agriculture in 133–148; characteristic features of: US power-sharing on the world stage 65–66; economic policy for 185–201; European Union's bloc imperialism 66–67; proposition and argument 60–61; Russian pole 72–74; theoretical debates on 61–65
New World Order 18
Nicaragua, US military interventions 16
NICIL see National Industrial and Commercial Investments Limited
NMWO see new multipolar world order
non-banks and financial instruments 123–124
Noriega, R. 32
North America 97
North American Free Trade Agreement 43
North Atlantic Treaty Organization (NATO) 49, 65, 73; Resolute Support Mission in Afghanistan 47
North Korea 46–47, 65
Novack, W.F. 16–17

OACP see Organization of Africa, Pacific and Caribbean
OAS see Organization of American States
Obama, B. 73, 172, 178; Administration 43, 45, 48, 49, 65, 158, 171, 177, 182; "Stream Protection Rule" 42
Odle, M.A. 117–119, 129, 130
OECS see Organization of Eastern Caribbean States
Office of International Cooperation and Development (OICD) 143
Office of the Leading Group for Promoting the Belt and Road Initiative (OLGPBRI) 127
Office of Trade Negotiators 110
Ogunseye, T. 53
OICD see Office of International Cooperation and Development
OLGPBRI see Office of the Leading Group for Promoting the Belt and Road Initiative
Operation Desert Storm 19
OPIC see Overseas Private Investment Corporation
Oracle 181
Organization of Africa, Pacific and Caribbean (OACP) 67, 97–99, 108; Group of States 99; Pacific 98
Organization of American States (OAS) 50; Inter-American Convention against Terrorism 35
Organization of Eastern Caribbean States (OECS) 98, 123, 163
Overseas Private Investment Corporation (OPIC) 71

Pacific OACP (POACP) 98
Pareto, V. 82
Paris Agreement on Climate Change (2015) 127
Paris climate accord 65
Paris Commune (1871) 82
Patriota, A.A. 64
patriotism 3, 40
PdVSA see Petroleos de Venezuela S.A.
Peloponnesian War 62
Pence, M. 71
People's Bank of China 128, 161
People's National Congress (PNC) 52, 54
People's Progressive Party (PPP) 52–54, 56, 156
People's Republic of China (PRC) see China
PEPFAR see President's Emergency Plan for AIDS Relief
Peru 17
Petito, F. 64
Petras, J. 114
PetroCaribe 151–165, 180; energy development alternative 151–152; Ministerial Council 152; US attempt to dismantle: destabilization of Venezuela 156–158; US–Caribbean Energy Summit 153–156
Petroleos de Venezuela S.A. (PdVSA) 156

212 Index

Phan-Gill, S. 47
Philippines 48
Pieterse, J.N. 64
Pigou, A.C. 82
plantation dependence economy model 86–87
Platt Amendment 15, 16, 21–22
PNAC *see* Project for the New American Century
PNC *see* People's National Congress
POACP *see* Pacific OACP
Polanyi-Levitt, K. 113
political economy, Marx's critique of 80–81
Pompeo, M. 51, 56–58
poverty alleviation 10, 123, 138, 143
PPP *see* People's Progressive Party; public–private partnership
PRC *see* People's Republic of China
preemptive military strikes 28–29
President's Emergency Plan for AIDS Relief (PEPFAR) 176
Primakov, Y. 62
primitive accumulation 19, 20, 191
Privy Council 190
Project for the New American Century (PNAC) 11, 25–27, 36, 57
property ownership 4, 88, 190, 193, 199
protectionism 3, 63, 82, 90, 191
public–private partnership (PPP) 169, 175
Puerto Rico: COVID-19 pandemic 188; plantation dependence economy model 87
Putin, V. 72

Qi, T. 163
Quad States 47

Ranis, G. 135
RCEP *see* Regional Comprehensive Economic Partnership (RCEP)
Regan, R. 90
Regional Comprehensive Economic Partnership (RCEP) 195
Regional Credit Bureau 125
Regional Credit Rating Agency (CariCris) 125
Regional Program for Monetary Studies (RPMS) 117
Reich, O. 32
Republican Party 48
Research Center for the Belt and Road Financial and Economic Development 129
Revised Treaty of Chaguaramas 119, 121
Rodney, W. 34
Roosevelt Corollary 15, 16, 22
Rowley, K. 162
Royal Bank of Canada 116
RPMS *see* Regional Program for Monetary Studies (RPMS)
Russia 2, 4, 7, 8, 14, 41, 49, 60, 63–65, 96, 104, 156, 176, 189, 193; and Belt and Road Initiative 71; capitalist development 89; and new multipolar world order 72–74

SADC *see* Southern African Development Community
Saint Lucia 50
SALISES *see* Sir Arthur Lewis Institute for Social and Economic Studies
Sanders, R. 155
SAPs *see* structural adjustment programs
Saudi Arabia 43, 156
Schulze, P.W. 62
SDGs *see* sustainable development goals
Seaga, E. 34
SED *see* US–China Strategic and Economic Dialogue
Seerattan, D. 124
Shanghai Stock Exchange 128
SIDS *see* small island developing states (SIDS)
Silicon Valley 141–142
Silva, S. 102, 103
Singapore 120
Sinopec 159
Sir Arthur Lewis Institute for Social and Economic Studies (SALISES) 117
small island developing states (SIDS) 3
Smith, A. 78
Smith, R. 134
Society for Worldwide Interbank Financial Telecommunication (SWIFT) 29
Sokolsky, R. 72
Somalia: US military intervention 19
South Africa 63

Index

South America 16–18, 22, 97; biofuels production in 142
Southern African Development Community (SADC) 98
South Korea 47, 48
Soviet Union *see* Russia
Spanish American War (1898) 16, 21
Sprague, J. 92
Steinberg, J. 27
Stiglitz, J.E. 3, 4
St Lucia: per capita calories consumption in 139
strategic global repositioning 9
Stronski, P. 72
structural adjustment programs (SAPs) 192
Stuart-Young, B. 163
St Vincent 32, 138
Sub-Regional Stock Exchange Mechanisms 125
Sullivan, M.J. III 18
Suriname 162–163, 189; Belt and Road Initiative and 22, 23; plantation dependence economy model 87
survival of the fittest 15
sustainable development goals (SDGs) 191, 196–199
SWIFT *see* Society for Worldwide Interbank Financial Telecommunication
Syngenta 141
Syria 46

Taiwan 159
Tapia, D. 23
TDC *see* CARIFORUM–EU Trade and Development Committee (TDC)
terrorism: in the Caribbean 30–31; definition of 28; war on 11, 19, 25, 27–36, 167, 181, 182
Terrorist Financing Tracking Program (TFTP) 29
Thatcher, M. 90
Thomas, C.Y. 2, 87–89, 118, 129, 130, 133–137, 140, 200
TIFA *see* United States–CARICOM Trade and Investment Framework Agreement
TikTok 181
TIP *see* Trade and Investment Program
TISA *see* Trade in Services Agreement
Toyota 43
TPP *see* Trans-Pacific Partnership

Trade and Investment Program (TIP) 143
Trade in Services Agreement (TISA) 196
Transatlantic Trade and Investment Partnership (TTIP) 49, 65, 196
Transpacific Partnership 48
Trans-Pacific Partnership (TPP) 43, 65, 71, 179, 195, 196
Treaty of Paris (1951) 96
Treaty of Tordesillas (1494) 79
Trinidad and Tobago 32–33, 162, 181, 189; Arthur Lok Jack Graduate School of Business 160; Belt and Road Initiative and 22, 23; CARICOM stock markets in 120; as CARIFORUM exporter 100; China-financed projects in 158–161; Double Tax Treaties 22; financial sector growth and region's economy 122–123; import substitution industrialization 86; Lake Asphalt 161; National Academy for the Performing Arts (NAPA) 160; neoliberal financialization 119; plantation dependence economy model 87; undernourishment in 138
Trump, D. 39, 51, 57, 156; Administration 27, 33, 39, 40, 42, 43, 46, 48–51, 53–58, 65, 66, 70, 71, 126, 157, 158, 167, 172, 176, 179–182, 186, 187, 196; 'America First' foreign policy" 3, 16, 40, 47, 48, 65, 72, 73, 176, 182; Trumpian nationalism 7, 14–16, 19, 48, 49, 186; Trumpism 7, 8, 10, 39–41, 44, 64, 176
TTIP *see* Transatlantic Trade and Investment Partnership
Turkey 63
Turner, S. 62

UN *see* United Nations
UNDCP *see* United Nations Drug Control Program
undernourishment 138
UN Family Planning Agency (UNFPA) 45
Union of Soviet Socialist Republics (USSR) *see* Russia
United Kingdom (UK) 16, 21: withdrawal from the EU 104–105
United Nations (UN) 41, 135; 2030 Agenda for Sustainable Development

127; International Ship and Port Facility Security 32; Security Council Resolution 1373, 30
United Nations Drug Control Program (UNDCP) 31
United Nations General Assembly 23
United Nations Latin American Institute for the Prevention of Crime and the Treatment of Offenders (ILANUD) 31
United Nations Population Fund 45
United States (US) 2, 10, 11; attempt to dismantle PetroCaribe: destabilization of Venezuela 156–158; US–Caribbean Energy Summit 153–156; Census Bureau 40; Congress 32; Council of Economic Advisers (CEA) 45; Defense Department 44; Department of Agriculture 138, 143; Department of Health and Human Services (HHS) 45; Department of Homeland Security (DHS) 44; Department of Justice (DOJ) 44, 45; Department of Veterans Affairs (VA) 46; economic power 7; Fact Sheet 41–48; Forest Service 143; global hegemony 97; imperialism 4, 9, 14; center–periphery relations and 19–22; rise and evolution of 15–19; invasion of Mexico and Central America 16; National Security Strategy (NSS) 179; National Space Council 46; National Strategy for Combating Terrorism 28; Patriot Act 29; policies toward the Caribbean 171–177; power-sharing on the world stage 65–66; relations with Cuba 16; Southern Command (SOUTHCOM) 52; State Department 33–34, 58, 157; State Department Counterterrorism Office 28; surplus capital 15; terrorism in the Caribbean 34; Treasure Department 29; Treasury Department 157; US–China relations on the CARICOM 177–180; Virgin Islands 188; war on terrorism 11, 19, 25, 27–36, 167, 181, 182; White House 41–47; "Young Leaders of the Americas Initiative, The" 172
United States–Caribbean Strategic Engagement Act of 2016, 173
United States–CARICOM Trade and Investment Framework Agreement (TIFA) 171–172
University of the West Indies 117
UN Security Council 47, 61, 179
US Agency for International Development (USAID) 57, 71
US–CARICOM Trade and Investment Council 172, 174
US–China Strategic and Economic Dialogue (SED) 178–179
US Trade Representative (USTR) 180

VA Choice and Quality Employment Act of 2017, 46
VAR *see* Veteran Appointment Request
VCP *see* Veterans Choice Program
Venezuela 17, 19, 47, 66, 174, 181, 182; division over 50–51; US destabilization of 156–158
Veteran Appointment Request (VAR) 46
Veterans Accountability and Whistleblower Protection Act 46
Veterans Appeals Improvement and Modernization Act 46
Veterans Choice Program (VCP) 46
Vietnam 48
Visa Lottery program 44

Walcott, J. 163
Walmart 181
Walras, L. 82
Warmbier, O. 47
war on terrorism 11, 19, 25, 27–36, 167, 181, 182; financial 29–30
Washington Consensus 156
WeFi *see* Women Entrepreneurs Finance Initiative
WFS *see* World Food Summit
WHO *see* World Health Organization
Wieser, F. 82
Williams, E. 140, 194
Williams, M. 124
Williams, T.O. 134
Women Entrepreneurs Finance Initiative (WeFi) 48
Working People's Alliance (WPA) 34
World Bank 10, 48, 51, 61, 89, 109, 119, 128, 165
World Food Summit (WFS) 138

World Health Organization (WHO) 49, 65
World Trade Organization (WTO) 65, 97, 100, 138, 144, 178
World War I 16, 22
World War II 18, 61–63, 83, 96, 105, 113
WPA *see* Working People's Alliance
WTO *see* World Trade Organization

xenophobia 40, 71, 107
Xianmin, W. 163
Xi Jinping 67, 161

Yaoundé Conventions 99

Zaga 15
Zephirin, M.G. 124

Milton Keynes UK
Ingram Content Group UK Ltd.
UKHW031501071224
451979UK00015B/147